TAKE CHARGE AND MOVE OUT: THE FOUNDING FATHERS OF TACAMO

True Believers and the Rise of Navy Strategic Communications

BY
LEWIS F. MCINTYRE

CASEMATE
Philadelphia & Oxford

Published in the United States of America and Great Britain in 2022 by
CASEMATE PUBLISHERS
1950 Lawrence Road, Havertown, PA 19083, USA
and
The Old Music Hall, 106–108 Cowley Road, Oxford OX4 1JE, UK

Hardback Edition: ISBN 978-1-63624-154-8
Digital Edition: ISBN 978-1-63624-155-5

A CIP record for this book is available from the British Library

Printed and bound in the United Kingdom by TJ Books

Typeset in India by Lapiz Digital Services, Chennai.

For a complete list of Casemate titles, please contact:

CASEMATE PUBLISHERS (US)
Telephone (610) 853-9131
Fax (610) 853-9146
Email: casemate@casematepublishers.com
www.casematepublishers.com

CASEMATE PUBLISHERS (UK)
Telephone (01865) 241249
Email: casemate-uk@casematepublishers.co.uk
www.casematepublishers.co.uk

Contents

Foreword

What is this thing called TACAMO? This is a question many people have asked over the years, as did I when I pinned on my Wings of Gold and headed across country to my first squadron, Fleet Air Reconnaissance Squadron Four (VQ-4).

Fast forward a few decades and I found myself commanding the U.S. Navy's Third Fleet in San Diego, California, in charge of the Navy from the West Coast to the International Dateline. Since retiring in 2017, I have had time to reflect on my journey, pondering how often I returned to my TACAMO roots, how much I learned from my leaders and my sailors. As a junior officer in the TACAMO community, I was given an amazing amount of responsibility and accountability, and quickly learned how to be, and not be, a leader myself, lessons that stuck with me throughout my career.

When I checked into VQ-4 in 1983, the "True Believers" in this book had already begun to rise to command in both squadrons. Fil Baca was in command of our sister squadron, VQ-3, at Barbers Point and Bob Downey was to take command of VQ-4 the following year. Other "True Believers" were in their department head tours, competing for future command. To me and my fellow junior officers, it was a foregone conclusion that there was an established TACAMO career path, limited only by one's own hard work and dedication to the mission, to our sailors, and to our country.

However, for those "True Believers" who blazed the trail for us, that career path did not then exist. They took a step and a chance on a TACAMO career, not knowing whether their feet would land on firm ground or empty space. The story of how and why those "True

Believers" took that risk and made the choice to remain in TACAMO is a vital part of our history not to be lost, the story of the birth of the TACAMO aviation community. These pioneers believed in the mission and our country, advocating for them and fighting for them. They put in the hard work required for the community to become a viable career choice and the cornerstone of our National Security it is today.

I have had the humble opportunity to accomplish several firsts in my journey from ensign to vice admiral. However, to paraphrase Isaac Newton, if I have risen higher than others, it is because I stood on the shoulders of those giants, the "True Believers" who led the way. My thanks to you, Lew McIntyre, for chronicling the birth of the TACAMO community and bringing together the stories of the "True Believers." Take Charge and Move Out!

VADM Nora Wingfield Tyson, USN (ret)

Dedication

This book is dedicated, first and foremost, to VQ-3 Crew Four members Andrew Barker, Bob Bond, David Cofer, Richard Eastwood, James Faul, William Juergens, Godfrey LeDoux, Christie Metcalfe, Daniel Miner, Dennis Mura, Monte Nichols, David Paige, Aubrey Russell, Mark Searing, Jack Strunk, and Andrew Yaroschuck, forever deployed following the tragic crash of EC-130 156176 on June 21, 1977, off Wake Island. This book is also dedicated to Vice Admiral Jerry O. Tuttle, who gave us our name, to Captain William F. "Bill" Coyne who gave us our vision, and to the TACAMO Community Veterans' Association, which has kept our history alive. Finally, it is dedicated to all the "True Believers" who built this community, especially Bob Downey and Bill Harsanyi who have gone before us, and to all officers and sailors of this magnificent community.

I also dedicate this to Karen McIntyre, my wife of 40 years, who is my strength, inspiration, and a meticulous editor, without whom this book would never have been written.

Introduction

TACAMO, which stands for "TAKE CHARGE AND MOVE OUT," is the Navy's strategic airborne communications program for directing and managing the nation's nuclear forces. TACAMO is the name of both the system and the forces that operated that system, an acronym coined in 1963 by a young lieutenant named Jerry Tuttle. With the success of its nuclear-powered submarine force and its ability to carry nuclear-armed missiles, the Navy needed a more reliable and survivable system of communications to reach a submerged nuclear missile submarine on patrol and supplement the shore communications sites. Vice Admiral Bernard F. Roeder, then director of Naval Communications, assigned the development of the system to Lieutenant Tuttle, underlining the handwritten phrase "take charge and move out" three times on the memo. The name stuck.

Lieutenant Commander Walt Reese from Naval Air Station Johnsville, Philadelphia, flew test flights in a WV-121 Lockheed Super Constellation to assess technical issues of antenna wire deployment using a five-mile target towing wire and reel in 1962 He encountered icing, lightning strikes, and once found himself interfering with Navy carrier flight ops between Virginia and Bermuda. The TACAMO Project at Johnsville was known simply as the #1 Chief of Naval Operations Priority Project.

Collins Radio of Dallas, Texas, had created a very successful line of high frequency ground and airborne radios, and was also a key provider in the Navy's shore-based Very Low Frequency (VLF) systems. That company designed roll-on vans for C-130 Hercules aircraft containing the radio receivers, transmitters, the high-powered 20-kilowatt VLF transmitter, and a five-mile trailing wire antenna.

Lieutenant Tuttle directed operationally-oriented testing in a Marine KC-130 (Bureau Number 148806), the prototype system, which he dubbed "TACAMO I" from Admiral Roeder's handwritten note. He flew on many of the flights in the North Atlantic Iceland–UK gap, the South Atlantic off Africa, and in the Western Pacific, his transmissions monitored and measured by navy communications stations and ships. Finalizing the design, Lieutenant Tuttle directed the development and delivery in late 1964 of four improved roll-on/roll-off communications systems, the TACAMO II system, to TACAMO Detachments at Agaña, Guam, and Patuxent River, Maryland. He then returned to his primary duties as an attack pilot, transitioning to the A-4 Skyhawk.

While TACAMO had a mission, it was not yet a community. It lacked officers returning for second and third tours, aspiring to command and bringing with them the customs, traditions and camaraderie that define a community. Unrecognized by the rest of the Navy as a warfare specialty, officers were encouraged to detach early for another tour in a recognized community. Mid-level department heads and commanding officers came from other communities. It was like an orchestra composed of the leading artists in their field playing together briefly, before moving on to permanent positions with other orchestras, led by "guest conductors," talented and recognized in their community, but who had never worked with this particular ensemble in the past.

The story of how this community came into being, against all odds, exists today as untold memories in the minds of the early pioneers who made that happen. One of the early commanding officers of one of these squadrons, during a time of great crisis, had the opportunity to inspire one of the great transitions of this community, indeed its birth. I feel obliged to document this event in TACAMO's history that unquestionably altered its historical course and assured its success for the next several decades.

That key event occurred when a cadre of very junior officers, assigned to VQ-3 and VQ-4 during the early and middle 1970s, imbued with an unshakable belief in TACAMO, chose second tours, creating that community so desperately needed. They knew full well that doing so might leave their Navy careers in a shambles before they had hardly gotten started. Their decision to stay with the program proved the keystone that established TACAMO as a warfare specialty, with its own unique career path leading to command. It became an unprecedented Navy success story with an evolving strategic operational capability.

This is the story of those courageous few "True Believers" who took that leap of faith, defying the conventional wisdom that to do so was professional suicide.

The ultimate success of the TACAMO program rests upon the advocacy and faith of this cadre, as well as everyone else who contributed to the success of the program. Here are their stories in their own words.

Lewis McIntyre
CDR, USN (ret)

PART ONE

The Beginning, 1968–1975

The proof-of-concept phase in the mid-1960s demonstrated aircraft could successfully transmit high-powered Very Low Frequency (VLF) signals capable of reaching great distances while deploying the miles of trailing wire antenna needed for these very long wavelengths. Four Lockheed C-130E Hercules carried the roll-on/roll-off TACAMO II vans with operating positions, radio equipment and hardware necessary to receive messages throughout the spectrum and relay them on VLF. Having successfully demonstrated that capability, the Navy purchased eight C-130Hs, modified them with the built-in TACAMO III communications suites, and re-designated the aircraft as EC-130Qs, the first fleet of dedicated TACAMO aircraft. The Navy stood up two squadrons in June 1968: Fleet Air Reconnaissance Squadron Three (VQ-3), the "Ironmen," in Agaña, Guam, and Fleet Air Reconnaissance Squadron Four (VQ-4), the "Shadows," in Patuxent River, Maryland, each with four of the new EC-130Qs. The four C-130Es were stripped of their TACAMO II vans, also given TACAMO III communications suites, and re-designated as EC-130Gs. These were assigned to VQ-4, bringing that squadron's allocation to eight aircraft, as the Atlantic Fleet then had the higher priority.

Developing hardware proved far simpler than developing a team of people to operate it, and the operating procedures were being written even as they were implemented (and sometimes afterwards). There was no precedent in naval aviation for what TACAMO did. The enlisted personnel and chief petty officers were easy to come by as, except for the specialized VLF transmitter and receivers, the communications and navigations systems they operated and maintained were common to many aircraft. Commanding officers were taken from the Fixed-Wing Patrol (VP) Anti-Submarine Warfare community as they were familiar with flying large multi-engine aircraft over great distances. Junior officers were offered the choice of TACAMO when they got their wings, initially without revealing what that choice entailed.

The big gap was in the mid-level leadership of lieutenant commander department heads. For front-running lieutenant commanders, eager to be promoted to commander and selected for command in their community, department head slots are highly sought billets in their own community. Department head slots in a new, unknown community put them at a serious disadvantage for selection. Competitive lieutenant commanders were unwilling to take such slots and detailers were unwilling to assign them.

Lieutenant commander is a unique position. Having achieved that rank, one is guaranteed a career, if one so chooses, and opportunity to compete for promotion and command. However, lieutenant commanders failing promotion to commander, being "passed over," had to leave the Navy at 20 years' service. In the interim, as all the choice billets are reserved for the still-competitive junior lieutenant commanders, good jobs are hard to find for those passed over. TACAMO department head slots were among those available to them as the promotable lieutenant commanders did not want them. Many of these officers served with distinction and made many contributions to the community. Others brought negative attitudes with them, bitterness toward the Navy, and a sense of personal failure that detracted from their leadership.

This gap in mid-level leadership was both a good thing and a bad thing for the community for many years. On the one hand, it left a leadership vacuum that allowed junior officers fresh from flight training to rise to very high positions of responsibility very early in their careers. On the other hand, the negative attitudes of many mid-level leaders discouraged junior officers from continuing in the community or even in the Navy. This would not change until TACAMO began promoting its own lieutenant commanders, returning them as hard-charging competitive officers in their own community.

There was an initial sensitivity about the nature of the TACAMO mission in the 1960s. The squadron names were misleading, VQ being airborne reconnaissance, associated with VQ-1 and VQ-2 which performed totally unrelated electronic intelligence missions, and officers newly posted to the TACAMO squadrons had no knowledge of what they would be doing. Despite this ignominious beginning, in the wardrooms of these backwater squadrons which had yet to promote a single lieutenant to lieutenant commander, were the 11 people who would break that mold, eight of whom would rise to command, three of whom would help create, then command as commodores, Strategic Communications Wing One, yet 20 years in the future. All would shape the community in very many ways.

CHAPTER I

An Island Paradise on the Edge of the War

Bill Harsanyi

Bill Harsanyi was a P-2V Neptune pilot who flew in Vietnam, transitioned to TACAMO, rising to become one of our first TACAMO-bred commanding officers. His story is written posthumously from notes and memorabilia by Vern Lochausen.

From a small town in West Virginia, I enlisted in the Navy. After boot camp, I got my rate as Aviation Electronics Technician, flying the Lockheed P-2V Neptune anti-submarine aircraft with Patrol Squadron Ten out of Naval Air Station Brunswick, Maine. During that time, we flew detachments to Iceland and Spain, hunting Soviet submarines. We lost an aircraft and crew that crashed and disappeared in 1962.

I returned home and attended West Virginia Tech, remaining in the active navy Reserve. In 1966, I was commissioned at Pensacola via Aviation Officer Candidate School and, in 1967, I earned my Naval Flight Officer Wings of Gold. My first fleet assignment was with VO-67 in Thailand, yes, in the Vietnam War. The squadron was just commissioned and our mission was highly classified. Today we can say that we flew our OP-2V Neptune aircraft over the Ho Chi Minh Trail that the North Vietnamese forces illegally used to bring troops and supplies though Cambodia and Laos into the fight in South Vietnam against our American and Vietnamese forces. We dropped sensors to detect their movements and monitored and reported what the sensors told us. I flew over a hundred combat missions and was shot down on one of those. Near the end of the squadron's existence after just 18 months, our skipper, Commander Paul L. Milius, was shot down and lost, ordering his crew to bail out. Though seven of his crewmen were rescued and another recovered, he was never found. Right before I left the squadron, we were flying missions in support of the Marines, besieged at Khe Sanh, locating the North Vietnamese division and providing targeting information for Air Force bombers, Navy close air support, and artillery.

I entered TACAMO via the Navy Communications School at Newport, Rhode Island, in 1968, reporting to VQ-3 just after it was commissioned at Naval Air Station Agaña on Guam. The roll-on/roll-off TACAMO II mission vans were slowly being replaced by the integrated Comm Central TACAMO III upgrades. Skipper Ed Preston had gone on to Naval Electronics Systems Command, working with Jay McCormick and Collins Radio on those new systems. With two sea duty tours under my belt and a healthy dose of Western Pacific experience, I was the detailed to Naval Postgraduate School at Monterey.

Barry Coyle

Barry Coyle had a notable career in TACAMO, beginning as a junior officer in VQ-3 and rising to squadron command after several squadron tours and an illustrious tour in Washington, creating the funding for the E-6. He retired as a captain.

I did not begin my service in TACAMO as a "True Believer." I became one after experiencing the challenges of flying the mission and completing demanding ground assignments, working alongside some of the finest officer and enlisted shipmates in the Navy and their families. My journey, from newly-minted naval aviator to a dedicated and lifelong TACAMO "True Believer," begins with my first tour in VQ-3.

A few weeks before I earned my Naval Aviator Wings in July 1970, our flight class went through squadron selection for our first tours. I really wanted to get into the Vietnam War, so Light Attack Squadron Four (VAL-4), flying the OV-10 Bronco twin turboprop in support of Navy Special Operations forces, headed my list. VQ-1, with a well-established electronic intelligence collection mission, and VQ-3, both homeported on Guam, also caught my attention. VQ-3, having just stood up two years before and operating brand-new EC-130Q aircraft, was very interesting, but there was no information on their mission. Lieutenant Mike Lloyd, recently detached from VQ-3 and assigned as an instructor at Naval Air Station Corpus Christi, was gracious enough to talk with my wife Tina and me about the squadron and Guam. Mike, too, would tell me nothing about the squadron's mission, beyond that it involved a lot of great flying. He and his wife spoke glowingly of life in the squadron and on Guam. Looking at the mysteriousness of the mission and the squadron's location, I assumed they were involved in some sort of intelligence work, which could lead to an intelligence subspecialty useful for future assignments. I submitted my preferences, VAL-4 first, VQ-3 second, VQ-1 third, followed by a couple of West Coast VP (patrol) squadrons. I graduated high enough to have my first preference considered, but there were no openings in VAL-4. I got my second choice and was off to VQ-3 and Guam.

There were six months of en route training, first Airborne Navigation School with Training Squadron 29 where I found myself with a fellow pilot from flight school, Jim Black, also ordered to VQ-3. This was followed by initial C-130 training with the 4442nd Combat Crew Training Wing at Little Rock Air Force Base, with Jim as my flying partner. Tina was to stay with her parents in Pennsylvania until I could locate suitable off-base housing on Guam, while Jim and I were off to San Diego for Survival, Evasion, Resistance and Escape and Deep-Water Environmental Survival Training schools. We boarded a Military Airlift Command flight at Travis Air Force Base for our flight to Guam, anticipating a lonely holiday season, since we knew no one. How wrong we were!

Our flight landed at Andersen Air Force Base, Guam, on December 23, 1970. I still remember stepping out of the air-conditioned cabin of that Boeing 707 into the 90-degree heat and 90 percent tropical humidity of Guam—and it was December and after midnight! It was like getting whacked with a hot, wet towel, but we acclimated to it very quickly in those days before universal air conditioning.

My sponsor, Lieutenant Tom Hollis, met me at the bottom of the stairs, with Jim's sponsor as well, for the drive down to Naval Air Station

Agaña. Tom was a senior lieutenant about two years into his tour at VQ-3. He was the Airborne Communications Officer (ACO) on Crew Five, and I was to be assigned to his crew. We went to the Duty Office for check in, and he dropped us off at the Bachelor Officers Quarters to get some sleep. He picked us up the following afternoon for the first of several progressive Christmas parties. In addition, the Officers Club hosted a nice New Year's Eve dinner and party, so there was no shortage of holiday celebrations. Jim and I were immediately treated like old friends and shipmates with the opportunity to meet all the officers in the squadron, and their wives, in an informal atmosphere.

The holiday half-day schedule gave Tom a chance to give me a good introduction and orientation to VQ-3 with briefings on the mission and operations, where I finally learned the TACAMO mission. Our job was to provide a communications relay to fleet ballistic missile submarines on patrol, as a supplement to the fixed shore sites. Our aircraft were equipped to receive messages on various radio frequencies and retransmit them using the aircraft's installed high-powered Very Low Frequency (VLF) transmitter. The squadron had a nice briefing book on how TACAMO fit into the overall strategic command and control system of the U.S., providing a robust and survivable command, control and communications network using ground and airborne communications systems. So, at last I knew the mission I was taking on! A far cry from the intelligence mission I had imagined.

The EC-130Q airplanes on the ramp were just 18 months old with that "new car" smell, entirely different from the empty cargo training C-130Es we had flown at Little Rock. The entire aft portion of the Hercules was filled with radio equipment, crew operator stations, and the large VLF transmitter and its reel machine for deploying the five-mile-long trailing wire VLF antenna. This permanently installed mission package weighed about 15 tons—a full cargo load for a standard C-130 Hercules. We would soon learn that flying these heavy Hercs was a different task than operating the light-weight training aircraft.

Each newly-reporting first-tour junior officer was assigned both ground and flight duties. On the ground side, we were typically rotated through three jobs of about 10 months' duration each during a 30-month tour, in different departments in the squadron, to give us a chance to work in several aspects of the squadron while growing in leadership and professional knowledge. My first assignment was in the Administrative Department as First Lieutenant/Security Officer, followed by a tour in the Maintenance Department as Material Control Officer—essentially the Supply Division for the squadron. I rounded out my tour as Flight Officer in the Operations Department.

For pilots, qualifications began with Third Pilot, Second Pilot, and ultimately Aircraft Commander, with top-rated pilots having opportunities for additional qualifications as Instructor Pilot and Post-Maintenance Check Pilot. The training programs for these positions included both local training flights and mission flights, flight proficiency events, evaluations and a minimum number of flight hours at each stage. Junior pilots also had to qualify as First Navigator. Naval Flight Officers (NFOs) also completed navigator training, then trained to become Airborne Communications Officers, the leader of the enlisted communications crew on mission flights. I worked hard on all my flight duties and was fortunate enough to achieve qualification as instructor, both as pilot and navigator, before leaving VQ-3.

All aircrew members were assigned to crews for mission flights. I was first assigned to Crew Five as Third Pilot/Navigator with Lieutenant Commander Chuck Krieger as Aircraft Commander, Lieutenant Stu Bell as Second Pilot, Lieutenant Tom Hollis as ACO and Lieutenant (junior grade) John Hamilton as Navigator/ACO trainee. Stu Bell was to make many contributions to TACAMO over the next 20 years. I stayed with Crew Five for about a year, qualifying as Navigator, then moved to Crew Six as Second Pilot under Lieutenant Commander Dick Mester as Aircraft Commander. I flew with them for about six months before returning to Crew Five, eventually becoming Aircraft Commander and serving with them until I left the squadron.

In addition to our regular ground and flight duties, all squadron officers below department head rank stood watches as Squadron Duty Officer about once a month to greet visitors, handle incoming messages, carry out inspections and security patrols, brief the Commanding Officer, Executive Officer and Operations Officer on daily activities, and fulfill other duties as required. The duty officer slept in the squadron so there was always an officer on board to handle emergencies or operational issues.

I served under three commanding officers while in VQ-3. Commander Bill Loeffler was skipper when I arrived, with Commander Rance Dunmire as Exec (executive officer). Unusually, Commander Dunmire served two tours as Exec before finally assuming command in mid-1972, as Commander Ken Kraus, senior to him, was ordered in out of sequence. Commander Kraus served as commanding officer without having completed an executive officer tour, also quite unusual. All these men had backgrounds in patrol aviation, having mostly flown P-2 and P-3 aircraft, accumulating 12,000 or more flight hours, a treasure trove of flying wisdom, and sea stories. They were all three outstanding leaders, each with different personalities and leadership styles, but all led the squadron effectively while maintaining high morale.

In general, the Navy selects its squadron commanding officers from the best qualified officers who have served multiple tours in squadrons and aircraft within their respective warfare specialty communities: VP, Carrier Anti-Submarine Warfare, Fighter and Attack, etc. But the Navy also has a large number of "miscellaneous commands," squadrons not associated with a specific warfare specialty that can be commanded by any qualified naval aviator. The VP community was assigned all the miscellaneous commands operating land-based, multi-engine aircraft, including the TACAMO squadrons. This system provided additional command opportunities for VP officers selected for command, but without an available VP squadron billet in that year. The Navy was then downsizing its patrol aviation force, retiring the venerable P-5M Marlin seaplanes and transitioning from the P-2V Neptune to the far more capable P-3 Orion, significantly reducing the number of VP squadrons. Miscellaneous commands became coveted prizes. They remain so today, but now TACAMO officers benefit from this system, with opportunities to command transport, training, and developmental multi-engine squadrons.

Although all my first squadron commanding officers were quite good, none of them knew what the future held for TACAMO. All three of my skippers at various times recommended I transfer to the VP community to ensure I was flying in a community that had both a storied history and guaranteed future, guidance I would have to consider in the future.

There were other notable senior officers who had an impact on my time in VQ-4.

Lee Pippins was a third commander in the squadron, but an NFO, in 1970 not eligible for command. He was the Communications Department Head and the senior ACO and navigator instructor in the squadron, with more than 10,000 flight hours. He and his wife were both great musicians and singers and Lee carried his banjo everywhere, including mission flights. My favorite memory of Lee occurred on my initial check ride for navigator, with him as the evaluator and the Exec as aircraft commander. It started out simple enough: just a night flight out to a specified geographic point, turn around and return to Guam, keeping the required charts and logs and providing position reports to the pilots. What could possibly go wrong?

When I had plotted my final land-based fix outbound and checked in with Guam Air Traffic Control to proceed "feet wet," Commander Pippins came up to the navigator's station and turned off all the electronic navigation aids. He said, "You have a simulated electrical failure. You have to complete the flight using only celestial navigation. If you hit the turn-around point and then bring us back to your last outbound fix, you pass the check ride. I'll be back aft. Call me if you need me."

He then went back to the communications compartment. The sextant was not my strongest talent or favorite navigation method, but it was a clear night with partial moon and plenty of good stars that gave a couple of good fixes on the leg out. But approaching the turn-around point, my star solution turned out to be quite large, requiring more than a little guesswork to determine our actual position. I began to sweat a little because if I didn't hit the turn-around point pretty close, I'd also miss the return to Guam entry point. But just as I gave the pilots the turn-around recommendation, we had a minor propeller malfunction that required an engine shutdown. Commander Dunmire declared an emergency and headed for home base on three engines. Commander Pippins returned to the navigator's station and said, "Okay, now we have an actual emergency. You can turn on all your navigation aids and get us back by the most direct route." So, with all the equipment back on, I was quickly able to determine our actual position: I had missed the turn-around by just a few miles, not bad at all, and plotted a course back home to Agaña for an uneventful three-engine landing. An exciting night, and I passed the check ride with high praise from Commander Pippins for good work during an actual emergency. He didn't even criticize my not-so-good celestial navigation!

Lieutenant Commander Charlie Gray was the Admin Department Head, a large, amiable man, well liked in the squadron. He had accumulated almost 20,000 flight hours, half of it in blimps until they were retired in the early 1960s. He then re-qualified as a multi-engine pilot, with a huge trove of flying knowledge and excellent sea stories. Charlie had a unique way of judging the duration of a mission flight. He would come into the planning room, take a quick look at the chart, then say: "That looks like a three-cigar flight," and pull out the appropriate number of cigars from his briefcase to put in a flight suit pocket for use on the mission. Yes, we smoked on the aircraft back then, ash trays at every crew station. Different times.

Lieutenant Commander Chuck Krieger was Maintenance Officer and Aircraft Commander of Crew Five with whom I flew for about 15 months. He was also a great instructor pilot who provided a lot of my training, having flown in both Patrol and Transport squadrons, and the only pilot in the squadron with previous C-130 experience. He was an outstanding pilot and leader.

We also had a number of officers finishing first tours that began in the original TACAMO proof-of-concept units, the TACAMO Detachment of VW-1 using the roll-on/roll-off TACAMO II vans carried in two slightly modified C-130E cargo aircraft. The four lieutenants who had served in this early TACAMO unit were pilots Ed Dufreche and Roger Granere, and NFOs Tom Hollis and Carl Swenson. They had all learned a great deal about the equipment and mission during those development times and the early months of operating the new TACAMO III EC-130Qs, passing their knowledge on to the new generation of junior officers.

The instruction and guidance received from senior enlisted personnel in the squadron greatly aided the junior officers' professional development.

In my ground jobs, I most remember Aviation Storekeeper First Class Rachuba, my senior petty officer in the Material Control Branch, who not only provided outstanding leadership for the sailors, but also taught me a great deal about aviation supply. In the airplane, we were blessed to have several senior flight engineers with multiple previous tours and thousands of hours flying C-130s. Aviation Machinist Chiefs Cotton Hope and Larry Barks, and Aviation Machinist First Class Gilliam, were flight engineers with whom I flew regularly. They, the communication crew and reel operators were happy to teach young pilots about EC-130 systems and maintenance and I soaked up as much of it as I could. I had a lot of respect for these hard-working enlisted flight crew members, many of whom would serve with me again in future TACAMO assignments.

From December 1970 to June 1973, the squadron was tasked to fly 50 percent coverage missions totaling about 360 hours a month, with at least one aircraft deployed away from Guam. About one third were orbital missions, retransmitting VLF exercise messages in restricted orbit areas.

Flying the EC-130Q on VLF transmit missions was quite challenging and tiring. To achieve the ideal antenna configuration, the aircraft had to be orbited using about 45 degrees angle of bank, just a few knots above stall speed. This required full attention, skill from the pilot and good back-up from the co-pilot and flight engineer. These orbit missions lasted from one to four hours, and the longer ones got very tiring. They had to be hand-flown for the entire duration because the autopilot on those early EC-130s was not capable of sustaining the orbit. These missions, especially the longer ones, were also very tiring for the communications crew down the back, because the increased G-loads multiplied the effort needed to complete every task.

Crew deployments generally lasted a week or so and included stops at three or four different Navy and Air Force bases on mainland Japan, Okinawa, Taiwan and the Philippines so, in addition to the interesting flying, we had many opportunities for travel, learning about these diverse cultures, shopping, and sampling the local food and drink. At least once a year, each crew was required to complete a Pacific island deployment to austere bases on Kwajalein, Wake Island and Midway. Although not as much fun as some of the other places we went, I always enjoyed these trips. All these islands had interesting World War II historical displays, great beaches and fishing, and gave the crews a chance to get to know each other better. These trips were frequently sweetened by a last stop either in Japan or Hawaii. The Hawaii stop was particularly coveted because it was good liberty in the U.S. and it gave us a chance to pick up stuff we couldn't get on Guam—fresh milk, never-frozen meat, fresh green lettuce, unadulterated beer, nice flowers for the wives, fresh fruit, etc.

In addition to the deployed operations, VQ-3 also flew several local communications training missions around Guam each month. These local mission flights gave the squadron a great opportunity to participate in a nice exchange program with the ballistic missile submarine communication crews, based in Guam's Apra Harbor. VQ-3 had a standing invitation to Submarine Squadron Fifteen for their radiomen and communications technicians to fly with us on any local missions conducted during a sub's in-port time; quite a few of them did so. Similarly, VQ-3 comm crews would visit the missile submarines pier-side to observe communications procedures on board. Sometimes, a sub would have to do a local shakedown at-sea test and a small number of VQ-3 communicators got to go to sea as well. These exchanges proved very valuable in improving procedures and performance of communications between the TACAMO aircraft and submarines on patrol.

In addition to our regular mission tasking and exercises, VQ-3 participated in a number of research and development activities. In May 1972, Crew Five was selected for another nifty research mission, a trip to Australia to test communications reception at extremely long range. We first flew to Royal Australian Air Force Base Amberley outside Brisbane, the main operating base for Australian C-130s, and flew one VLF transmit mission out of there. We also had a couple of days of liberty in beautiful Brisbane and got to sample Australian wine and steak for the first time. We then flew cross-country up to Darwin. While Amberley had been super modern, the base at Darwin looked like it came straight out of a World War II movie, though well-maintained and with modern equipment on hand to support aircraft operations. The outdoor bar at the very nice Officers Club was covered by camouflage netting and tended by a retired sergeant major who had endless stories from his service going back to World War II. Very cool.

Darwin in those days was more like Dodge City, with one paved street, no building taller than two stories, filled with gritty opal miners, oil field roughnecks, shipyard workers, fishermen, cattle station employees, truck drivers, etc. Very interesting and also good liberty, but a place where you needed to be careful, for sure. We flew a couple of VLF transmit missions out of Darwin.

Another research chore we did was to collect data on aircraft and trailing wire antenna performance during orbit transmissions. This task required the co-pilot to jot down altitude, angle of bank, airspeed and drogue tension every 90 degrees of turn during an orbit, something which came up quickly at 45 degrees angle of bank! We were filling in these fields on paper templates as fast as we could write and throwing the pages on the deck to be collected after the orbit was complete. The navigator also collected a different set of position data for these forms. The squadron sent boxes of these completed forms back to the Applied Physics Lab, Johns Hopkins University, every month to be used to develop the next-generation TACAMO IVB communications suite.

In early 1973, the Commander-in-Chief, U.S. Pacific Forces, added a requirement for VQ-3 to have an aircraft and crew on 30-minute alert at Naval Air Station Agaña whenever there was no mission crew airborne. With the Vietnam War winding down and the Cold War heating up, strategic readiness was an increasing concern. This alert requirement was implemented without much difficulty but was a scheduling headache. This capability was only used a couple of times for exercise/test purposes.

Finally, the squadron also flew pilot training flights, post-maintenance check flights and various miscellaneous flights that added to the amount of time spent flying by all aircrew personnel.

There was then a lot of good-natured, though sometimes not-so-good, give-and-take between aircrew of VQ-4 and VQ-3, which continues to this day, about who was working harder and flying more. After all, VQ-4 was tasked with 100 percent airborne, not 50 percent, but to do that, they had eight aircraft and 12 crews, while VQ-3 had four aircraft and six crews, so the flight hours per crew were about the same. Certainly,

VQ-4's operations generated a little more stress because of the necessity to make every take-off on time in order to maintain continuous airborne coverage. VQ-3 could be a little more relaxed with most of our missions and we could delay a mission to fix a minor maintenance problem or avoid some ugly weather. I finished my 30-month tour just short of 1,600 pilot hours and just over 800 navigator hours—about the norm for first-tour pilots in both squadrons. So, for sure, nobody was sitting on their duffs!

Unfortunately, in January 1972, VQ-4 lost one of its eight aircraft. An explosion and subsequent fire in an outboard fuel tank in EC-130G Bureau Number 151890 shortly after takeoff on a mission flight forced the crew to make an emergency gear-up landing in a farmer's field just across the Chesapeake Bay from Patuxent River, Maryland. Because of the remarkable flying skill of the crew, they all survived the accident with nothing more than minor injuries, but the fire and damage from the landing were so severe the aircraft was scrapped. This left VQ-4 with only seven aircraft, adequate to conduct continuous airborne operations and other squadron missions under ideal conditions. However, a major modification program, TACAMO IVB, would soon take several aircraft out of service for extended periods. The loss of '890 would eventually have a significant impact on TACAMO operations, drawing VQ-3 down at times to just a single aircraft to support VQ-4's 100 percent tasking. During my time in VQ-3, however, we were not affected, retaining four planes throughout my tour.

In the early 1970s, Guam was a pretty isolated place. In that environment, the squadron became your family. We all lived within walking distance of each other and families spent much off-duty time together. Both the Officers Club at Agaña and the much larger one at Commander, Naval Forces Marianas Headquarters, the "Top of the Mar," served excellent meals and provided various bands for music and dancing, not to mention weekly Happy Hours. The island of Guam had some spectacular beaches and coral reefs for swimming and snorkeling, and a large network of caves to explore. There were many World War II sites and monuments and we got to see Japan's last soldier, Sergeant Yokoi, surrender to U.S. forces in 1973 after eluding capture for 30 years! Many of the officers in the squadron bought off-road motorcycles, riding into the jungles, hills, and the isolated beaches of Guam at least a couple of times a month. There were a number of excellent restaurants in the civilian community serving a variety of international cuisines. We got to see one of Bob Hope's famous USO Shows. Because of Guam's isolated location, one of the best recreational deals provided to Navy folks stationed there was a once-per-year free flight for a vacation in the Far East. My wife Tina, and I, and Tom Hollis and his wife Ellie, teamed up for one of those trips in early 1972, going to Japan to tour Tokyo, Nara, and Kyoto before spending three days at the 1972 Winter Olympics in Sapporo, one of those fantastic travel opportunities you fall into in the Navy. Tina and I also took one of those flights the following year on a wonderful trip to Hong Kong and Thailand. Guam might have been small and isolated, but it was never boring if you took advantage of the opportunities available. Sharing all these activities with our squadron mates and families drew us all closer together and most of us made lifelong friends there.

Guam also offered employment opportunities for spouses. Tina and I did not have children and she landed a job as a government civilian in the Supply Department at Andersen Air Force Base, part of the team that ordered, inventoried and issued the bombs used by the B-52s stationed there. This was no small task since we were dropping thousands of bombs each week on North Vietnam during my entire time on Guam. Trained as an accountant and bookkeeper, Tina found the details of this work very satisfying, but was always a little appalled at the sheer number of weapons being used in that air war. Bombs came into the naval base at Apra Harbor, near the south end of the island, and a continuous stream of trucks delivered them to Andersen. These trucks provided us a stark reminder that the U.S. was engaged in an ugly shooting war, with many of our friends involved. Tina's cousin was a B-52 pilot deployed to Guam for a few months while we there. Visiting with him and Tina's co-workers gave us the chance to meet people on the island that other Navy folks did not.

As the saying goes, all good things must come to an end; my tour in VQ-3 was certainly a good thing. I had held ground jobs and flying positions of increasing responsibility and challenge, traveled extensively, been exposed to outstanding leadership and mentoring, and been surrounded by great shipmates, many of whom became lifelong friends; hard to imagine a better first tour.

Much has been written by other contributors to this book about the seemingly slow growth of the community and development of experienced TACAMO commanding officers and senior enlisted leaders. In June 1973, TACAMO was only five years old as a formal Navy squadron. First-tour officer attrition, especially among pilots, was high, as it was throughout the Navy in those years, but a goodly number of folks who served in VQ-3 during those first five years would return to the community to build the numbers needed for us to provide our own experienced department heads and, eventually, commanding officers. From my VQ-3 wardroom, Bill Harsanyi, Andy Riddile and myself would all become TACAMO skippers, and Andy would become the first commodore and wing commander. Frank Kockler, Stu Bell, Charlie DuBois, Dan Johnston, and others would make major contributions in the years to come. Many enlisted personnel also returned for multiple tours. The situation was the same in VQ-4. We were definitely growing our own, even in the very earliest days of the program, though we were not yet aware of our future.

As the end of my tour approached in June 1973, it became time to start thinking about my next assignment. Both the commanding officer and executive officer advised me to change communities to VP with a back-to-back sea tour. This didn't sound like a good idea to me, but I was still considering it when my detailer offered me orders as a Naval Reserve Officer Training Corps (NROTC) Instructor at the University of Pennsylvania, from which I had graduated four years earlier on an NROTC Scholarship. So, naturally, I eagerly accepted the opportunity to go back and teach there, and Tina was thrilled to be going back to Philadelphia as well.

So, with orders in hand, we departed Guam and VQ-3 in June for the next Navy adventure. I was not yet a TACAMO "True Believer." Indeed, I had not even decided if I was going to be a career naval officer and was actually leaning toward completing my initial obligated service and resigning to pursue a civilian career. However, that wonderful tour in VQ-3 planted the seeds from which a "True Believer" would sprout a few years down the road.

Andy Riddile

Andy Riddile was another junior officer, contemporary with Bill Harsanyi and Barry Coyle in VQ-3. His career took him through several squadron tours and extensive experience at the highest levels of national strategic command and control, serving in the National Emergency Airborne Command Post and the White House Military Office. He rose to command VQ-4 and became the first commodore of the newly-established Strategic Communications Wing One. He retired as a captain.

When I joined the NROTC at Rensselaer Polytechnic Institute in 1965, I had no plans whatsoever to make the Navy a career. My high school buddies were headed to Vietnam. I preferred to serve as an officer in the Navy as my father did in World War II. He was a gunnery officer on an armed freighter in the Mediterranean Sea. So, NROTC seemed the way to go. When I subsequently requested entrance into the NFO program, I still did not intend to stay in the Navy past my obligated time commitment. I finished Training Squadron Ten second in my class of about 25, thinking I might consequently have a good chance to be assigned to the aviation community of my choice. I requested assignment to Fleet Air Reconnaissance Squadron Two, homeported in Rota, Spain. I was attracted to the aerial reconnaissance mission and to its homeport in Europe. VQ-2 flew the EC-121M Super Constellation, magnificent at the time, and there were rumors of the coming EP-3E Aries. I couldn't pass that up. I promptly received orders to Fleet Air Reconnaissance Squadron Three. VQ-3 was only one number away from VQ-2, but it was almost halfway around the world to the east, homeported at Naval Air Station Agaña, Guam, and, as I was to learn, VQ-3's mission was entirely different to that of VQ-2.

I wasn't going to be flying reconnaissance missions at all. I was going to serve in the Navy's only strategic aviation mission, oddly called TACAMO. It was a mission vital to United States national security, yet poorly understood or appreciated by most everybody, including officers at the Navy's most senior levels. The secrecy surrounding the mission did not help this state of affairs.

There were other challenges to TACAMO readiness. To a harmful degree, the early community served as a pasture for failing officers. When the two squadrons were still new, squadron mid-level leadership was at times weak. The best junior officers bailed out of the community at their first opportunity. There was no viable career path yet established for the community. The commanding officers of my first squadron were fine gentlemen, but all came from other communities to command TACAMO as an "associated command." Typically, these first commanding officers did not fully understand the technicalities of the mission. Without a full appreciation of the significance of the role of TACAMO in national security, and with no understanding of its future, early commanding officers commonly guided talented junior officers out of the community. Further, the middle-grade officers also came from a variety of communities, many of them having failed to promote, and were lacking in motivation and appreciation of the mission. The standing up of the two squadrons was at times chaotic, with no clear source of leadership at all levels, and no established career path for junior officers other than to start over in another community or leave the Navy entirely. This resulted in a constant and critical loss of operational experience and mission expertise during that first decade.

My first stop on the way to VQ-3 was the Communications Officer (Afloat) Course at Newport, Rhode Island; not so technical, not particularly challenging. Daily, there was a fountain spewing champagne at the Officers Club at lunch. I would remember this later when the Navy had insufficient funds to adequately support the TACAMO mission. My second stop on the way to VQ-3 was VQ-4's Replacement Training Division at Naval Air Station Patuxent River, Maryland. Patuxent River is about a 65-mile drive from the center of the nation's capital. In 1971, it could have been a thousand. One of Lexington Park's features was a strip joint named "The Office," a name that allowed patrons to be somewhat honest about their whereabouts, "working late at The Office." At VQ-4, I received highly technical training on equipment operation for which I would be responsible as an Airborne Communications Officer. The mystery of the EC-130 mission capability was revealed. I learned a deep appreciation for the radiomen and avionics technicians who served as instructors. It was there I decided I would leave the most technical understanding of the equipment to the enlisted operators.

My last stop on my way to Guam was Survival, Evasion, Resistance and Escape School at Warner Springs, California. It occurred to me there that someone in authority believed there was a threat to those who performed the TACAMO mission. Noted.

The heat at Warner Springs was a dry heat. The heat in Guam was not. I still remember an immediate inability to breathe properly when the transport aircraft's door opened at Andersen Air Force Base in May 1971.

My experience at VQ-3 began inauspiciously when I stole the submarine squadron commodore's combination cover at a Dining-In during the first week of my arrival. The commodore and Commander Loeffler apparently chose to laugh it off, rather than crush me, fortunately for my future career! VQ-3 skippers Loeffler and Krause seemed to me to be good leaders. Skipper Dunmire, however, was more inspirational. He saw something in me I did not yet see in myself. Over many years, we kept running into each other and we became friends. Rance Dunmire's command tour at VQ-3 was his introduction into what turned out to be a long run in various other aspects of strategic warfare.

It eventually struck me that among squadron personnel there was a certain lack of mission understanding. Out of respect for those in VQ-3 who at the time dedicated themselves to the mission, I will not dwell on the various clues I saw of a certain casualness that permeated even the aircrews. I was a young pup at the time and could not have fully understood why, even beyond this apparent dismissal of mission commitment, that VQ-3 and VQ-4 commanding officers were not normally the first choice for squadron command. Also, there was a lack of material support. There was little coherent guidance, written or otherwise, on the operational procedures or even on the operational concept. Exactly how were we expected to fight this strategic war? Not even the most knowledgeable, most committed personnel had a full understanding of the big picture of strategic warfare. I was easily daunted by all of this;

as a fresh-caught lieutenant (junior grade), it was a far bigger problem than I could even begin to take on.

In the early 1970s, the drug and alcohol abuse problem in the Pacific Fleet became serious enough to receive far too much national media attention stateside. The Navy responded in 1973 by establishing Counseling and Rehabilitation Centers around the world. I could make a difference here, at least locally. I answered the call to help launch such a center in Guam, which we established with great fanfare. Shortly thereafter, I received permanent change-of-station orders to overhaul the counseling center in Subic Bay, Philippines, which directly supported the Seventh Fleet, fighting the war in Vietnam. Although Commander Dunmire warned me that leaving my first squadron tour early to do something so out of the ordinary for an NFO would not strengthen my record, helping sailors with substance abuse problems struck me as a problem well bounded and necessary.

CHAPTER 2

The Seed is Planted

Ken deGraffenreid

Ken deGraffenreid was a junior officer in VQ-4, with first-hand exxperence of that squadron before and immediately after the sea-change wrought by Bill Coyne in attitudes and professionalism. After two tours he transitioned to the reserves, and though he was no longer active in TACAMO, his civilian career took him to the highest levels of national policy and command and control, President Reagan's Senior Director of Intelligence Programs on the National Security Council Staff, working with such notables as Oliver North. He retired as a captain in the Naval Reserve.

I'm not at all sure I qualify as a "TACAMO Founding Father," but I certainly asked for a second TACAMO tour. My Navy career differed from the other "True Believers" in that I left the regular Navy for the Reserves after my second VQ-4 tour, retiring many years later as a captain. This was for an opportunity to pursue a broader national security policy career, and a very tough call, but, surprisingly, my career circled me back many times to TACAMO-related issues and support. As a result, much of my contribution to the success of TACAMO occurred later, in several White House and senior Office of the Secretary of Defense billets, and in various contractor relationships. Sometimes this support was very much behind the scenes, but it was always, I believe, motivated by a true belief in the TACAMO mission and in the encompassing area of survivable national command, control, and communications. All of this I first learned from the people, the pioneers, and experiences in my two TACAMO tours.

My remembrances take us back a little farther in time before there was a whole lot of thought given to TACAMO careers, perhaps giving perspective to some of the "Founding Fathers" observations and to the issue of why the "one and done" first tour TACAMO experience had become the unfortunate norm. And I would offer a word about the contributions of those who left.

I was a Naval Reserve Officer Training Corps (NROTC) regular type at Purdue University, graduating in June 1967, and was "stashed" at the old Naval Air Station Glenview, a fine old base near Chicago. In August, I started flight school, got my pilot's wings in October 1968 and, just because I thought they looked cool, put C-121s VQ-1 or 2 on my dream sheet! The detailer must have said, "Have we got a live one here," and I've always suspected that's how I got VQ-4. One would have expected some details of the TACAMO mission to which he assigned me, except no one seemed to know a whole lot about that subject.

My whole flight class went to Training Squadron 29 for Navigation School, an annoyance at the time as we were ready to get to the fleet. However, in the early days in VQ-4, a pilot had to fly a full two-week deployment on the navigator's table in order to make second pilot. In addition, my first aircraft commander insisted each pilot, including himself, navigate for a leg on each long deployment, and also that the navigators and Airborne Communications Officers (ACOs) be fully familiar with basic airborne co-pilot duties. Most of all, he also taught a valuable lesson: you could never know too much about the aircraft or the international flying we were doing.

I also went through the Air Force C-130 Hercules training at the 4442nd Combat Crew Technical Training Wing at Sewart Air Force Base, Tennessee. Absolutely first rate: old-time senior instructor pilots who had been flying the C-130 since the mid-50s, although I'm not sure they always knew what to make of three newly winged Navy ensigns and lieutenants (junior grade) going to a mysterious something called TACAMO. They taught us how to fly the airplane, including short-field landings, airborne pallet extractions, and low-level work, handling the C-130 like a fighter. They also taught that same lesson I would hear again when I got to VQ-4: one can never know too much about the plane and its systems. Their ideal was that a pilot should come to have the same knowledge as a senior flight engineer!

When I arrived at VQ-4 in April 1969, 10 months after the unit had been commissioned, things were very much in a start-up situation. The EC-130Qs with the built-in TACAMO III communications suite were just arriving and I was ordered to Lockheed Marietta, outside Atlanta, to pick one up; it smelled like a new car. The C-130Es with TACAMO II vans were en route to Collins for TACAMO III installation to become EC-130Gs.

Crews were just forming, trying to define the mission as it was understood at the time, which wasn't much. Full deployments were much sought after and generally once a month. With only a few airplanes on board, the pace, naturally, was modest; Happy Hour at the Bachelor Officers Quarters bar started pretty early almost every day. After a few months, however, I got assigned as third pilot to a good crew and things picked up. I loved the flying, the travel and life in the squadron.

When I arrived, we had three EC-130Qs (Bureau Numbers 156170, 156173, and 156174). Eventually, 156175 showed up, completing the Q-bird inventory. Over the next few months, newly designated EC-130Gs (Bureau Numbers 151888, 151889, 151890, and 151891) rejoined the squadron. Interestingly, an old VR-1 C-130F model (Bureau Number 141806), used in earlier TACAMO development, was often seen around as a logistics bird.

All the aircraft carried the squadron letters "HL," along with large red and yellow sparks, on the tail, "VQ-4" above the main landing gear door, and the VQ-4 logo, "The Shadow" from the 1950s radio show, near the crew entrance hatch. Each also carried a random side number under the cockpit.

I arrived in a squadron filled with outstanding young aviators and navigators. Some had been in the first-generation TACAMO vans with the VR-1 TACAMO Detachment and were VQ-4 plank owners or arrived just after the squadron stood up. A number of the pilots, although junior in rank, had accumulated many flight hours in C-130s flying with transport squadron VR-3 supporting Military Airlift Command. Several of the younger navigators also had thousands of hours of valuable worldwide experience in that squadron. This experience among the junior officers was critical to getting the TACAMO mission off the ground, especially since the initial mid-level lieutenant commanders from VP did not bring these essential skills to the mission. However, many of the VR-3 veterans came without a more traditional naval officer orientation since, in those squadrons, pilots and navigators only flew and did not really have "ground" jobs, the Air Force model. This lack of strong leadership and management experience at the department head level was an early TACAMO vulnerability which ironically became an advantage as junior officers rose to fill the vacuum.

Most of the newly arriving junior officers possessed outstanding leadership and aviation skills that carried the squadron in the early years, in the absence of guidance and example from their seniors. Many later TACAMO types may not recognize some of their names: Paul Koch, John Stanley, Dunton Wyatt, Carl Williams, Dick Wagner, Hal Willard, Larry Traskos, Larry Phillips, John Ramshur, Norby Kerwin, Denny Rutledge, Andy Gabriel, Sam Murray, Bob Haynam, Denny Oberg, John Magurn, Bob Myers, Stan Walz, and Al Johnson. None of them ever returned to TACAMO and only one or two even stayed in the Navy, but these guys laid the foundation stones in basic TACAMO deployment, operations and communications: safe international flying, random basing, devising the complicated theater-wide communications plan, alert systems and remote logistics. This foundation gave the next group—Bill Coyne, Fil Baca, Ed Hampshire, Andy Riddile, Kermit Ayers, Vern Lochausen, and others—something on which to build. They did a great job with little guidance and established the TACAMO tradition of a strong and independent junior officer corps which continues to this day. And they had a lot of fun doing it.

When I arrived at the squadron, the mid-level officers were a collection from various Navy backgrounds, almost all passed over, and generally lacking enthusiasm, interest in the mission, or leadership skills. Unfortunately, this serious shortcoming did not improve as new lieutenant commanders arrived. I believe this was a significant factor that worked against retaining outstanding talent for TACAMO. There were some notable exceptions. One was Lieutenant Commander Wally MacNab, who was probably the finest natural pilot with whom I have ever flown, having flown Corsairs in combat in World War II and recalled from the Reserves for Korea. He stayed in the Navy, but policy precluded his promotion beyond lieutenant commander. He was the Naval Aviation Training and Operating Procedures Standardization (NATOPS) officer, responsible for all flight crew training and standardization when I checked in, a true gentleman and an inspiration to the junior officers.

Our first two skippers seemed to me, as a novice lieutenant (junior grade), somewhat aloof at a time when the newly developing squadron needed enthusiastic, mission knowledgeable, and energetic leadership. Our next two skippers, Walt Thomas and Chic Wilson, were more broadly experienced, more interested and focused on the mission, and brought some much-needed enthusiasm.

The VQ-4 sailors were invariably great, even as the Navy was going through the end of the Vietnam War. The maintenance shops kept our aircraft flying as the squadron surged to eight aircraft and very soon supported 24-hour-a-day, 100 percent coverage. Our ground crews and aircrews worked harder than anyone to make TACAMO real. There was great opportunity all around. We had surface force radiomen with wings in friendly competition with aviation electronic technicians as operators. We had aviation electricians as flight engineers. Our chiefs were simply outstanding, both in the divisions and on flight crews. Many were also memorable characters, as it should be.

My own experience focused on the flying and I was blessed with getting my own crew early on, even as a lieutenant (junior grade), something that was to become a TACAMO hallmark. I became an enthusiastic instructor which led to my becoming the aviation safety officer in early 1971. We set up a reinvigorated Safety Office and program, with outstanding sailors from each of the divisions and aircrew positions, set on creating a real safety program under the banner that the safest flying is also the most mission-effective and combat-ready flying. Under this new philosophy, finally taking hold throughout the Navy at the time, safety wasn't the opposite of operational readiness, it was critical to it. Key to our effort was robust attention to incident reporting; we learned a lot. Our office tackled the drafting of a new and effective pre-mishap accident plan. The old one went back to the VR-1 days and was poorly written, comical, and obviously cribbed from another squadron. As a result, we were as ready as possible in January 1972 when an EC-130G (Bureau Number 151890), deploying with a 15-man mission crew, experienced an explosion and port wing fire, though the pilots successfully crash-landed it on Maryland's Eastern Shore with no injuries. They landed in a cornfield owned by Mrs. Bessie Gore and the Dorchester Volunteer Fire Department arrived to put out what was left of the fire. Our team successfully investigated this major strike accident. The cause of the fire was later determined to be the reset of a circuit breaker, pulled on the preceding flight due to fluctuating fuel quantity indications from the port wing outboard tank. The flight engineer, unaware it had been intentionally pulled, reset it, and the fault caused electrical power to be introduced into the fuel sensor, igniting the fuel.

Incidentally, this accident left us with a treasure in the form of an intact, but no longer flyable, Mission Communications Suite. Rather than scrap this valuable asset, we installed it in a building behind the hangar as a full-fidelity communications system trainer, in the Replacement Training Division, capable of performing most of the functions of the TACAMO III aircraft system, except for transmitting Very Low Frequency (VLF). Funding for establishing such a facility would have cost nearly as much as another aircraft and been unthinkable, but once in place it was much easier to keep current with the aircraft. Today, the descendants of that crash survivor live on today as the System Integration Laboratory, across the street from the old Replacement Training Division, a full-fidelity "E-6B without wings" used for initial integration of new systems without impacting aircraft availability, and two Mission Avionics Systems Trainers at Tinker Air Force Base used for crew and maintenance training.

Why did so few officers from these early TACAMO years choose not to attempt a TACAMO career or even remain in the Navy? This contrasted sharply with enlisted retention during these same years. I would give two reasons among many that could be cited.

The first was poor leadership, failing to sell the TACAMO mission to junior officers as a viable career path during this early period, often selling patrol aviation instead as the most desirable next tour.

The second was simple failure by seniors to ask officers to stay. One example: when a senior lieutenant, my highly respected former aircraft commander, announced he was leaving the Navy, I asked why. His answer, obviously painful to him, was that while he liked the TACAMO work, and his fitness reports reflected he was doing an outstanding job, no one ever asked him to stay. As a result, the Navy and TACAMO lost a fine and creative officer, a common enough occurrence in those early days.

But all the while, we learned more about the mission and where we fit in the big picture, doing, for example, reciprocal visits with the folks from the National Emergency Airborne Command Post, call sign *Nightwatch*. We also participated in a major strategic communications exercise by deploying most of the squadron to Mildenhall Air Base. Eventually, we set the stage for continuous airborne coverage.

One strange incident foreshadowed my later involvement with TACAMO. We were summoned to an All Officers Meeting for a hush-hush threat briefing by the Naval Investigative Service and Navy Intelligence which rather graphically depicted the human intelligence operations being run against the squadron at our overseas deployment bases. Everyone gulped and we became instant "True Believers" in the Soviet threat to TACAMO. If the Navy did not yet understand the value of TACAMO to the U.S. nuclear deterrent, the Soviets clearly had figured it out.

By the time I departed the squadron, things had improved considerably in terms of the mission, but we had a long way to go, especially in the area of officer morale, and particularly at the Bureau of Personnel detailers' level whose oft-repeated advice was to "get a warfare specialty" in another community.

Bob Downey

Bob Downey was a senior lieutenant in VQ-4, with a previous tour in VW-1 weather squadron on Guam, where he first came in contact with TACAMO. Bob, with Fil Baca, were the first lieutenants in six years to be promoted to lieutenant commander. After VQ-4, Bob had a second squadron tour in VQ-3, a carrier tour as communications officer, and a tour with the Airborne Warning and Control

System E-3A, before becoming the first TACAMO-bred commanding officer to lead VQ-4. He had a number of follow-on tours in Naval communications, retiring as a captain. Bob Downey passed away during the spring of 2017. His section was reconstructed from a brief biography he provided the TACAMO Community Veterans Association, command history, and personal recollections of his executive officer, Ed Hampshire.

In January 1964, I enlisted, reporting to Great Lakes, Illinois, for boot camp. Very soon I was in a huge auditorium where we all took the General Classification & Arithmetic Test. I thought I had loused up the testing as I had scored "only" 64 and 70. I asked an officer if I could try again; he replied that I did not need to retake the tests, my cumulative score would enable me to go to the Naval Academy or any College that had an NROTC curriculum. However, both of those programs required one to be single through graduation and I was engaged to be married to my spouse Patty.

I instead requested the Naval Aviation Cadet program, got orders to Pensacola, and earned my Naval Flight Officer (NFO) Wings of Gold and a commission as an ensign. Patty and I were married and we went to Guam where I flew into the eyes of typhoons with VW-1. In addition, we also flew to Chu-Lai, south of Da Nang, and alternate flights between Hanoi and Haiphong, tracking P-3 aircraft to ensure they did not go "feet dry" over North Vietnam. I accumulated over a thousand hours with VW-1 and my son Jack was born on Guam. My ground job was Legal Officer.

During my tour on Guam, I saw an ugly C-130 aircraft with all sorts of antennas on the exterior. This was the VW-1 TACAMO Detachment, run by Lieutenant Commander Ron Carlson as officer-in-charge, who would later turn over command in 1968 as VQ-3 stood up with its first commanding officer. Right there, I set my plan to fly in the futuristic EC-130. Ron Carlson and I also flew in the Super Constellation Typhoon Trackers and remained lifelong friends.

Following VW-1, I was stationed at Glynco, Georgia, for shore duty, where our daughter Tina was born. I then got orders to Patuxent River as a lieutenant with VQ-4, flying as ACO and navigator on the Hercules I had fallen in love with on Guam. My job was special communications officer, setting up landline teletype circuits and broadcasts for squadron command and control of deployed aircraft, and evaluating crews' post-mission performance, under Lieutenant Commander Jim Moore as department head. Lieutenant Fil Baca and I also worked together as a team, developing mutual respect that lasted throughout our careers.

I detached from VQ-4 in 1973 for the Naval Postgraduate School at Monterey to get my bachelor's degree, so I missed the tumultuous Bill Coyne years. While at Monterey, I failed to select for lieutenant commander, along with Fil Baca, still in the squadron. That was the norm, as no senior lieutenant had yet been promoted to this critical grade. I chose to challenge this decision, mailing a letter directly to the selection board highlighting my two proven subspecialties. The next year, both Fil and I were promoted, in an extremely rare above-the-zone selection.

Fil Baca

Fil Baca was also a senior lieutenant in VQ-4, having served his first tour with the A-6 community in Whidbey Island. He along with Bob Downey, were the first lieutenants to be promoted to lieutenant commander, and earning a master's degree in Monterey and a carrier tour, he became the first TACAMO-bred commanding officer of VQ-3. After a tour heading the TACAMO program at OPNAV, he retired as captain.

The early days of TACAMO were filled with a lot of uncertainty and finding our way. Most Navy people had never heard of TACAMO, and many even in today's Navy are only slightly aware of it. The Navy had two VQ special mission squadrons in the early days, VQ-1 and VQ-2, which were electronic warfare squadrons in Atsugi, Japan, and Rota, Spain, rather large squadrons with EC-121 Super Constellations and A-3 Skywarriors. With the arrival of VQ-3 and VQ-4, uninformed Navy folks would presume these were more of the same electronic warfare type squadrons and it became common place for those wanting to appear knowledgeable to say that TACAMO meant a "Tactical and Monitoring" squadron. When we explained that TACAMO stood for "Take Charge and Move Out," there was an unbelieving and incredulous stare. It was both fun and funny in a sort of perverse way, "Fun 'n' Zest" Navy style!

Time would correct this misperception and elevate TACAMO to its justified importance and stature.

I was transferred from A-6 Intruders on Whidbey Island to VQ-4 TACAMO, an outfit of which I had never heard, in 1972, which seemed at the time to be a dumping ground for officers with no career path. The commanding officers came from VP squadrons, and most were ultimately selected for captain, but the lieutenant commanders had all failed to select for commander, and not a single lieutenant, such as myself, had ever been selected for promotion to lieutenant commander; it just wasn't in the cards. I was one of the first to fail selection for lieutenant commander, along with Bob Downey and a few others in 1973, and others failed the following years. Pilots chose to get out as soon as possible, most to pursue careers as commercial pilots, and the NFOs pursued a variety of successful alternative careers. I had been enlisted for seven years as an aviation electronics technician repairing radar altimeters in helicopters and flying as the radio operator in P-2V Neptunes and had already committed to a Navy career. Quitting the Navy was not in my genes, despite my commanding officer saying I should get out while I was young enough to pursue another career since the lieutenant commander promotion rate was a miserable five percent for "second looks."

The year after that failure was agonizingly bitter for me, as it is for all facing a similar demise. Those seeking to make a Navy career were considering other pursuits including a change in warfare specialty, transferring to other squadrons such as VP, VA (attack), VF (fighter) and the "real" VQ, anything but TACAMO! There was a definite loyalty and concern among the lieutenants with frequent talks and idea sharing on how we might make our career opportunity better. Several of us talked and sought ways to improve selection for junior officer promotion rates through telephone calls to our detailers and letters to the Bureau of Personnel, both official via the chain of command as well as by personal notes. We gradually began to see movement, not only for our efforts personally, but also with support from our commanding officers. It was not easy, but, in collaboration with other communities, such an effort had contributed to both the formal designation of NFOs, formerly Naval Aviation Observers, with their own unique wings and a path to command that had been formerly denied them. A lot of the junior officers were beginning to believe a defined career pattern for TACAMO might emerge, and a certain camaraderie blossomed and gained momentum among them; there was more than just Happy Hour to look forward to and the feeling was good. Maybe there was some good brewing in this mix. Morale seemed to be on the rise as Bill Coyne took the helm.

The Operations Control center in the hangar office spaces came under my purview. I was scheduled to go out on a navigation training mission and I knew in advance the results of the lieutenant commander promotion selection board, my dreaded and final "second look," would be coming out that afternoon and we weren't scheduled to return to home plate until later that night. I asked Denny Arneson, a good friend, to watch for the message and my name and, if selected, to send me a message announcing the good news. If I had not been selected, he was to send nothing. Our flight path took us south along the East Coast to the Caribbean and then northeast along the edge of the Bermuda triangle. We stopped in Bermuda, refueled, made a run on the Exchange for stereo components, trinkets, Mateus wine, and some goodies for the trip back to home plate, taking off for home early in the afternoon.

After a few hours, I had not received the message announcing the selection board results and I started justifying why: maybe Denny hadn't been able to get through; maybe the list was postponed; maybe communications were interrupted. I asked the radiomen to check and recheck and still nothing. Instant depression. I told my student to just maintain course until landfall and, if he needed me, to send for me. I started to feel very depressed that I had failed the final opportunity to select for lieutenant commander. We continued on, landed late in the evening and pulled into the parking spot by the hangar to wait for customs. I was in no mood for questions from anybody, particularly from a small, pompous, inquisitive, arrogant, nasty, offensive United States Customs agent seemingly devoid of any semblance of genteel ways or decorum.

Whenever our aircraft returned from out-of-country, customs agents came aboard to look at our customs declaration forms and sign off on those who are cleared. We had two U.S. Customs agents come aboard that evening, which was highly unusual. The lead agent took my form and asked me if that was all I had to declare and I responded in the affirmative. Then he challenged me again and asked what "else" I had brought back from Bermuda. He asked me more than once if that was all that I had to declare and I looked at their customs form again and announced that I was in no mood for this harassment! "A case of Mateus is all I have to claim!"

Then he asked me again "Are you sure?" I told him I was absolutely sure, whereupon he accused me in so many words of lying. At that point, Bill Coyne, the Exec (executive officer), came aboard and asked what was going on. He asked me in no uncertain terms if my customs forms were accurate and I told him unequivocally yes! Then he grabbed my arm and said I had to calm down before I got in real trouble. I demanded he get his hands off my arm!

My anger meter was pegged in the danger zone. Assault upon a superior officer was in the making. The whole crew was wide-eyed in amazement, although I suspect that at least some had an inkling of what was going on. Suddenly, my bride appeared on the plane followed by Bruce Cloud, my commanding officer. I was so blind with rage that I didn't see what my bride was holding—gold lieutenant commander shoulder boards! It took a few seconds for my "hard drive" to compute and compile until this became one of those Significant Emotional Experiences you learn about in Aviation Safety School. I was selected for promotion! The whole crew applauded and whooped and yelled. I was in a daze! I hugged my bride, the executive officer, the commanding officer, the customs agent. I exited the plane to find a lot of squadron friends outside waiting for me. What exhilaration, thrill and happiness! VQ-4 had produced a lieutenant commander! TACAMO had arrived! We all went to my house and had a grand pre-wetting down party!

Bob Downey, though no longer in the squadron, also got picked up on the same board, also as a "second look." The squadron had finally promoted two lieutenants! I subsequently received orders to the Naval Postgraduate School at Monterey, California. My career seemed to be back on track after only a minor speedbump.

Ed Hampshire

Ed Hampshire was a senior lieutenant in VQ-4, having served as a flight instructor in the Training Command after earning his pilot's wings. Like Bob Downey and Fil Baca, after Monterey he took a carrier tour as communications officer, then became executive officer of VQ-4 under Bob Downey, then commanding officer. After his command tour, he took the helm of the TACAMO program office at the Naval Air Systems command before retiring as a captain.

My story of how I decided to stay in TACAMO is a fairly simple, evolutionary and uncomplicated tale. I can't point to any big "Ah Ha!" moment. I just did my job as well as I could and waited to see how the Navy repaid me

How I initially chose VQ-4 in the 1970s was a bit round-about and, like others found, shrouded in secrecy, or more likely ignorance, of its then-new mission, but that choice determined what my future in the Navy would look like, so I guess I should start at the beginning.

I was one of the very few student pilots who was married during flight school and that shaped my decisions, because I had another person to whom I was accountable, not just myself. I was a very good pilot and always on the "Captain's List" for excellence. My flight grades determined my choice of pipeline to follow; mine were high enough that I could freely choose among helicopters, multi-engine, or jets, rather than getting what was left over. I chose multi-engine aircraft just because it seemed to be the safest of the three: helicopters crash with distressing regularity, especially in a warzone, and jets get shot down or crash on the carrier. I didn't want to make Sherry a widow while we were still newlyweds. Sherry and I talked about this decision at some length and she emphasized I should choose what I wanted to fly. She didn't want me to be disappointed in my choice later if I chose because of her.

There was no hesitation or regret on my decision and I enjoyed every moment of my thousands of hours flying the Hercules. A little later in my flying career, I always had a very small thought in the back of my head about what my flying career would have looked like had I gone jets. I might have been killed, like 14 out of 19 of my flight school class, shot down or crashing in Vietnam. A seed of survivor's guilt would then take root when I thought about not taking "my turn in the barrel" as they did. I never mentioned this to Sherry because I didn't want her to feel responsible for any regret I might have for taking a different path. This is how it all played out in real life.

As you can see from the attrition of my flight school class, the Navy was losing pilots like crazy in Vietnam. They were trying to keep their seasoned and experienced pilots in the war so they selected several of us newly-designated aviators to be sent back to the training command as "plow-back" flight instructors. This allowed the Navy to keep its seasoned pilots in combat, rather than rotate them to shore duty in the training squadrons. I often wished I could have gone to an operational squadron right after receiving my wings to relieve one of those seasoned pilots to come back as an instructor in my stead, rather than their staying in combat. During this time, I was Lew McIntyre's instrument instructor in T-28s before he transferred to the NFO pipeline. He was later to be my navigator and ACO and we came to share a common love for TACAMO throughout our Navy careers and beyond.

When I finished my tour as an instructor pilot, I was pretty much guaranteed my first choice of duty. I was offered three assignments that would have been "in country" in the Vietnam combat zone with the resulting tax-free pay and possible early promotion. All three were one-year tours of duty: light attack squadron VAL-4 flying OV-10A Broncos; a secret unit called the Trails, Roads, Interdiction, Multi-sensor squadron performing low-level night attack in very highly modified P-2H Neptune aircraft; and the highly classified "Ghost" squadron (VO-67) flying modified P-2E Neptunes dropping sensors along the Ho Chi Minh trail. Bill Harsanyi, who went on to TACAMO and later became a commanding officer of VQ-3, was shot down in VO-67 but parachuted out and survived. The squadron was decommissioned shortly thereafter due to heavy losses.

I was also offered two different assignments with shore-based patrol squadrons flying P-2Vs or the then-new P-3 Orion, or carrier-based anti-submarine squadrons flying S-2 Trackers, deploying for only six months in the Vietnam combat area.

Finally, almost as an afterthought, I was also offered a tour in another ultra-secret squadron, VQ-4 flying EC-130s, stationed at Naval Air

Station Patuxent River, Maryland. My detailer couldn't tell me anything about this squadron except where it was stationed and what aircraft it flew. This squadron had the highest national priority for people as it was expanding in size. This really might be "an offer I couldn't refuse" as he looked into the requirements for pilots needed in this squadron. The squadron was about to run short of pilots since standing up in 1968, with the initial cadre either leaving or being involuntarily extended. They needed pilots like me with over 1,000 hours who could be upgraded quickly to aircraft commander to replace them. This squadron sounded like a definite possibility because of the aircraft it flew and the possibility of becoming an aircraft commander in about a year.

I took my T-28 cross-country flight to Patuxent River one weekend to check this out. I contacted the squadron and told the Exec that it looked like I might be receiving orders to VQ-4 and would they consider a visit with a tour of the squadron and aircraft for me? I was met by Lieutenant Joe Slattery and shown around the squadron, the base, and the local area including a Happy Hour at the Roost Restaurant. The real squadron mission was never mentioned because I wasn't cleared for it. Joe was a furloughed Pan American airline pilot who came back on active duty for a couple of years until the airline could call him back to work. He was a great teller of sea stories and loved the squadron. I really liked what I saw that weekend so the decision to accept those orders was pretty exciting. Maybe Joe was just recruiting his own relief so he could go back to work for the airline but, at any rate, he sold me. The rest, as they say, is history.

I received orders to VQ-4 via the U.S. Air Force C-130 school at Little Rock Air Force Base, Arkansas, assigned to the 4442nd Combat Crew Training Wing as a student aircraft commander learning to fly the C-130 from the left seat, not the right seat as a co-pilot. Wait a minute, did I just say 4442nd Combat Crew Training Wing? What does this VQ-4 squadron really do anyway, that I have to go to "Combat Crew" training, and why do I need to go through explosive decompression training in an altitude chamber to fly this EC-130? What did I get myself into? I won't even have anything to shoot back with if someone shoots at me. To deepen this mystery, the Air Force C-130 "gods" had never even heard of an EC-130Q. Oh well, my bed was already made for me in VQ-4, so I might as well enjoy the ride wherever it might take me. And oh, by the way, who knew the Air Force had so many Combat Crew Training Wings? I was assigned to the 4442nd one. This U.S. Air Force must be really big!

I arrived in VQ-4 and about one year later I was an aircraft commander with my own Crew Seven. Also on Crew Seven were Lew McIntyre, who was my navigator, and Chuck Fitchet, another "True Believer" who later became commanding officer of VQ-3. What a great time that was! How could anyone have a better flying tour? The dedication of the flight crews was remarkable. We had a very high priority mission to do and we worked tirelessly to make sure we did it, and we had fun too. That was one real key to my continuing in the TACAMO mission, the pure fun. As one of the commanding officers said, "If you're not having fun doing it, then you aren't doing it right." And I was, at least 90 percent of the time. The hardest part was being gone for so many holidays and special family occasions. I went one year with being deployed for every possible holiday in the year and every family birthday or anniversary too. That's why they call it sea duty!

My first billet in the squadron was Avionics Division Officer. It was here I learned what a poorly engineered and integrated mission system we had in the EC-130. Even the documentation in the technical publications was terrible. If it weren't for the onsite technical representatives from Collins Radio and Lockheed Aircraft, the squadron would have failed to meet its mission tasking many times. The conventional wisdom was that TACAMO and the EC-130 was a temporary solution to a survivable communications system that would be built around land-based Extremely Low Frequency sites and space-based blue-green lasers. The Navy didn't want to spend a lot of money on a temporary solution. What do you mean, temporary? Nobody told me that when I accepted orders to VQ-4. I just found it hard to really believe this mission was just all temporary. It was easier to believe the reason for the poor documentation and engineering/integration was that the lead systems command for the TACAMO Project was Naval Electronics Systems Command, the agency which built communications systems, rather than the Naval Aviation Systems Command, colloquially called NAVAIR, whose main business was integrating electronic systems into aircraft. The haphazard way our TACAMO aircraft were put together would ultimately influence my efforts to change this throughout my navy career, as I will relate.

I was also assigned to fly many of the development/test flights on the TACAMO IVB system out of Addison Field, Texas, where Collins Radio was doing its integration and flight tests. I believe I have the dubious distinction of losing the first TACAMO IVB five-mile-long trailing wire antenna and drogue in an orbit due to "yo-yo." Yo-yo is a vertical oscillation of the drogue that eventually breaks the wire. This problem was not understood until Dr. Lawton from Cornell Aeronautical Lab instrumented a drogue to find out. The old TACAMO III wire was a quarter inch in diameter and the only way you could lose one was to have it ice up so much the weight exceeded the tensile strength of the wire. The much smaller TACAMO IVB wire was much lighter per surface area than the old wire and generated enough lift to make "flying" easier for the same relative wind over the wire, initiating the yo-yo maneuver leading to wire breakage. The solution was to keep the wire stalled in the orbit by varying the bank angle of the aircraft.

We learned many other significant, but unanticipated, things during the TACAMO IVB development flights. This system provided a very high-speed extension of the long trailing wire antenna, better than a mile per minute, with attendant high rotation speed of the reel assembly. We learned the hard way, though not as hard a lesson as it could have been, that the spinning reel assembly acted as a very powerful gyroscope that resisted banking turns during extension, generating a torque-induced precession force powerful enough to stretch or even break the mounting bolts holding it to the deck. That precession force was also strong enough to pitch the nose of the aircraft up toward a stall, or down into a steep dive, depending on the bank angle direction. That was one scary flight when we discovered this. We could have lost the aircraft had things not gone our way. This was replicated a few years later when VQ-3 suffered a severe overspeed due to reel failure and loss of control; had they turned the aircraft, the reel assembly might have been ripped out of the floorboards by precession forces. More experimentation gave us the lesson learned: don't start to orbit until the wires are out.

The TACAMO IVB system had some real improvements to the engineering/integration over the TACAMO III system, much more power, with a better antenna and signal processing. Collins Radio was great at building electronics and radios, but aircraft integration was a different ball game, a game in which they were relative newcomers. But wait, was the Navy really spending a lot more money on TACAMO for a new communications system in spite of its "temporary" mission? I saw the first hint the Navy would keep the TACAMO mission going into the foreseeable future.

My next billet in the squadron was Personnel Officer, maintaining the service records for all squadron personnel under the Administrative Department. While in this billet, we established a Personnel Reliability Program, like that used for personnel handling nuclear weapons, to ensure the squadron only received personnel of the highest caliber to fill aircrew and key positions in the squadron. This was a labor-intensive and expensive program for the Navy to implement, giving close scrutiny to possible candidates for the squadron. We had priority one manning to keep the squadron as close to 100 percent as was possible. This was at a time when most Navy units were manned at 65 to 70 percent so this was a big deal. I thought to myself, "Why would the Navy expend this much manpower on a 'temporary' unit? There may be a future in this TACAMO mission after all." I decided to just keep watching to see how many valuable resources the Navy would commit to keep the "interim" TACAMO mission going. What alternative did the Navy have to TACAMO? None!

My next billet in the squadron was as Assistant Operations Officer. This was a great billet, very rewarding being able to affect change with ideas that would help improve our operational survivability and efficiency. Another benefit of this job was that I was able to schedule my crew's itinerary on our two-week deployments. I could finally see the "big picture" of how we fit into the strategic communications networks and the command and control of our nation's nuclear forces. The Extremely Low Frequency system was off to a very slow start and the blue-green laser remained elusive. I left the Operations Department with a positive outlook for the future of TACAMO.

The last billet I had in VQ-4 was my most enjoyable and the most fun as a pilot. I was designated as the Naval Air Training and Operating Procedures Standardization (NATOPS) Officer and Pilot Evaluator; I was responsible for certifying each pilot for their position. I had been a Pilot Instructor for more than a year and this job seemed like a dream job to me. I was also in charge of, and responsible for, the EC-130 NATOPS Flight Manual, the bible for flying the aircraft. However, ours was basically a knock-off of the U.S. Air Force "Dash One" Flight Manual Tech Order for the C-130E, only approximating the performance of our EC-130s and with different engines. The notes at the bottom of the charts even referred to the Air Force "Dash One" Tech Order. We were trying to squeeze every minute of flight time out of our EC-130s, in case we were extended in flight to Prudent Limit of Endurance, so it would have been nice to have actual performance charts for our aircraft. When we were using small civilian airports with shorter runways for random basing, it would have been nice to have actual take-off and landing performance charts for our aircraft at the weights at which we routinely operated. After several attempts to get our own flight manual from NAVAIR, we finally succeeded by demonstrating how our old manuals could lead to a loss of an aircraft and crew, irreplaceable national strategic assets. We then had actual flight tests run with our EC-130s and a major review and change to the old flight manual. The Navy finally spent the money required for TACAMO to have an accurate NATOPS Flight Manual for our EC-130s. It proved to be a major revision, good for our series of EC-130Gs and Qs. The new flight manual reinforced my growing belief the Navy would keep the TACAMO mission going into the foreseeable future. What alternative did the Navy really have available to phase out TACAMO in 1974? None.

While I was NATOPS Officer, we started to get deliveries of the TACAMO IVB aircraft. I developed the required transition training and qualifying of each TACAMO III crew before that crew could take a mission in the new configuration. The NATOPS evaluators for each crew position would develop their transition criteria and we would fly with each crew for five flights out of Bermuda (better weather).

The NATOPS crew took the first production TACAMO IVB aircraft to Bermuda for 30 days. The squadron would then rotate TACAMO III crews through Bermuda to fly with us for training and qualification during the required number of flights. It turned out the whole NATOPS crew exceeded the allowable flight time for a month doing this transition training, but we didn't realize it until later and had to stop flying for about a week.

I also took the aircraft to the Pacific for the first-ever TACAMO IVB transmission there.

In mid-1973, I had served my obligated service to the Navy and I was tempted to get out and go fly for the airlines as many of my contemporaries had. But I was still having fun, so I decided to complete my three-year tour in VQ-4 and, ultimately, I was extended through March 1975 for pilot experience continuity. My detailer and I decided on the Naval Postgraduate School at Monterey for my master's degree as my next duty assignment. I was a prime candidate with an electrical engineering undergraduate degree. Could it be that the Navy believed in me enough now that it was going to invest more time and money into my further education? Perhaps I really did have a future in the Navy after all. Maybe a tour in TACAMO wasn't a "kiss of death" as I had heard many times in the squadron. Besides myself, there were also several other officers from VQ-4 who had received orders to Monterey, including my perennial sidekick, Lew McIntyre, Fil Baca, Dan Lashbrook, Denny Arneson and Al Shuff. The Navy was certainly investing in so many TACAMO officers going to Postgraduate School.

I thought back to my time spent as the Avionics Division Officer and saw the mess of poorly engineered, integrated, and documented mission systems in the EC-130. I therefore chose to go into the communications engineering curriculum, electronic engineering with a communications technology design emphasis. I hoped someday, with those qualifications, to be in a position to exert a positive influence on the design of TACAMO systems, making the lives of the sailors in the squadrons better and the systems more reliable. After all, I fully expected the TACAMO mission to be around long enough to make that contribution.

Mike Davidson

Mike Davidson was a junior officer in VQ-4 who initially intended to leave the Navy after his obligated service. But the fates had other things in mind for him, a tour with the Bureau of Naval Personnel, and ultimately commanding officer of VQ-3 shepherding the transition from the EC-130 to the E-6. The actual transition, originally scheduled to be under his watch, was to occur under his executive officer Vern Lochausen's tour. He went on to become Commander of the Joint Interoperability Test Command at Fort Huachuca, where he retired as a captain.

The Selective Service System instituted a draft lottery around 1970 to call to service men born between 1944 and 1950. My birth date came up, lottery number 151. With a number lower than the mid-point and West Virginia having the highest percent of Vietnam casualties, I planned on serving, but not on the ground. The Navy recruiters had been to my liberal arts college several times but hid under one of the staircases to keep a low profile from the various campus protest groups. I passed the aptitude testing and went to Naval Air Station Willow Grove for a weekend flight physical and swearing-in. I gave my draft board the sad news the following Monday—I was a member of the U.S. Naval Reserves.

In September 1971, I reported in to "Poopieville" in the old clapboard barracks area of Naval Air Station Pensacola. Eighteen months later, I earned my wings as a naval aviator with verbal orders to VQ-1 on Guam. Not my first choice at all. I wanted multi-engine aircraft time to prep for an airline career, but also wanted to be close to my wife's family and my own in the eastern U.S.. One of my advanced flight training instructors had been in VQ-3 on Guam but wouldn't tell me anything about the mission. He suggested I look into VQ-4 at Patuxent River. A friend finishing at the same time had verbal orders to VQ-4 but wanted to fly P-3s, so we agreed to a swap. The detailer bought into it and I was headed east via Little Rock Air Force Base to master the EC-130 Hercules, affectionately known as the "Herc."

VQ-4 proved challenging for a first-tour aviator. I was Commander Bruce Cloud's Public Affairs Officer, and his Exec, Commander Bill Coyne, wanted the skipper's picture in every weekly edition of the base newspaper. Also, the *Hometown News* program kept a steady stream of VQ-4 sailors at my desk. The Bermuda detachment was standing up and our Journalist 1/c spent time getting to know that place and writing stories about the crews' adventures.

I then was assigned to the Safety Department, spending six weeks at Aviation Safety School in Monterey, California, learning how to investigate accidents and run a good squadron safety program, for the fliers and ground folks alike.

My last VQ-4 job was the Quality Assurance Officer. This position was one of several situations which had me leaning toward an airline career; I was still a reserve officer and ambivalent toward the Navy. I was offered a choice of flight training, or the Bureau of Personnel, then still located in Arlington, Virginia, and a stone's throw from the Pentagon. I asked both the commanding and executive officers for advice. The Exec suggested going back to flight school as an instructor, breaking out as number one and getting my performance record on track again. My commanding officer saw things differently. He advised going to the Bureau, getting to know the Navy from a headquarters position and learning the "system." Plus, working the detailer for my next assignment would be a piece of cake. The Bureau assignment offered a location close to my home and my soon-to-be former spouse and our son. So, off to Arlington and the Bureau.

Lew McIntyre

I came to VQ-4 in 1972, having earned my NFO wings after graduating from the Naval Academy. After VQ-4, I got my master's degree from Monterey, along with Fil Baca, Ed Hampshire and Bob Downey, then took a tour with the Operational Test and Evaluation Force. I followed the lead of those three, our first command selectees, taking a carrier tour with Carrier Group One. I did not get a command tour, but went on to the National Emergency Airborne Command Post and the Joint Strategic Target Planning Staff at Offutt AFB, where I retired as a commander in 1990. I returned to TACAMO as a contractor, supporting the community as an engineer until 2020.

I entered the Naval Reserve as an airman recruit in April 1965, a few weeks after my 17th birthday while still a junior in high school. I came by that decision because the money my father made as a cab driver, even with generous scholarships, was not likely to cover college costs. The Naval Air Reserve offered an attractive program called "2×6," two years of drilling reserve, one weekend drill a month and summer active duty periods for reserve boot camp and "A" school technical training, then two years of active duty beginning as a third class petty officer, followed by two years of reserve duty. This was compatible with my graduating from high school if I weren't called up for the Vietnam War then heating up. I would be able to start college on the GI Bill just two years behind my contemporaries with two years' technical training and experience, preparing me for an engineering curriculum. I scored quite respectably on my aptitude tests and my reserve unit, Air Wing Staff-67 at Naval Air Station Atlanta, got me to sign up for several officer programs. I went to boot camp at Naval Air Station Olathe, Kansas (Yes, there was one!), during my summer break and, when I returned, I had a letter from the Bureau of Personnel stating that, if I was interested in attending the Naval Academy, to travel to Charleston, South Carolina, for my physical exam. Had I signed up for that too? Yes, I had indeed, one of the many things I signed that first weekend after swearing in. The Reserves more than adequately solved my college problems and gave me many fun weekends in Atlanta during my senior year.

I graduated from the U.S. Naval Academy with the class of 1970 and got my wings as an NFO in 1972, standing second in the class and getting married along the way. I came to TACAMO by an unusual route, from the Basic Jet Navigation pipeline, the source for A-6s and EA-6s, in the early 1970s, the premier communities for NFOs. However, as was typical of the Vietnam War drawdown, there was only one A-6 seat available and the number one guy got it. I had a choice of RA-5C Vigilantes or something called "VQ-4." As I had worked with a commander who had some unpleasant experiences in the RA-5C "Ensign Eater," I opted for VQ-4. The instructor coaching us on our pick opined that "they must have stood up an East Coast Replacement Air Group (RAG) for VQ-2 in Rota, Spain. They fly A-3s and do cool spook stuff." Kind of reminiscent of what others were told. TACAMO was an unknown entity.

The en route training included communications school in Newport, Rhode Island, and in one of the course books I found a picture of an EC-130 making a Jet-Assisted Takeoff, indicating it was a TACAMO bird attached to VQ-4. It turned out to be EC-130G 151891, in which I was to have my first and last TACAMO flights, and still survives today in the museum at Pensacola. Hmm, so they had C-130s; I wondered what for. I was soon to find out, because VQ-4 was not the VQ-2 RAG; they had no A-3s, but they had lots of EC-130s, all equipped with sextants for celestial navigation. Did I mention that Basic Jet Navigation did not include celestial navigation in the curriculum? It turned out I and two other "nuggets" had been in the same pipeline. I, at least, had taken shipboard celestial navigation at the Academy and had kept my *Dutton's Navigation and Piloting*. I held school call with the others to go over the theory of celestial navigation, how to determine the geographical position of a star, how to precompute a fix, and how to figure out where you were. Interestingly, all three of us later became navigation instructors or evaluators!

Navigation became one of my flying passions, though it was, I think, one of the harder jobs in the aircraft. It began on the day before the flight, an hour spent laying out the preflight for a 10-hour flight. During the overwater part of flight, often six or eight hours from "feet wet" (going oceanic) to "feet dry" (landfall), the navigator had the "nav," usually without relief; overland, the pilots had the nav. There was something very satisfying, however, telling the pilot that he was at his landfall waypoint, the needles coming to attention pointing directly ahead, and the mechanical distance indicators clicking up to within a mile or so of where you thought you were. This was especially satisfying after a morning launch from Lajes in the Azores back to the U.S., making landfall at St. John's, Newfoundland, after eight hours of very rudimentary navigation: Sun Line of Position (SLOP) for a speed line, and Pressure Line of Position (PLOP) for a course line. We called it "slopping and plopping." I later used that as navigator's pre-check for my students.

I was assigned to Crew Seven under Ed Hampshire, my old instrument instructor from T-28s, with the only other "ring-knocker" in the squadron, my classmate Chuck Fitchet. We had some serious fun on that crew. Ed introduced me to Heineken beer, colloquially known as "Green Heinies," in Lajes. And there were some stories about Chuck Fitchet, our third pilot Fernando Anduze, and me, along with an Air Force colonel and a fire extinguisher in Mildenhall that are best left unsaid!

My initial duties were as Communications Division Officer, responsible for about 30 radiomen. I worked under Fil Baca, my assistant department head, who became a lifelong friend and mentor, another of the "True Believers." Here, I came to grasp the TACAMO mission, carefully documented in several classified safes, and a lot of the supporting ground communications infrastructure that terminated in our duty office in a chattering teletype machine. It was through this crude but effective network that we successfully maintained 100 percent coverage, based mainly on voice over high frequency and teletype broadcast over a first-generation satellite, the Lincoln Labs Experimental Satellite, LES-6. I qualified as ACO and was tasked to solve a problem with the satellite system we had on board the aircraft. I worked closely with Wendell and Jack Metcalf, and Dudley Stewart, in the Naval Electronics Systems Test and Engineering Facility vans behind the hangar, to solve that problem, forming a lifelong friendship with all three.

I was reassigned to the maintenance department as Avionics Branch Officer under Ed Hampshire, my division officer, to help bring in the TACAMO IVB system, a huge improvement over its TACAMO III predecessor: a tenfold increase in power and sophisticated signal processing made the downlink much more robust. It also added a second short wire for better efficiency and an improved long wire reel. Because of the frequency, wavelengths for the downlink required deploying between three to five miles of long wire, and about a mile of the short wire, and getting those wires deployed quickly was critical. My shop "swing shift" supervisor was Aviation Electronics Technician Jim Amsden, a veteran of the '890 crash, and someone with whom I was to work with 40 years later at NAVAIR.

My tour was not without heartache and setbacks. My Pensacola marriage fell apart after only a few years and I had a professional setback in the squadron while Bill Coyne was skipper. I was responsible for all communications material, the largest such account in naval aviation and a position of great responsibility. We had had several incidents in which this material was not handled properly and I put out a memo saying that the next ACO to have a communications material incident would lose his driver's license. As fate would have it, it was to be me. Bill Coyne gave me the opportunity to throw my communications supervisor, Radioman First Class Denny Reed, "under the bus" for the incident, perhaps testing me to see if I would try to avoid the responsibility. This I refused to do, though I knew it meant losing my ACO designation, just so recently earned, and probably the end of my career. I was reassigned as Navigation Officer, the lowest status job in the squadron. Coming coincident with my pending divorce, I spent a few weeks feeling acutely sorry for myself.

But if I was to end my career as a navigator, I would at least end it well. Hewlett-Packard had just brought out a new programmable calculator that allowed you to store a complex series of key strokes on a magnetic strip, a hand-held computer. I spent several weeks determining the math for calculating a star shot. It basically involved just determining the range and bearing from where you thought you were to the point of the earth directly below the star, its geographical position. With that done I cranked in the keystrokes, recorded them, and I had an automated celestial precomputation program.

Celestial navigation usually involved precomputing three stars and measuring their elevation with the sextant. Manual precomputation was so time-consuming that one could not do this more than once an hour. However, with my calculator, I had no problem doing a star-shot every 30 minutes and often did so over an eight-hour overwater navigation leg.

I found myself in the Training Department, as Navigation Training Officer, and among my first students was Vern Lochausen. At that time, it seemed every navigator had his own way of keeping a log and some procedures were well known and used by some, but not others. I decided, before I left the Navy, that I would pass on all my navigation expertise among my students. I emphasized to all of them that the "dead-reckoning" position, that location where you thought you were, was more important than any individual fix. Twenty years later, when I attended Vern's change of command as our third commodore in Tinker, he, not knowing I was in attendance, used that in his speech, on the importance of always maintaining a good dead reckoning position, not only in navigation, but in all things, where you think you are versus where you are. Apparently, I made an impact!

I captured everything I had learned into the Navigation Standard Operating Procedures, which became the guide for all navigation training. It was to be my swan song before rolling to civilian life in 1975, but two things happened that year that ended my time in limbo. In January, though I only had six months left, Bill Coyne called me into his office and asked me if I would like to be an ACO again. Of course, the answer was yes and I had the opportunity to qualify as mission commander as well. I quickly went through the syllabus and got a crew. When fitness report time came around, though I didn't rank as high as I had before, it was still a pretty good "fitrep," with no mention of the incident that should have damned my career. Then my orders to the postgraduate school at Monterey came through. My career was out of ground effect and flying again. Not trying to shift responsibility onto my enlisted communications supervisor for the incident turned out to be the best choice I could have made in a bad situation; I subsequently was to work with Denny Reed 20 years later when we were civilians.

One of the most enjoyable aspects of TACAMO was the enormous responsibility it placed on very junior people, young in years. Imagine being a mission commander, just a few years removed from college and flight training, in your early to mid-20s; you have a 15-man crew at your command, your very own multi-million-dollar Hercules at your disposal, and a vital nuclear command and control mission to perform, 3,000 miles of tenuous communications removed from any supervision of the commanding officer and department heads. It was truly a "Take Charge and Move Out" experience, akin to having one's own command. This heady responsibility was one of the deciding factors in my choice to return.

I had the pleasure, as did Fil Baca, Chuck Fitchet, Ed Hampshire, Mike Davidson, Vern Lochausen, and Andy Riddile, to serve under Bill Coyne through his turbulent tour as commanding officer, a watershed for TACAMO. Before him, we were kind of a "McHale's Navy" outfit, a backwater allowed pretty much to do our thing. Bill brought new standards of professionalism to the squadron and, as you can expect, not everyone was happy with the changes.

Vern Lochausen

Vern Lochausen was a California boy who became a junior officer in VQ-4 in 1974, and my first navigation student in my new role as navigation instructor. Vern had a tour as an NROTC instructor and three squadron tours, rising to command VQ-3 through the initial operations of the E-6. He became the third commodore of Strategic Communications Wing One, then retired as a captain. He continued to support the community as a senior contractor to the present, and is very active in the TACAMO Community Veterans' Association.

To understand my story about being a "True Believer," it is first necessary to understand my state upon entering the community in the summer of 1974.

Born in Los Angeles County in a then rural farming and dairy community, I discovered at age 10 that my dad had been a flight engineer on B-17 Flying Fortresses in World War II. He didn't share as much about the war as he did about airplanes. Together we built a plastic model of a B-17 from a kit, and then we made a trip to the Los Angeles County Museum for my birthday that year. The aviation "hook" was thereby set. Dad and his father were in the trucking business as small business owners, the latter since 1924 and Dad joining him after the war in 1946. So, there was another hook set, big rig trucks. However, as I was ready for junior high, we moved from Los Angeles to Milton, Florida, primarily to escape the rapidly increasing growth and stressful tempo of Southern California.

Living under one of the aerobatic areas used by Naval Air Station Whiting Field, we often sat on our Florida patio and watched the T-28s performing all the classic maneuvers. The "hook" was really set then. In my early high school years, my first mentor entered my life. Lieutenant Bill Stanley was an instructor pilot in T-28s and I knew him from church and two fraternal organizations to which he had introduced me, Toastmasters and Naval Aviation. From Hannibal, Missouri, Bill answered my question about how I get to "Fly Navy" by saying, "Get the grades and the activities and get that Navy scholarship, same as I did to escape my small town." And it happened that way, at not-so-nearby Ole Miss (University of Mississippi) where this southern California kid was a bit out of place.

Excelling at Ole Miss as battalion commander, like at Milton High, and as class officer and club president in Advanced Studies in Aerodynamics, I won those orders to Aviation Indoctrination at Pensacola. Within a month the Naval Aviation Medical Institute "NAMI Whammy" hit. Vietnam was over. The pilot pipeline opening was narrowing and I had "excessive refractive vision errors." "Two choices for you, young man," my advisor said, "Surface Warfare Officer School or Naval Flight Officer." Within a few days, I decided I could do the latter; if I didn't have the stick, I would at least be flying. On to Training Squadrons 1, 10 and 29, getting my first choice at each. At Training Squadron 10 graduation, I coined our class moto: "NFOs do it better in the back seat."

At Training Squadron 29 I met my next two mentors, Lieutenants Bill Wilt and Norm Tindall, both of whom would be my VQ squadron mates in the future. Both were pilots, but these guys actually knew navigation and they talked about how cool it would be to fly the oceans in the Herc. Therefore, I chose VQ-4 TACAMO, like everyone before me, without knowing what that phrase stood for, nor the mission.

I checked in at Naval Air Station Patuxent River, otherwise known as "Pax River," when there was not even a McDonalds and the only grocery was an old A&P Market. My skipper was Bill Coyne. A steely-eyed pilot with a booming voice and forceful leadership style to match, he was, in a word, the epitome of the hard-driving but gentlemanly "Colonel Frank Savage" of *Twelve O'clock High* fame. He encouraged me to give it my all and get qualified fast, because something called 100 percent airborne coverage was coming, a vital mission. Briefly, I was the senior

"Bull Ensign" for a few days until a slightly more senior guy checked in and I had to surrender the flag and oversized bars to him. My first encounter with the junior officers in the Shadow Squadron was a salty Lieutenant Lew McIntyre who ran the Navigation Office. He issued me a pocket watch in a wooden box and a navigation bag full of stuff, and said, "Now, Ensign, we will do some dry swims before you see the flight line." What a pain that was! I just wanted to go fly. "Fix, dead reckoning ahead, alter heading, that is your routine to follow and the rest will come along as you work with it," he said. He had me plan a mission, laying it out on a large map, then he gave me pieces of paper with time, course, speed and fix information to plot and log till I arrived at destination. If I stayed within 10 miles of the real track, which he had on another chart, I passed and could go fly.

Finally, the day came when I was on the actual flight schedule for a pre-deployment shakedown flight just off the coast. Returning from that short familiarization hop, I was riding high until I charged up the ladder well on the commanding officer's side of the hangar from Maintenance Control to check in with my department head. Then it happened: the skipper "had my ass."

"Ensign, did you guys transmit VLF while you were out there?" Proudly, I proclaimed, "Yes, sir! And it was awesome to orbit and all." He quickly replied, "You guys probably cost me my fourth stripe! Didn't you know a Russian AGI was in port in Baltimore? Go tell your mission commander to get up to my office right now!" As I ran back down to Maintenance Control, I was thinking, "My career is toast and what's an AGI?" It was an intelligence collection ship. So, I learned you need to check out all the conditions and mission parameters before you go flying; Bill Coyne Lesson #1. Somehow, I survived that encounter and learned to arrive at the weekly All Officers Meeting early enough to get a standing place along the wall, so the lieutenants would sit or stand in front of you and insulate you from the "Skipper's Wrath." Every meeting I learned more as the more flippant officers were taken to task for not thinking or not acting. More Bill Coyne Lessons learned. That 100 percent stuff was not intuitive and so I filled my little green gouge book with what to do and what to not do. Vicarious learning beats an ass-chewing any day. The first law of thermodynamics, learned at Ole Miss as a math/physics major, also applied to All Officer Meetings: if the heat is on you, it is not on me.

By the time I had been a lieutenant (junior grade) for less than a year, I was a mission commander, leading a crew around the Atlantic on independent operations. I inherited New Yorker Lieutenant Frank "Godfather" Caruso's well-trained Crew Ten, "The Godfather's Men." Fortunately, he taught me all that pilot stuff, requiring me to sit every seat and learn what each crewman did. As the navigator, I was taking a turn in the right seat, making radio calls and air reports, and running the checklists from the navigator's seat. I learned a lot of flight deck stuff from master flight engineer T. K. Klosterman, including how to run the radar. Flying as an NFO turned out to be pretty dang cool. With a great series of radiomen, techs, and reel operators, I quickly learned all about the mission, communications, hydraulics and VLF trailing wire operations, as well as maintenance; our crews were self-supporting, with all aviation maintenance rates represented. We could, and often did, change engines and propellers while deployed. Once Skipper Coyne had guided us through standing back up to 100 percent, establishing an alert on Bermuda, and standby alert at Pax, he brought us into the fold of the administrative side of the Navy. We stood our first administrative and material inspection. Commander Tactical Support Wing One, our new wing command, was all over us for few days. I vividly recall the All-Hands field days and the pre-personnel inspections, not to mention getting our airplanes and office stuff set up, reviewed by the Head Shed, and ready for inspection. In the end, VQ-4 did very well on this endeavor.

Looking back on it after more than four decades, I now see that the squadron and the community had finally arrived! Bill Coyne had scared the hell out of the misfits and lazy non-performers. He had set and enforced a standard, developing the procedures and rules for everything as we went along. He embraced good ideas and dismissed bad ones. He had charmed some of his department heads, chastised others, and endeared himself to some of the wives by being as open as he could about our operations. At one point, he held an evening reception for all the wives, officer and enlisted, to tell them what the squadron was about and how well we had done because of the work their husbands had done, at home and deployed "on the road." It went well until one wife said, "You mean he gets paid extra to go on those trips?" As they say today, "Too much information."

One thing Bill Coyne had instituted that did not sit well with the crew, nor long survive his departure, was the requirement for all flight crew to wear a canary yellow "dickie" ascot inside the neck of their green flight suits. On the day of Bill Coyne's departure change of command, I was with my crew in Bermuda, on crew rest and about to assume the alert. "TK" Klosterman and I swam out to Nonsuch Island and dove down to a wooden shipwreck sitting there in shallow water. Our mission: to deep-six the offensive yellow dickies. The new commanding officer had made it known they would no longer be required. We tied them to the vertical ribs of the wreck, and, as they waved in the current, you could see the words we had written across them in black Magic Marker: "So long Sweet Ole Bill."

Virtually all the rest of Bill Coyne's procedures and processes remained, some for decades and even into the transition from the EC-130 to the E-6B. Many of these procedures he adapted from his days as a VP squadron mission commander and the rest he and his cadre of smart guys invented: Ed Hampshire taught us how to fly a two-wire orbit and Kermit Ayres created the model for deployment budgeting and expense accounting. Some folks relaxed too much and the new Exec, another commander from the VP Navy, reminded them we were on step and not looking back. For a variety of reasons, I became severely cross-threaded with him, though I maintained my professionalism throughout his tour. He was smooth, but not the pro and the gentleman leader Bill Coyne had been. I began to make my plans for my exit to shore duty, but he, by now the commanding officer, tried to have my tour extended and my order to University of Texas NROTC cancelled. With nothing to lose, I went in his office for a "serious discussion" of our mutual issues. My orders stayed intact but my detaching fitness report was not up to my usual high standards.

Bill Coyne: Commanding Officer, 1974–1975

Bill Coyne came from the patrol anti-submarine warfare community, flying P-5M seaplanes, P-2V Neptunes and P-3 Orions. He took command of VQ-4 in 1974 and established a high-standard of professionalism, which many did not appreciate at the time, and attempted to establish TACAMO as a recognized warfare specialty. This last effort failed, because no one was returning for a second tour in the community, but his vision inspired that cadre of "True Believers" to take the chance and make it happen by returning to TACAMO. From VQ-4 he went on to Naval Air Forces, Atlantic (AIRLANT), where he retired as a captain. He earned a law degree and pursued a second career as a lawyer. He actively supports the TACAMO Community Veterans Association in that capacity. Bill was inducted into the TACAMO Hall of Fame in 2015.

"Good morning, Commander. I have been advised by your detailer that you have screened for alternate command and will receive orders to Fleet Air Reconnaissance Squadron Four in Patuxent River sometime in the summer. This is a major accomplishment in your career and I am proud to be the one who gives you this news. Good luck in your new assignment."

As I was returning to my office in the "E" Ring in the Pentagon, I pondered the meaning of those words, uttered just moments ago. Little did I know at the time how those words would change my whole world as a commissioned officer and aviator in the United States Navy. While I was pleased and proud beyond words, my innate inquisitive nature led to the inevitable question, "Why an alternate command selectee?" How were these decisions made? What did I lack in my career as a warfare specialist in Anti-Submarine Warfare flying with various patrol squadrons? Could it be that the selection was made on the basis of a program fit, not on the pecking order of squadron billets, and therefore not an alternate command per se? I never found the answer to those questions. It was of no consequence because, in the end, whatever fate guided this decision, it resulted in the most gratifying tour in my Navy career: challenges met and meaningful accomplishments made by a squadron of focused, highly skilled professionals. They taught me the true meaning of dedication and professionalism.

The Special Mission (VQ) designation was also perplexing to me. I expected a squadron whose mission was primarily focused on electronic surveillance, as were the other two squadrons with that designation, VQ-1 and 2, flying EA-3s, EC-121s and EP-3s collecting electronic intelligence. If so, I surmised it was multi-engine, required experienced navigational skills, probably a communication package that was a cut above VP requirements, and required a comprehensive knowledge of associated surveillance tactics. However, my orders did not assign me to any schools in this genre.

I was mistaken. The Navy's choice to designate the TACAMO squadron as VQ could have been misdirection, just as the mission name itself; plausible, because one story ran that our aircraft were borrowed from the Marines to practice tanker tactics, referring to the orange VLF antenna drogue that nested just below the "beaver tail" under the rudder, for support of Navy multi-engine refueling. More likely, the Navy just did not want to define a new squadron designator for what was envisioned as a temporary stop-gap program.

I made no further efforts to research the TACAMO mission, nor did I receive any information from the squadron as to their mission. It was not unusual for me to react in this manner as I was one of those unique aviators who believed the Navy, specifically my detailers, knew best, so I always went with the flow. I recall that when I was ordered to the Pentagon it was to be in support of the SARS effort. I assumed this to be Search and Rescue (SAR), not far-fetched to me because of my VP background and carrier experience. It turned out that SARS stood for Selective Action Reports System, in the OP-90 Planning, Programming, Budgeting System.

After my Pentagon departure, I was off to Little Rock for training in the C-130. I took to this aircraft, a love affair to the end. This reliable platform and its stability in the orbiting maneuvers served the TACAMO mission well and positioned it as a thoroughly tested strategic asset until airframe age forced the transition to the E-6A. Training complete, I reported on board for duty. After a cordial welcoming on board, I was initially assigned as the Maintenance Officer, since I had arrived with several months overlap with the executive and commanding officers. I determined later that there are sensitivities associated with a third command selectee on board who was not assigned to a specific responsibility. Maintenance Officer seemed to be a good "stash" for me, though there were several mid-level senior Limited Duty Officers assigned to the department, such as Lieutenant Commander Don Disharoon, who were thoroughly trained and uniquely qualified for the position. I accepted this tasking without reservation, notwithstanding my desire to receive additional qualification as an ACO to have a reasonable grasp of the challenges faced by this position. That would have been a most unusual ticket for a pilot to have punched, since that is an NFO qualification.

At the time of my arrival, the squadron had been maintaining 100 percent airborne coverage for several years. This meant that 24 hours a day, seven days a week, there was always one aircraft airborne somewhere in the Atlantic area, ready to provide communications to the missile submarine force. Elaborate procedures and communications protocols and networks had evolved to provide highly reliable command and control to direct the off-going airborne aircraft to fly to Prudent Limit of Endurance, the TACAMO watchword, until the relieving aircraft or a ready duty alert replacement aircraft could launch. But 100 percent airborne coverage required a minimum number of aircraft to sustain this effort. The TACAMO program was undergoing a major modification program to the TACAMO IVB configuration and, a year earlier, the squadron had lost one airframe, though fortunately no people, when 151890 suffered a fire in flight and crash-landed on the Eastern Shore of Maryland. Even after borrowing from our sister squadron, VQ-3, which did not at that time maintain 100 percent coverage, our aircraft assets fell below the critical number required. So, not long after my arrival in the squadron, the order to stand down from 100 percent airborne coverage was issued, to facilitate transitioning the squadron to the TACAMO IVB platform.

It was a devastating event for the commanding officer, Bruce Cloud. This officer ran the 100 percent airborne operation with great skill, pride in ownership, and an unquenchable fire to prove the system. He was an avid reader, impeccable researcher, and a well-respected representative of the TACAMO program to his superiors and to several commands in Europe. The finesse of achieving a sustained continuous airborne coverage with limited aircraft and a restrictive supply pipeline was remarkable in itself; to retreat from this finesse seemed to be a step in the wrong direction. I was privy to a great deal of information from my Pentagon tour about competing programs, like Extremely Low Frequency Project *Sanguine* and the blue-green laser, and it gave me pause to consider that I might be the one overseeing the final stand-down on my watch. I can only imagine what the "one and done" junior officers were feeling at this time. Hindsight is great, but funding alternatives are difficult. I can't help but wonder what the outcome might have been had the Navy considered purchasing or borrowing aircraft to go through the Collins company's refit program without having to interrupt a well-orchestrated strategic system of 100 percent coverage. One could speculate that uncertainty about the program's future was in the decision equation.

Random flights at about 50 percent airborne coverage were now the order of the day. Crew rest at various stops was increased as each crew relinquished their aircraft to an awaiting crew and then enjoyed leisure awaiting the next crew in with an aircraft to take them home. Frequent make-up flights out of Pax River were common and provided great flexibility to Prudent Limit of Endurance limitations. While it was less stressful, the loss of focus on the absolute necessity to keep an aircraft in the air 24 hours a day had a negative effect on morale, as pride of achievement transitioned to a country club existence. Because of this change, and the fact that fewer aircraft were available to the squadron, the pressure was perceived to be lessened to meet routine scheduled flights. Cannibalization, borrowing good parts from non-flying aircraft to repair another, was in excess of 100 per month and the supply system could not meet the challenge. Flyable aircraft would come in for mandatory checks and would be stripped for parts, requiring weeks to get them flyable again. This took a great deal of effort to correct. Thanks to the Air Force, the C-130 parts found their way back into the TACAMO aircraft and I mandated that I had to specifically authorize the removal of any working part from an aircraft, eventually reducing the cannibalization rate to less than one per month. This provided the new commanding officer greater aircraft availability during the transition to the TACAMO IVB aircraft

A major turning point amid this debacle happened in October 1973, when the Arab–Israeli Yom Kippur war took a turn for the worse; Soviet intervention appeared imminent and an elevated global defense condition was declared, requiring 100 percent coverage that could not be provided by airborne assets. The crisis demanded improvisation and the answer was the TACAMO War Watch. For 12 hours before a scheduled flight, an aircraft and half the crew would bring up circuits on the ground, ready to launch if necessary. At the end of this period, the aircraft and full crew would fly an airborne mission and recover, then the other half of the crew would post the War Watch, after refueling the aircraft, for another 12 hours. Therefore, TACAMO was able to provide 100 percent communications coverage, though not airborne. As arduous as this routine was for several weeks, it did much to reverse the deteriorating morale and reminded all hands of the mission's criticality. Our ability to improvise to achieve what seemed to be the impossible was not lost on the senior Navy leadership.

Following my change of command, the squadron settled back into a reluctant, but accepted, reduced mode of operation. Various operational changes and new deployment sites enhanced TACAMO's flexibility and strategic response. The squadron's workload was greatly increased as not only VQ-4 personnel participated in the TACAMO IVB training programs, but also VQ-3 personnel, who would transition after us on Guam.

It is accepted that each commanding officer brings their own perspective and goals to the table when they assume command. Few, in my experience, have the same outlook on how to achieve their goals. Some are pure operators or technically highly capable, others have great strength in people skills, and some have unassailable belief in the mission. All have one over-riding goal, however: getting the job done safely, economically, and at the least personal cost to the men and their families. My predecessor, Bruce Cloud, because of his background and personal network with officer detailers, was the perfect spokesperson and advocate to attempt to achieve the squadron's designation as a warfare specialty, with an established path for junior officers from division officer to department head and to command, with shore duty billets providing enriching complementary experience. During his tenure, he frequently solicited help within his network and hosted visits from the detailers' offices to brief and listen to the concerns of the junior officers about their career potential in TACAMO. He faced an uphill battle, because the counterargument was that TACAMO could not be a warfare specialty until enough officers chose to return to it, while the junior officers did not want to bet their careers this would happen. Better for them to continue the "one and done," transition to a back-to-back sea duty tour with VP and leave TACAMO in their wake. However, a seed was planted, both in the Bureau and in the minds of a few officers, even though it would take about five years to come about. I also believe the efforts he made in support of his junior officers did not go without notice or effect.

As the months passed, the squadron continued its transition and routine operational schedule, as well as participating in a series of ongoing joint exercises which were to measure TACAMO's capability to achieve its perceived capabilities. These included active participation with the Air Force "Looking Glass" mission, flying the EC-135 out of Offutt Air Force Base, Nebraska. While the rumors persisted that "Looking Glass" might replace TACAMO, underlying technical issues with the EC-135 deemed this rumor would remain just that. The TACAMO IVB modification program that had so devastated our operating schedule had given us 10 times the transmit power of the EC-135, an improved dual wire high-speed antenna system, and a more robust VLF downlink. Further, the EC-135 could not perform the specialized orbit of the EC-130, which severely limited its ability to communicate with submarines. Ironically, the follow-on to the EC-130, the E-6B, would replace the EC-135 to take over the "Looking Glass" mission 25 years later.

Immediately prior to the change of command, two new events unfolded, supporting the theory that TACAMO had a major role to play in the long-term Navy strategic goals and joint force operations. The squadron was notified that it would transition from the direct administrative control of Commander, Naval Air Forces, Atlantic colloquially AIRLANT, to a newly-established intermediary, Commander, Tactical Support Wing One. In addition, the order to return to 100 percent airborne operations was issued. Both of these events were met with mixed emotions. Since its inception, VQ-4 had enjoyed an unusual autonomy free from most administrative oversight, reporting operationally to the Commander-in-Chief, U.S. Forces Atlantic (CINCLANT) as well as direct liaison with various entities in Washington. At one time, a direct line in the commanding officer's quarters connected me directly to the National Military Command Center. Adding more reporting responsibility, and the administrative oversight it entailed, was viewed by some as impairment to the squadron's efforts. Nevertheless, this change in the Navy's attitude toward TACAMO must be viewed as positive. If nothing else, TACAMO was now a part of the normal chain of command which afforded more day-to-day recognition and oversight responsibilities, especially with regards to maintenance and supply parts. TACAMO had always enjoyed a Force Activity Designator One status, the highest priority within the Navy for logistic support, but there had been no "big stick" to guarantee consistent immediate response to its needs. Tactical Support Wing One's commodore happily wielded that stick for us.

This change could also be viewed as the next step towards designation as a warfare specialty as it identified TACAMO as a squadron among squadrons. Again, fate moved its hand toward a positive outcome as the commodore was a brilliant, no-nonsense, traditional Navy officer who made it his prime objective to understand the squadron's unique circumstances and to add his capabilities to all others in ensuring the program's success. In a gesture of unusual foresight, he deferred to the operational decisions coming down directly to the squadron from CINCLANT in return for a requirement to keep him informed of any events significant to AIRLANT's responsibilities. He was VQ-4's first wing commander, and Commander, Tactical Support Wing One continued in that role until TACAMO stood up its own wing, Strategic Communications Wing One, when both squadrons relocated to Tinker Air Force Base after E-6A transition in 1992.

The order to return to 100 percent airborne coverage also engendered mixed but positive reactions. The TACAMO IVB transition was not complete. There were TACAMO III aircraft still awaiting mod and personnel to be trained. Some, but not all, TACAMO IVB crews could operate either configuration. In addition, the squadron maintained a ready alert aircraft and a standby aircraft, with crews for both, around the clock. Again, the magnificent support and understanding of the mission by CINCLANT brought about a concession that made it possible to meet the new operational plan. The much higher power and robust downlink of the TACAMO IVB system allowed VQ-4 to intersperse into the schedule a limited amount of Patuxent-to-Patuxent flights in order to accommodate crew schedules, training, and efficient aircraft utilization. This compromise was akin to a mining mission when the crew could not release some mines so they threw out the toolboxes knowing the enemy would still have to sweep the field. TACAMO was still in the air 100 percent of the time. The mismatched crew arrangement fell hard on all personnel for, during this period, some crewmembers had to make more frequent deployments, some back-to-back, and, in some cases, assume immediate ready duty status while home-based. Using the tried-and-true aircraft crew rest turnover plan was impossible, dropped early in the deployment schedule because of the mixed crew qualification. This management of aircraft modifications would be repeated many times in the next 40 years, with TACAMO Improvement Program Phases I and II, the E-6A transition, the E-6B transition, the E-6B Block I

Modification, and a number of other programs waiting in the wings as TACAMO marches toward the third decade of the 21st century.

Ultimately, the final event in my purview, modifying the alert cycle, established a pattern of operations that made strategic sense, offered a better deployment cycle for the crews, ensured better alert launch response, and created a valid counter to an adversary's threat to the East Coast of the United States.

Alerts until this time had been replacement aircraft not keyed to an immediate threat, with about an hour's response time. Crewmembers stood them in their quarters, on or off base, until called in to launch. Often, ready alert launches were delayed because a critical crew member could not arrive within the one-hour requirement. This loss of coverage was counterproductive to morale, as well as leaving a gap in response capability. Lexington Park was growing, with more traffic and crew members living further away. Placing the ready alert crew on base exacerbated the time crews were away from their home and or families. Accordingly, VQ-4 requested, and CINCLANT approved, placing the ready alert plane and crew in Bermuda. Crews would stand the ready alert during their deployment. The ready alert crew was capable of being airborne within minutes, more responsive to threats. The crew had a longer turn-around time between deployments and, when at home, they had more time for themselves and family. As in all positive improvements, not all things went smoothly. The issue of shore duty and sea duty created a deployment restriction for ground maintenance personnel needed to support the Bermuda aircraft.

One would now consider that, with successful deployment of the TACAMO IVB aircraft, the program's future within the Navy's long-range planning was more secure. Ed Hampshire, a mid-level lieutenant mission commander, deployed a TACAMO IVB aircraft to the Eastern Pacific area which went off flawlessly, appraised by the operational commanders to be a major accomplishment of the system's capability. Ed would later return to TACAMO by choice, command a TACAMO squadron, be promoted to captain, and serve as the system's project manager in Washington, one of the "True Believers." Additionally, during my tenure as commanding officer, two second-tour senior lieutenants, Fil Baca and

Bob Downey, both passed over for promotion to lieutenant commander, were subsequently reselected and promoted, returning to TACAMO to ultimately become the first "home-grown" commanding officers of VQ-3 and VQ-4 respectively, and both making captain. They too were "True Believers." This appeared to be the turning point the officers and men needed to see, to know their unbelievable efforts in the past were recognized, that these efforts were not in vain, and that TACAMO might have a future.

The TACAMO IVB transition was completed, and my tour was coming to an end with two more major modifications and the electromagnetic pulse hardening programs on the horizon. All this bode well for the future of TACAMO, but that was not yet apparent to the junior first-tour officers who chose to continue their career in a community that did not yet exist, making a perilous decision to bet their careers on an uncommitted policy. There are no words, actions or way of conveying how much the country owed these officers for their role in the future success of the TACAMO program. It is even more meaningful when one recognizes their foresight, belief and extraordinary performance at a time when belief in the future career potential of TACAMO required an unquestioned leap of faith.

VQ-4 was honored for its accomplishments during this transition period by winning its first Battle Efficiency "E" award from AIRLANT for administrative and operational excellence.

In retrospect, did the TACAMO program suffer for lack of "home grown" senior officers? The answer is both yes and no!

TACAMO probably did not suffer greatly during this period from "alternate command" commanding officer/executive officer selection from the VP community, as much of the experience of aircraft deployment scheduling, maintenance, training and crew concepts were common to both missions. Fifteen years later, as a third-year law school student, I came to understand the logic of how the Navy assigns senior positions based on experience, performance, and fit, even in the absence of previous assignments in the warfare specialty. My professor noted that upon graduation and acceptance to the bar, no matter 10 minutes later or 10 years, you are assumed capable of doing the job. Regarding Navy practice, that concept is borne out by the practice of assigning fighter/attack officers selected for prospective carrier command to command deep-draft replenishment ships in preparation for taking command of a carrier. However, the VP-raised TACAMO commanding officers' lack of familiarity with the intricate TACAMO technical issues restricted their ability to maximize TACAMO's potential.

The real loss came as junior officers exited the community after a single tour, taking their operational experience with them, a continuous hemorrhage of corporate knowledge of these unique issues. There was a particular problem at the mid-level management, the senior lieutenants and lieutenant commanders. While alternate command was a viable and necessary means of generating the necessary commanding officer and executive officers, the mid-level department heads were all too often lieutenant commanders passed over for promotion and command in other communities, with no future but a mandatory exit from the Navy after 20 years' service. While many nevertheless served with distinction, others were reluctant to rock the boat, and a few were no longer even interested in rowing it!

At the time I took command, the squadron was approximately six years old. Second tour lieutenants and lieutenant commanders should have been rising up, mission-experienced officers ready to take the reins and grow the TACAMO concept. That had not even begun to happen by the time I arrived in the squadron in 1973, though during my tour the first returnee, VQ-3 veteran Andy Riddile, checked aboard for his second tour in TACAMO. This "True Believer" would later rise to TACAMO command, make captain, and become our first home-grown commodore, commanding Strategic Communications Wing One, but that was 20 years in the future

Why did this growth of a seasoned cadre of experience leaders not happen? The simple answer was that TACAMO was not yet recognized as its own unique community, an essential element in the United States' strategic deterrence arsenal. Many still considered airborne transmission of high-powered VLF signals from a specialized aircraft, using a complex orbital maneuver for best water penetration, to be a cumbersome and unreliable method of providing highly reliable communications to the ballistic missile submarine force. They considered TACAMO to be an interim program, soon to be superseded by Project *Sanguine* land-based Extremely Low Frequency sites and water-penetrating blue-green lasers, neither of which ever lived up to expectations. And interim programs did not merit a warfare specialty that would lock junior officers into a career path supporting a program that likely would not exist when they rose to command. Accordingly, most of the junior officer "bright stars" assigned to the TACAMO program up to the late 1970s chose "one and done," departing TACAMO to seek their future in the more promising field of VP aviation, or as civilians.

Loss compounds as the years wear on. If left unchanged from this inauspicious beginning, the TACAMO program could not have achieved the status it enjoys today and indeed might not even exist. The turning point came in the coming of the "True Believers," those officers who steadfastly believed "one and done" was not an option.

How was I to know that in my wardroom were eight future TACAMO commanding officers and captains? Fil Baca, Bob Downey, Kermit Ayres, Andy Riddile, Ed Hampshire, Chuck Fitchet, Mike Davidson, and my Bull Ensign, Vern Lochausen, would all rise to command, and Kermit and Vern would join Andy as our first three commodores, commanding Strategic Communications Wing One.

PART TWO

TACAMO in Transition, 1975–1980

The TACAMO transition began in 1975, driven by four significant events:

- The first was Bill Coyne's leadership which established a new standard of professionalism and optimism for the community. He had also begun a program of flying captains and admirals from Naval Air Forces, Atlantic and Commander-in-Chief, U.S. Forces Atlantic, and various other commands on operational missions, for a first-hand view of TACAMO in action; this increased the understanding of the mission at the highest levels.
- The second event was the return of the first cadre of second-tour TACAMO officers, beginning with Andy Riddile and Ken deGraffenreid to VQ-4, and myself and Bob Downey to VQ-3. We brought experience into the mix and a strong sense of purpose. Cross-fertilization between the two widely separated squadrons began to percolate.
- The third significant event was the promotion of our first lieutenant commanders, Fil Baca and Bob Downey, which, though this happened on an unprecedented second look, demonstrated to all junior officers that this indeed could be a successful career path.
- The fourth was the pending deployment of the Trident missile submarine with greatly increased range and capability. Plans to effectively employ this new weapon system included close scrutiny of the TACAMO mission, how they operated, and where they were located. This was to have a major impact on VQ-3 as the Pacific was no longer to be the secondary theater.

CHAPTER 3

The First Retreads

Lew McIntyre

We had a small cadre of TACAMO contemporaries at the Naval Postgraduate School in Monterey, California: Denny Arneson, our premier technical expert, Dan Lashbrook, Al Shuff (the real owner of my call-sign "Zig-Zag"), Fil Baca, Ed Hampshire, and myself. We were all in different curricula, but we socialized frequently and considered ourselves "TACAMO Detachment West." We were all coming up to graduation in 1977, the subject of second tours a hot topic for discussion. Denny, Dan and Al were strongly sold on VS, carrier-based anti-submarine warfare built around the new S-3 airframe. Fil, Ed and I inclined toward returning to TACAMO. I don't know how Fil and Ed's conversations went with the detailers, but mine was acrimonious; he ended up saying words to the effect, "All right, I'll give you the damned orders to VQ-3, but don't come crying to me when your career is in shambles!" And he hung up.

That was how the three of us became "True Believers." This was the leap of faith and, no, it was not easy. The day I departed Monterey, June 21, 1977, the radio reported a Navy C-130 had been lost off Wake Island. It was VQ-3's '176, lost with all of Crew Four. I was to have relieved Jack Strunk, the aircraft commander of that flight.

For a variety of reasons, the Pacific in the 1960s and 1970s was a lower priority of operation for the fleet ballistic missile submarine forces; consequently VQ-3 was a lower priority than VQ-4. For VQ-4, the Pentagon in Washington and the operational and administrative commanders, CINCLANT and AIRLANT in Norfolk, were only a few hours' drive from Patuxent River. For VQ-3, the operational commander, Commander-in-Chief, U.S. Pacific Forces (CINCPAC), and our primary customer—Commander, Submarine Forces, Pacific—were in Hawaii and our administrative commanders, Fleet Air Wings Pacific and Naval Air Forces, Pacific (AIRPAC), were in Atsugi, Japan, and San Diego respectively. A visit to any of these organizations required weeks of planning to go by EC-130, a trip that might be cancelled at the last moment due to weather or aircraft availability. Casual trips to the Pentagon were out of the question.

Morale was at a low ebb following prolonged single-aircraft operations exacerbated by the sudden loss of their shipmates with Crew Four. That crew's number was retired and is maintained on the Ready Board in Operations as "Forever Deployed" to this day. The officers frequently complained that VQ-4 got all the support, so there was no point in doing more, but many of the junior officers in the wardroom were to have long careers in TACAMO: Bill Wilt would see the squadron through its many challenges ahead; and Rich Adamo would complete Test Pilot School in Patuxent River, fly many TACAMO test flights, and end up in the TACAMO Program Office in Naval Air Systems Command (NAVAIR). Many of the enlisted men also played big roles in TACAMO and Naval Communications; for example, Chief Radioman Donnie Decker, Master Chief Radioman Dunn, and Aviation Electronics Technician Bret Sylvia, who become the TACAMO Configuration Manager at NAVAIR 20 years later.

I was Assistant Training Officer under Bob Downey until he moved up to Operations. We revitalized the training program, bringing in the Navigation Standard Operating Procedure I had written in VQ-4 to ensure all students got the same training in log keeping, chartwork and celestial basics.

We had been found deficient in a recent Administrative Inspection for not having a Personal Qualifications System, then the Navy standard checklist for training in a variety of positions. This was not a fair "gig" for VQ-3, because VQ-4, as model manager, should have been tasked long ago with developing that training. We had a lot of arguments with various crew positions, all centering around "Why are we doing this? Why isn't (pick one) VQ-4/NAVAIR/AIRPAC doing it?" In short, anyone but us. I must admit I had a strong desire to beat my former squadron to the punch with this one. I got copies of the VP (patrol squadron) Personnel Qualifications System and, this being about 1978, we had a new high-tech tool to use for this project. Naval Air Station Agaña had just received a programmable Selectric typewriter that stored the document on a magnetic card about the size of an IBM punch card. Problem was, there was only one on the island, in the base commanding officer's office, and nobody knew how to use it. I worked out a deal for my yeoman third, among our first females, to go over, learn how to use it and train others, in exchange for having priority for this project. I set to work with a pad of yellow paper and the P-3 Naval Flight Officer (NFO) syllabi and in a few weeks she and I had presentable drafts of the Navigator and Airborne Communications Officer (ACO) Personal Qualification System. Pilots and flight engineers worked off the relevant P-3 syllabi to tailor them to the EC-130, particularly for the orbit. Communicators and flight techs took my ACO package as point of departure and expanded on it, and the reel operators; well, they just rolled their own. No model for them to follow! A year later, we submitted it to VQ-4 for the model manager's approval and then to AIRPAC. A job well done!

The squadron stayed at single aircraft ops, then began to climb back up to three. Bob Downey moved to ops and we began trying for 50 percent coverage, remembering that VQ-4 had instituted 100 percent coverage largely on its own. If we could not attend submarine debriefs at Submarine Pacific Headquarters, we could participate in individual boat debriefs with Submarine Squadron Fifteen on the USS *Proteus* (a submarine tender) at nearby Apra Harbor.

And in 1979, the choices made by the "True Believers" were vindicated and TACAMO became a warfare specialty in communications. We now had a career path!

Also in 1979, we received word the squadron would relocate to Naval Air Station Barbers Point in Hawaii in 1981 and receive new EC-130Qs and people to expand to eight aircraft, over 600 personnel, and support 100 percent coverage by 1983. Just a few minor changes, folks! I was tagged to lead this transition with Warrant Officer Ken Aymond.

I had taken a course while on Guam on Program Evaluation and Review Technique, developed by Hyman Rickover to manage the Polaris submarine and missile development and integration. Some of you may recognize it today as Microsoft Project, which did not exist then, nor did computers on which to run it! I had to do it manually so I went to the base exchange and bought every large pad of graph paper, every color of colored pencils they had, and dozens of rolls of scotch tape, along with index boxes and 3×5 cards, and began to connect the dots of how to relocate a squadron, along with all the maintenance items on Guam that were there because we were. And how to bring in two different aircraft configurations, TACAMO Improvement Programs Phases I and II, and crews trained in each; and, oh yes, I could only send people back to the States for training if they had a year left in the squadron and I could not bring a person in on permanent-change-of-station orders to Guam then immediately send them back to the States for six months of training. A lot of moving parts.

I can't say enough great things about Ken Aymond. He was the brains of the operation, identifying all those critical threads, determining the multitude of items that Naval Air Station Agaña had because VQ-3's EC-130s were there—tugs, check stands, power carts, the list was endless and mostly forgotten over the past 15 years of TACAMO operations there—and he documented them all. All I did was take careful notes. He and his wife Lee would later become godparents of my two children.

Somewhere along the line we would have to stand up a detachment at Barbers Point, which would grow and ultimately transition into the squadron, while the facility at Guam would shrink to detachment then wink out of existence. Oh, yes, and we were to stand up to 100 percent coverage, a task that ultimately would fall to my former department head, and fellow "True Believer," Fil Baca. My "Navajo Indian Blanket," as they jokingly called my multi-colored, scotch-taped graph paper timelines at the transition planning meetings, was meticulously done and redone by hand, from scratch, whenever something changed. They served as the roadmap for a very challenging transition from backwater to mainstream, and the term "Navajo Indian Blanket" continued long after I left VQ-3, a term the squadron used for any complex schedule.

Along the way, I had a delightful squadron wedding for me and my wife Karen, compliments of Skipper Dave Thompson, my best man, fortunately not one but two days after my bachelor party, the latter carefully plotted by Lieutenant Bob Lake and the Exec, Commander Bob Niederstadt. Photos of said party, taken by Jim Dear, our intelligence officer, kept reappearing in his intelligence briefs for the remainder of my time in VQ-3 to remind me of those things I did not remember. Karen and I had a delightful two weeks in Japan for a honeymoon, far off the beaten tourist path since I had some proficiency in Japanese at that time. This included a visit to Hiroshima's Peace Park, perhaps a somber thing to do on one's honeymoon, but something I think everyone in the nuclear business should do.

Right before I detached to return stateside, Boeing came by the squadron, marketing something they called the "ECX," a 707 airframe to replace the EC-130. Jets? What heresy! How can it orbit?

Bob Downey

Following promotion, graduation and an assured naval career, I was assigned to the USS *Midway*, based at Yokosuka, Japan. We made one of the first Indian Ocean deployments, earning the Battle Efficiency "E" award and two awards of the Green "C" for communications excellence.

The USS *Midway* was in Yokosuka, "cold iron" on a Friday night in August 1976 when we got the word to recall all ship's company and get underway for Korean waters. The North Koreans, armed with hand axes, had killed unarmed U.S. Army personnel after they had entered the Korean demilitarized zone to chop down a tree blocking the view. We got underway early on Sunday, the air wing flew aboard from Misawa, along with General Singlaub. On arrival, we bombed the Korean demilitarized zone, and operated non-stop, 24 hours a day for two weeks

You may recall this "incident" or have read about it. Subsequently, we chopped the tree down without interference.

I was the first, but by no means the last, TACAMO officer to bring our extensive hands-on communications expertise into fleet communications.

Following USS *Midway*, I requested orders to VQ-3 on Guam, as Training Department Head, with Lew McIntyre as my assistant. VQ-3 suddenly had not one, but two second-tour officers and, by all accounts, they had needed this badly. Morale was at a low ebb after protracted single-airplane operations. VQ-4 had begun borrowing aircraft from VQ-3 to support the TACAMO IVB transition, and the loss of 156176 and Crew Four forced the squadron into single aircraft operations. When I arrived in 1977, Lew and I found the training program in a shambles. Many NFOs and pilots had not achieved qualification as ACO or aircraft commander and some were being held back for personal reasons. Though Bill Wilt, the Naval Aviation Training and Operating Procedures Standardization (NATOPS)/Safety Officer, later returned as another "True Believer" to play a major role in VQ-3's later expansion on Guam, the remaining NATOPS instructors and evaluators were of the "one and done" mentality, hoping to leave the squadron early with great fitness reports to begin their real career in VP or civil aviation. It was not in their interest to expand the pool of qualified ACOs and aircraft commanders and the squadron did not need more. With the support of the executive officer, Commander Hugh "Barney" Barnhill, we began the slow process of changing that mentality, beginning with enforcing the rule that every flight had to be a training flight with some syllabus element signed off. The squadron had instituted something called a second navigator, an intermediate position not recognized by NATOPS, which we abolished. If a navigator trainee was on the crew, he had to have a dedicated instructor who could not double as the ACO. The prospect of extra deployments helped change the mindset of the instructors and we began to qualify people.

Our main challenge in training was to prepare for the new TACAMO Improvement Program Phase I modification. This basically was a digital switch system called the Time Domain Multiplexer that allowed us to exchange teletype hardware among the various radios; they had formerly been "stove-piped" into hardwired configurations. Fortunately, this training program proved to be easier to execute than it had been to plan as the system was easy to operate and greatly improved the flexibility of the communications suite.

Commander Barnhill, after his change of command, subsequently assigned me as the Operations Officer. We undertook a number of initiatives to rebuild a "can-do" spirit in VQ-3. Though we only had two mission birds at the time, once I directed the launch of both (one east and one west of Guam), "zip-lip" with flashing lights from the tower, to deploy their wires 500 miles in their op areas and transmit.

As the third mission bird arrived, along with a KC-130F logistic support and bounce bird, we began the slow process of building up toward 50 percent airborne coverage. The outfit was beginning to feel like a functioning squadron again. We participated in major command and control exercises. In one case, Lew McIntyre doggedly cleared a trailing wire reel mis-spool with an unscheduled flight the day prior to the exercise, successfully clearing the problem, but only after deploying about a third of the last wrap from the drum. I asked him what held the wire on the drum. His answer? "Just tension, nothing else." He went on to successfully prosecute the exercise.

We left VQ-3 a far better squadron than we found on our arrival, self-confident and ready to take the next major steps that would put them finally on an even footing with their formerly "big sister" squadron, VQ-4. It had taken 10 years, but VQ-3 had arrived. I detached to be the Navy Liaison Officer at Tinker Air Force Base, Oklahoma, to support the Airborne Warning and Command System E-3A. I had no idea at the time what a momentous role that airframe and that Midwest Air Force base would play in TACAMO's future.

CHAPTER 4

A New Professionalism

Andy Riddile

As Director, Subic Counseling and Assistance Center, in Subic Bay in the Philippines, my experience turned out to be personally and exceptionally rewarding. I remember fondly each of the staff of 16 sailors I was fortunate to lead, each highly capable and decidedly disciplined, some still lifelong friends. I also still have a substantial pile of personal letters from the skippers of deep-draft warships thanking me for what my counseling center crew and I were able to do for them and their sailors. We did indeed make a difference. I have been told the Subic Counseling and Assistance Center subsequently served as a model for the modern Correctional Custody Unit. Thanks to my boss, Rear Admiral Don Shelton, Commander, Naval Base Philippines, I received a Navy Achievement Medal from Admiral Mickey Weisner, Commander-in-Chief, Pacific Fleet. These were great leaders. I was able to work closely with Admiral Shelton who once told me he slept better when I stood the watch. To be sure, standing duty on a Friday night in Subic Bay in the early 1970s was an experience unlike most any other; anything, virtually anything, was likely to happen. I left the Philippines with a sense of accomplishment, though it was an accomplishment unrelated to strategic warfare.

The decision to return to the TACAMO community at this point in my career was enormous as I was the first to make such a decision. There was no one to consult. I did not paint the entire Navy with my rather uninspiring experience at VQ-3. I was grateful for the superb leadership I had at Subic, where the Navy allowed me to make a difference. I was self-confident. Even though I would occasionally indict Navy leadership for various perceived sins during my career, I always had an abiding faith in the Navy overall. I would be recognized for doing the best I could with what I was charged to do.

So, off I went to TACAMO again, this time with VQ-4, Naval Air Station Patuxent River. In 1975, I found things at VQ-4 improved considerably over that which I had left at VQ-3. I caught just the last few months of Skipper Coyne's command. It was immediately clear he had established a cultural change at the squadron. He understood that naval officers respond to the challenge of high standards with increased professionalism. There was a better-defined operational concept. There was more commitment among the aircrews. He established the aircrew position of Mission Commander, now available to Naval Flight Officers. A rigorous Mission Commander training syllabus, capped with challenging check deployments and a dreaded Mission Commander Board held in the office of the commanding officer, certified that pilots and flight officers each had a broad and deep understanding sufficient to ensure competence in command of an aircrew.

However, there was still no warfare specialty laying out a career path for junior officers. Poor material and personnel support occurred even with special designations from higher authority intended to ensure sufficient support. Worse, there was still no comprehensive understanding of strategic warfare. This time, as a second-tour lieutenant, expected to know something, I set out to learn it all. No longer was I satisfied to leave the in-depth technical understanding of the aircraft to the enlisted operators as I had on my first tour. As the Communications Department Head, I was in a good position to learn mission equipment, procedures, and operational concepts—some of the big picture. Portions of some 14 publications provided various and sundry pieces of disjointed guidance to aircrews. Some might remember the "Pink Pearl", for example, higher authority's operational procedures publication, most of which was falling apart, held together with rubber bands, the directions contained within sometimes in conflict; and, altogether, there were still missing guidelines. The Air Intelligence Officer, Gerry Thomas, and I pored through everything we could get our hands on that was relevant to our mission operating procedures and the background for those procedures. We found materials in squadron files, at Atlantic Fleet Command, Submarine Force Atlantic, in various organizations in the Pentagon (Navy, Air Force, and the Joint Staff). We worked to piece it all together, including background, but leaving out the irrelevant and incorrect. The result was the TACAMO Operating Procedures Manual. This manual served as the first single, authoritative source for everyone who needed to know what to do and why when operating in support of TACAMO Atlantic. This new publication, signed by the commanding officer, institutionalized the various operational tactics. During this process, I learned much about United States strategic warfare in terms of concepts, authorities, capabilities, and procedures. I learned what happened on board deployed ballistic missile submarines, U.S. Air Force strategic bombers and intercontinental ballistic missile silos, and at the command centers serving the Unified Combatant Commanders and the Chairman of the Joint Chiefs of Staff. I even learned a little about what happened at the White House. Based on this knowledge, I developed a mandatory classified course of instruction on this vital information for junior and mid-grade VQ-4 officers.

With dismay during this time, I watched certain commanding officers maneuver to resist the initial assignment of female aviation officers to the squadron. One tactic was to insist that, since male aircrew officers were required to undergo Survival, Evasion, Resistance and Escape training, and since women were not allowed in that training, women could therefore not be allowed to serve in the squadron. Not having experienced the historical bias against women, I could not begin to understand why women could not serve as equals in the TACAMO community. Fortunately, senior decision makers in Washington decided assignment of women to TACAMO was appropriate and so ordered it. Women, both enlisted and officer, have since been freely assigned to the community and served with great distinction.

As the new Executive Officer, Commander Wes May walked into the wardroom for the first time and immediately ordered all hats be removed from the table. Now! A marker: that he was not someone with whom to trifle. A Rhodes Scholar, he continued his tour instilling discipline in the wardroom. He was not universally popular but, like Skipper Dunmire, Skipper May saw something in me that I began to feel stirring. Toward the end of my tour, he designated me as his Executive Assistant, sitting at a desk in his office.

My commanding officers now relied on me as one who had a broad understanding of U.S. strategic command and control. I became committed to TACAMO and to a career in the Navy, a "True Believer." It had become an honor to serve in TACAMO.

Mark Herkert

Mark Herkert came to VQ-4 as a junior officer in 1975–1978, and after a 7-year hiatus that included tours as a recruiter, on the USS Coral Sea, the Naval Postgraduate School, he returned to TACAMO with VQ-3, and played a major role in setting up Strategic Communications Wing One and the squadrons at Tinker AFB. After retiring as a commander, he continued working with Wing and is now the executive assistant to the Commodore.

I joined the Naval Reserve Officer Training Corps (NROTC) on a fluke. During freshman orientation at the University of Wisconsin, my mother saw a man wearing a Navy uniform and went over to talk with him. Turned out he was the executive officer of the NROTC unit and the next thing I knew, I was signed up as a contract student. At the conclusion of my freshman year, I was offered and accepted a scholarship. NROTC provided an opportunity for me to earn my private pilot's license through a "Flight Indoctrination Program" and I fell in love with flying. My goal became to fly the P-3 Orion, as my uncle was a P-3 Naval Flight Officer (NFO). Upon graduation and commissioning, my wife Shirley and I headed to Naval Air Station Pensacola, Florida, for Aviation Indoctrination and Primary Flight Training. Shirley and I found an apartment on East Larua Street in Pensacola, only to find there had been a number of females murdered on the street in the past few months. That, and lack of employment for Shirley, led us to jump at the chance to move to Corpus Christi, Texas, to continue training. I attended Basic and Advanced Flight Training there while Shirley worked as a nurse at the local hospital. It was during this time I learned of the death of my college roommate, Ensign Michael Strole, in a Navy training aircraft accident in Michigan. His picture is now displayed in the University of Wisconsin NROTC hall of fame dedicated to members who died on active duty.

Upon getting my wings, I received orders to VQ-4 at Naval Air Station Patuxent River, Maryland. We drove via Wisconsin to visit relatives, arriving at Patuxent River with Shirley far advanced in her pregnancy; we were fortunate to secure base housing.

August 27, 1975 will always be in my memory as the day I completed my EC-130 third pilot check ride and the day on which our son Bryce was born. A year later, Shirley would work in the same base hospital in which Bryce had been born. After that, life took on a very hectic pace. I was assigned to Crew Two with Lieutenant Paul Jackson as Aircraft Commander and Lieutenant Mark O'Leary as Second Pilot. They took me under their wing to teach me about the TACAMO mission while we flew between Patuxent River, Bermuda, Europe, Canada and the eastern U.S. over the next year. I have many memories of standing alert in Bermuda, including a great memory of Shirley joining me there when I was the Officer-in-Charge of the squadron's detachment. I had some really great instructors over the years, especially the flight engineers, reel operations and communications team sailors. I will never forget Chief Radioman Fisher. He would cook the first meal out of Patuxent River. He prepared the sauce while he was watching football at home the Sunday prior to departure; the worse his team did, the hotter the sauce. After one very abysmal loss by his team, the sauce was too hot for anyone to eat!

It was during my three-plus years in VQ-4 that I became a "True Believer" in the TACAMO mission, the urgency that we be always airborne, capable of relaying our strategic messages. I remember many missions deviating from the planned flight plan to avoid adversary aircraft or ships in the vicinity. I remember a three-engine alert launch from Bermuda, and a two-engine landing there, and many bumpy rides dodging Atlantic thunderstorms.

I also remember the pride I felt at being able to properly fly the orbit, a not-so-simple task of trying to keep a constant strain on the wire by varying angle of bank, slowly increasing in altitude so as not to run into turbulence from your own aircraft and keeping one's speed just above power-on stall, often in pitch-black night with no visual horizon. During this tour, I earned designations as Aircraft Commander, Mission Commander, and Instructor Pilot.

I also served in many junior officer ground jobs, the best ones being Aircraft Division Officer, Quality Assurance Division Officer and Model Manager. My fondest memories, second only to seeing my son crawl, walk, run and saying his first word ("airplane"), was of the sailors, enlisted and officer, with whom I had the pleasure to serve. They believed in the mission, in the aircraft and in each other. They were professionals. They were there for each other. I was not sure I wanted to make the Navy a career, but knew that, if I did, I wanted to return to TACAMO for my next sea duty.

My skippers during my VQ-4 tour were Commanders Laurel Pederson, Wes May, Bryan Anderson and Floyd Painter. They were good skippers, some were great leaders, but they had no TACAMO background, nor did any of the middle-grade leadership, the lieutenant commander department heads. TACAMO was not a warfare specialty. The only two lieutenants I remember making lieutenant commander during my tour were Stu Bell and Ken deGraffenreid.

Ken deGraffenreid

I left VQ-4 in April 1972 and reported to the Defense Intelligence Agency, also working on my Master of Arts in national security studies, including strategic nuclear issues, at Catholic University. I visited the squadron occasionally to give an intelligence lecture and to get a little extra flight time, as I was flying proficiency in T-28s and S-2s during that tour. Part way into my shore duty tour, the detailer offered the choice of a non-flying billet on an aircraft carrier, or another TACAMO tour, surprisingly positive, saying that the Navy needed second-tour TACAMO pilots very much. Thus, I followed Andy Riddile as the very first batch of second-tour junior officers in TACAMO.

When I went back through C-130 training, now relocated to Little Rock Air Force Base, prior to my second tour, the old timers were gone and the training was programmed "paint-by-number" instruction which sometimes actually discouraged aircraft systems knowledge.

I returned to VQ-4 in the summer of 1975, bringing my earlier experience, wider exposure to national, Pentagon, and especially threat issues, and a more developed understanding of nuclear command and control.

The squadron was not the same as I had left, far more focused, serious, professional, and shipshape in very many ways. The mission was being coherently addressed and VQ-4 was flying hard. It was good to see these improvements.

I made lieutenant commander shortly after returning and was given the Naval Aviation Training and Operating Procedures Standardization (NATOPS)/Safety Department, substantially improved from my earlier time thanks to the fine work of Kermit Ayers, Fil Baca and others. In this and so many other areas, far from being able to rest on my "second tour" status, I realized I was going to have to measure up to a new standard. Fortunately, my flying skills were still intact and the squadron was full of a new set of great characters. I got a crew and loved it. I did have the sense that some people kept a little distance from anyone who had not personally gone through the Bill Coyne "growth experience." Fair enough. And I mastered the new billet, instituted under Bill Coyne, of Mission Commander.

In early 1977, I had to make a tough decision, to stay in TACAMO and the regular Navy or to pursue a new national security opportunity. I took the latter and, after a few months waiting on another background investigation, joined the staff of the Senate Select Committee on Intelligence and started a new career. I also walked across the ramp and joined the VP Reserves, flying the P-3 for many more years. Nice plane but the motors are on top, and it can't back up like the Herc.

Both these moves led me back to TACAMO issues repeatedly for a number of years. In my civilian life, I wound up on the National Security Council staff of the incoming Ronald Reagan administration which was committed to rebuilding American strategic power through "peace through strength." Together with many other "True Believers," we worked hard on the issues of funding, new EC-130Qs, the E-6, nuclear hardening, and much else, during the 1980s. When I left the White House, I went to a special project on national continuity survivability, always running into Paul Jackson, Andy Riddile and other TACAMO veterans who were now spread throughout the strategic communications world. It seemed to me that, at a practical level, TACAMO had arrived.

In my Navy Reserve life, after my flying days sadly ended, I wound up on the Navy staff at the old OP-65—the strategic nuclear shop. TACAMO again! I finished my Navy career on the Chief of Naval Operations Executive Panel and worked with CIA Director Jim Woolsey on a major study on assuring connectivity to Navy nuclear forces. As a contractor, I later worked with the first four Strategic Communications Wing One commanders on special survivability issues, during which, as a reserve captain, I got a few hours flying the E-6.

Godspeed TACAMO. Keep 'em flying.

Barry Coyle

After leaving Guam in June 1973, we transferred to the University of Pennsylvania in Philadelphia. Tina quickly found a banking job in the city while I became immersed in a very busy three years at Penn. I did no work there directly associated with TACAMO, but all three of my primary duties there contributed to my future assignments in the Navy and TACAMO.

First and foremost, I was a Naval Science instructor, teaching Naval History and Naval Operations and, later, Leadership and Management. One of the modules in this course dealt with career patterns in naval aviation, surface ships and submarines, such as alternating sea and shore assignments, the detailing process, and what billets were considered good and bad. As Senior Advisor, I got to know the Bureau of Personnel detailing staff well while helping my "middies" negotiate initial assignment orders, all good knowledge for my later career decisions.

Second, I earned a Master's Degree in Business Administration with a major in Management Policy and Planning and a minor in the then-new field of Information Systems. This would shape all my future shore duty assignments.

Third, I participated in the Navy proficiency flying program to maintain basic pilot skills. As a multi-engine pilot with over 1,500 flight hours, I was assigned to fly the S-2G Tracker and the C-1A Trader, not only for training but for actual logistics support and personnel transportation missions, qualifying as Aircraft Commander and Instructor Pilot almost immediately. Three years of flying experience honed and matured my decision-making and instructional skills. I also flew midshipmen on indoctrination flights in T-34 Mentors as flight leader, due to flight time and experience, along with five others. That was a fun summertime duty assignment, two or three flights a day, six days a week, with only a few days off between the midshipman classes. It was very nice to go back to flying a basic, single-engine airplane through aerobatics and other maneuvers, further sharpening my flying skills.

As my NROTC tour drew to a close in 1976, I had some decisions to make: First, whether to stay in the Navy at all and, if so, what to do for my next assignment? Not easy decisions, either one. Tina really wanted me to leave the Navy and settle down in Philadelphia, since her own career in banking was now well established. Many employers came to the Wharton School to conduct interviews with graduating MBA students, giving me excellent prospects for civilian jobs. At the same time, I was working with my Navy detailer to see what he might have to offer for my second sea tour, either a second squadron tour or a tour aboard an aircraft carrier, the conventional wisdom at the time favoring the ship tour as a broadening experience. TACAMO was calling, however, as the Navy had a shortage of second-tour EC-130 pilots and the detailer offered me a second squadron tour at VQ-4. After lots of research, discussions, thought and hand wringing, I finally decided to accept orders to VQ-4 at Naval Air Station Patuxent River, Maryland.

It was at that moment, when I accepted those orders to VQ-4, that I became a TACAMO "True Believer." After leaving NROTC duty in late August, I completed C-130 refresher training at Little Rock and reported to VQ-4 in November 1976. During my time away, major changes had taken place in both the aircraft and communications equipment and in personnel assignment practices, but the first thing I noticed was the huge size of the squadron. When I left VQ-3 in 1973, the squadron had about 30 officers and 250 enlisted personnel. In 1976, VQ-4 had 100 officers and almost 600 enlisted—one of the Navy's largest squadrons. Quite a change!

By late 1976, Naval Air Systems Command (NAVAIR) had completed installation of the new TACAMO IVB communications suite in all VQ-4's aircraft, centered around a new Very Low Frequency (VLF) transmitter with power output increased tenfold to 200 kilowatts, with a much more efficient two element antenna system: the five-mile-long trailing wire antenna as before, but with a new short trailing wire antenna, about a mile in length, both with new, heavier wire. The TACAMO IVB suite also included many new radios and upgrades to the communications crew operator station. The flight deck also received welcome upgrades, including updated communications and navigation gear, a modern autopilot, and updated cockpit instrumentation. There was a lot to learn as I began my re-qualification in the EC-130.

The fluid aircraft inventory situation throughout this tour made flying and maintaining the aircraft very challenging. When I arrived in late 1976, VQ-4 had eight aircraft assigned—the three remaining EC-130Gs of the 151 series, three 156 series EC-130Qs delivered in 1968, and two new EC-130Qs in the 159 series, procured to replace the airplane lost in 1972. The remaining EC-130Qs were assigned to VQ-3 or were completing TACAMO IVB upgrades. There was great hope that, once the IVB mods were completed, squadron inventories would stabilize above minimum levels.

Two things happened in 1977 to dash that hope. First, the early aircraft had developed cracks in the center wing box structure, a major structure in the aircraft fuselage to which the wings were attached. This cracking was caused by the EC-130s continuously conducting mission operations at the C-130's design maximum gross weight, as well as pilot training involving many take-offs and landings with the heavy-weight TACAMO aircraft. The center wing boxes on all TACAMO EC-130s, except the two newest ones, would have to be replaced as expeditiously as possible, a complex repair process that took a minimum of six months per aircraft. For the next three years, one or two aircraft were out of operational service for this rework.

Second, in June 1977, VQ-3 lost an aircraft in a crash immediately following a night mission take-off out of Wake Island, killing all 16 members of Crew Four. The exact cause of the accident was never determined. This crash, with the loss of so many shipmates, caused great sadness and shock throughout the TACAMO community. The loss of one more aircraft greatly complicated inventory management to support reworks, modifications and operational requirements. There were several times during my VQ-4 tour when we were reduced to six operational aircraft for months at a time. Although NAVAIR quickly ordered a replacement aircraft, it was not delivered to VQ-4 until February 1979.

There were other adjustments to inventory as well. The squadrons had long been trying to convince NAVAIR to provide them with a cargo C-130 to be used for internal logistics support and pilot training, to ease the load on the scarce mission aircraft. The cracked center wing boxes added ammunition to this argument and in late 1978 NAVAIR agreed to provide each squadron with a KC-130F on loan from the Marine Corps. These aircraft were stripped of all their refueling equipment and provided to the VQ squadrons as basic cargo planes in September 1978. To further help ease the training burden on the mission aircraft, VQ-4 began using KC-130 simulators in 1977, first at Marine Corps Air Station Cherry Point, North Carolina, and later at Marine Corps Air Station El Toro, California. VQ-3 joined in this simulator program as well.

With all these aircraft adjustments, by the end of my tour, VQ-4 was operating four different series of EC-130 aircraft and the KC-130F, plus the simulators. All of these had significant differences between them in aircraft systems, instrumentation and procedures, making flying them safely a challenge for the pilots. Our Naval Aviation Training and Operating Procedures Standardization (NATOPS) team, responsible for flight training and safety, developed and maintained a Differences Manual that had to be reviewed before every flight to make sure pilots remembered everything about the aircraft they were assigned to fly that day. Also, Ed Hampshire had published an excellent Orbit Data Manual which provided excellent engineering information about the workings of the dual trailing wire antenna system and procedures for both the reel operators and pilots to deploy the antennas for maximum effectiveness. These in-house manuals plus the thick Navy NATOPS manual meant that flying in VQ-4 required a lot of constant study!

Two changes in overall Navy personnel policies had an impact on manning in the TACAMO community. The first of these was the shift to augmented flight crews from the minimum crew concept that had been in effect during my first tour. This was driven by the Navy's campaign to fix its abysmal naval aviation safety record, caused in part by inadequate crew rest between missions. This led to new crew rest regulations and to larger crews on aircraft like ours flying very long missions. So now our officer crews consisted of three pilots, a navigator, and an Airborne Communications Officer (ACO). The ACO was also a qualified navigator and the pilots were freed of navigator duties. The communications crew and reel operators were also augmented. The additional crew members allowed people to rotate out of their positions and rest during long flights, some of which were up to 14 hours long.

A major change was precipitated by the Bureau's decision to make NFOs eligible for squadron command in 1974. This change generated the Mission Commander concept in the VQ and VP communities. In this concept, the pilot aircraft commander or the NFO ACO, whoever was senior, would be designated as the crew's Mission Commander. While the aircraft commander retained overall responsibility for safety-of-flight on crews with an NFO ACO/Mission Commander, the Mission Commander, whether pilot or NFO, otherwise had overall responsibility for mission completion and crew leadership. This arrangement provided NFOs an opportunity to develop operational leadership skills, leading to squadron command. A specialized Mission Commander training syllabus was developed to ensure both pilots and NFOs had a base of shared knowledge to properly serve in this important position.

The Navy's professional development ladder was one thing that hadn't changed. Second-tour lieutenants were still assigned to jobs in different departments to continue the career-long process of learning as much as possible about the squadron, but to jobs with much more responsibility and many more people to lead. My ground jobs, in order, were: the Avionics

Division Officer in the Maintenance Department, the largest division in the squadron with over 100 personnel; Assistant Operations Officer; and Safety Officer. After my promotion to lieutenant commander in October 1978 and a six-week assignment to Naval Postgraduate School Monterey for Aviation Safety Officer School, I was assigned my first department head billet as NATOPS/Safety Officer. My fellow second-tour TACAMO officers—Bill Harsanyi, Mike Davidson, Ed Hampshire, Stu Bell, Andy Riddile, Chuck Fitchett, and Frank Kockler—also began filling these important jobs. Bill, Ed, Stu, Chuck and I would all complete our first department head tours during this second tour in VQ-4. The squadron also had a new generation of outstanding first-tour officers, many of whom would become multi-tour TACAMO senior leaders and "True Believers" themselves. Some of these included Vern Lochausen, John Brouillette, Kris Strance, Mike Clemens, Jim Molino, Pete Schlumbrecht, Terry Cush, and Joe Sereno. The squadron was also fortunate to have a large number of enlisted personnel and chief petty officers who had served prior TACAMO tours and were able to share their knowledge and experience with us on the ground and in the air.

The biggest and best professional development news during this time occurred in April 1979 when the CNO approved the Bureau of Personnel's plan, long in development, to establish the Airborne Strategic/Electronic Warfare Communities (VQ-3 & 4/VQ-1 & 2) as Aviation Officer Communities. This meant officers could now serve multiple tours within their warfare specialty squadrons with a clear path to compete for command of those squadrons. There could have been no better news! All of us early TACAMO pioneers, who had gambled on TACAMO eventually becoming a viable career path, were now rewarded for our faith and enthusiasm, and an opportunity for command was open to the new generation of officers. It would be a couple of years before the first TACAMO commanding officers would be selected, but all of us "True Believers" felt vindicated. Our gamble had paid off and our dream had come true.

In the aircraft, the development ladder remained pretty much as previously described, with the addition of the Mission Commander qualification. As a second-tour pilot with almost 2,000 total pilot hours, 1,400 of them in EC-130 Hercs, I quickly advanced to Aircraft Commander and Mission Commander with a crew, as well as qualifying as an Instructor Pilot for the both the aircraft and simulator.

All aircrew officers also stood watches. VQ-4 used watch teams that stood watch in the squadron Operations Control Center for a week. Each crew got this rotating assignment roughly every three months. The mission commander would be the squadron Command Duty Officer and the other four officers on the crew would stand eight-hour Squadron Duty Officer watches.

Leadership and mentoring remained strong during these years. The COs I served under in VQ-4, Commanders Wes May, Brian Anderson, and Floyd Painter, the latter the first NFO to command VQ-4, all had different leadership styles and personalities, but each led VQ-4 very effectively through a series of challenges that included the aircraft modifications and reworks, introduction of simulator training, and various personnel issues, all while maintaining 100 percent airborne coverage, an extremely high operational tempo, and outstanding safety record. When Commander Anderson completed his commanding officer tour, he was assigned to the Bureau where he led the effort to finalize and implement the Strategic/Electronic Warfare Specialty plan.

Below the commanding officers, we also had fine leadership that ensured the squadron functioned at a high level. I especially remember the two Maintenance Officers, Lieutenant Commanders Ray Mensch and Bruce Davidson, both VP officers with an extremely difficult and demanding job in those years. Just getting aircraft ready for the fast-moving flight schedule was often a challenge, but they also had to manage routine aircraft inspections, repairs, modifications and reworks, not to mention managing about 400 of the squadron's 600 people. They always seemed a little stressed, but got the job done. Finally, we were also getting experienced TACAMO leadership in key squadron billets, with Bill Harsanyi as Ops Officer, and Andy Riddile, followed by Frank Kockler, as Communications Department Head. Ed Hampshire, followed by Stu Bell and then myself, held down the NATOPS/Safety Department Head slot. Chuck Fitchett would become Ops Officer later in his tour. Things were definitely looking up for the development of a professional TACAMO community as the early "True Believers" became more senior.

During my VQ-4 tour, the squadron's mission was to maintain continuous airborne communications coverage in the Atlantic area. This meant one aircraft airborne all the time, normally deployed, plus one on 30-minute alert. The squadron used a complex deployment schedule, developed by Lieutenant Commander Paul Tillson, to optimize aircraft endurance, crew rest, and aircraft maintenance, based on a planned mission duration of 10.5 hours, with crew rest and alert periods multiples of two and four times that, respectively. Crews deployed for two weeks to fly multiple scheduled missions and two alert periods, one before and one after the deployment. However, a normal mission flight included three hours of preflight and two hours of post-flight, plus any unscheduled extensions of the flight and post-flight maintenance, all of which came out of the scheduled 21-hour crew rest time, so actual crew rest could get very short!

If the relieving aircraft had a problem, such as weather or maintenance, that delayed its take-off, the airborne aircraft would be directed to remain airborne until its Prudent Limit of Endurance, the dreaded PLE, extending the flight up to two hours, also cutting into the rapidly disappearing crew rest period. I have a lot of flights in my log book in excess of 13 hours, the longest being over 14 hours.

As in VQ-3 earlier, most of our mission flights were airborne listening watches, but some were also VLF transmit missions in an over-water operating area to extend the antennas, orbit and transmit any received messages.

With 14 crews, the start of a deployment came up about every six weeks, although individual crew members would sometimes get doubled-up to fill for someone unable to fly on another crew. Typical deployment began with a mission flight from Pax River, terminating at Naval Air Station Bermuda for the first 42-hour alert period, with a permanent detachment there to help with turnarounds, maintenance, fueling, etc. The crews stood alert in the bachelor officers' quarters and enlisted barracks or, during nice days, at recreational places near the aircraft. The requirement was to launch as quickly as possible after notification. My best was a no-notice alert launch, from a dead sleep, in record time; everything went just right that morning. Alert launches were not popular because they added extra missions and flight time to an already grueling deployment schedule, but, sadly, they occurred fairly frequently.

After the first alert period, the crew would depart to fly several missions, each terminating at a different location, then returning to Bermuda for the second alert period. The final mission would take us home to Pax River. VQ-4 used a wide variety of deployment bases: several bases in England; Scotland; Spain and the Canary Islands; Lajes Air Force Base in the Azores; several in Canada; and bases all up and down the East Coast. We got plenty of travel and liberty time in interesting places! During these years, we implemented several new mission flight profiles and procedures designed to minimize predictability and observability.

Life in VQ-4 revolved around crew scheduling. Crews deployed for two weeks every six weeks and stood a week of watches in the Operations Control Center every quarter. Even leave was scheduled by crew in a block that didn't interfere with deployment or watch commitments. The Operations and Training Departments worked hard to keep crews together as long as possible, but transfers, promotions, training pipelines, and other factors drove a certain amount of turnover on each crew. I was fortunate in this regard. When I checked in to the squadron, I was assigned to Crew Eleven and stayed with that crew for my entire tour, replacing Lieutenant John Urban, one of the finest first-tour officers I ever knew, as Aircraft Commander and Mission Commander when he completed his tour. Earl Alexander was the Navigator on the crew when I joined. He moved up to ACO and took over as Mission Commander when I left. He and I became good friends and had many adventures together in flight and on liberty.

An interesting aspect of life in VQ-4 was also driven by crew scheduling. Crews on opposite schedules would be deployed when the other was home and vice-versa. It was possible to go a year or more without meeting maybe a third of the officers in the squadron.

In addition to deployed mission operations, VQ-4 also flew occasional missions from Pax River to some operational areas nearby where we could extend the trailing wires and transmit when required. Most of these local operations were flown in support of various exercises. There were other types of flights as well: post-maintenance check flights; logistics support to deployed crews; and, of course, pilot training, adding to the approximately 750 mission hours. With the squadron flying over 1,000 hours per month, each of our aircraft was accumulating almost 150 hours per month at a time when the huge Air Force fleet of C-130s was averaging 35. We were definitely burning the service life candle of our aircraft at both ends.

With 55 pilots in the squadron, the pilot training load was never-ending, including syllabus flights and annual check-rides. Instructor pilots took the brunt of the non-deployed flying hours. Most of the aircraft commanders were also instructor pilots, but we still ended up with a couple of instructional hops every week when at home. In addition, all the second and third tour aircraft commanders became designated as simulator instructors. We used the KC-130 simulator at El Toro to do a portion of all syllabus training as well as annual NATOPS evaluations for both pilots and flight engineers. This program took a lot of strain off the real aircraft but was also an ordeal because of the distance from Pax River. A typical simulator evolution included an instructor pilot, instructor flight engineer, two pilot students and one or two flight engineer students. We would fly commercially to Los Angeles on Sunday to do five 8-hour days of training at El Toro through the week that included ground training as well as daily flights in the "box." Often the instructors did additional work with the simulator staff to improve the software to better simulate EC-130 flying characteristics. At the end of the week, we'd fly back home for what was left of the weekend. Despite the travel time, these trips were enjoyable both professionally and personally. The simulator facility was first-rate, modern, and the training always valuable. There were many great restaurants and bars in the El Toro area as well as good sight-seeing. Simulator instructors got one trip about every two months, squeezed in between deployments and other duties. In my last 12 months in VQ-4, between deployments, simulator trips and schools, I spent nine months away from home.

One unfortunate operational event occurred during this tour. On January 7, 1979, the squadron experienced another aircraft accident—this time with the KC-130F. The aircraft was on a "Sleigh Ride" mission picking up squadron personnel returning from Christmas leave in various locations. The aircraft was on a leg from Chicago to Indianapolis on a cold, blustery winter day, with heavy snow that morning, the runway icy with a strong, gusty crosswind.

Just as the airplane touched down, a very strong wind gusted across the runway, causing the aircraft to tip up and slide to the right on the icy runway. The number three propeller struck the runway and shattered, ripping the propeller assembly and gearbox off the engine. Shrapnel from the propeller punched almost a thousand holes in the adjacent number four engine, right wing, fuel tanks, and fuselage. Miraculously, there was no fire and no injuries. It took five months to repair the aircraft and restore it to full operational capability. This was the last significant aircraft mishap in the TACAMO community during the C-130 era.

Flying in VQ-4 was extremely challenging. The fast-paced schedule, the exhausting deployments, pressure to maintain 100 percent airborne coverage, five different series of aircraft, and the North Atlantic weather all combined to ensure that pretty much every flight required your full attention. I wish space permitted discussion of some of the more interesting and hair-raising flight operations I encountered!

Unlike my first tour on Guam, VQ-4 was not in an isolated location. While Pax River was out in the country in southern Maryland, it was just two hours away from the major metropolitan areas of Washington, Annapolis and Baltimore, with all their attractions. Some squadron officers lived in on-base housing, others had bought or rented homes in the local community. Many spouses were employed locally or in one of the nearby big cities, and people were involved in many activities that did not include squadron personnel, so the squadron was not as cohesive as VQ-3 had been on my first tour. Certainly, there was not as strong a feeling of "shipmates are family" in VQ-4, although we all made friends there with people we saw frequently. The squadron sponsored the usual picnics, parties, and hail-and-farewell events, and the base and the local community provided plenty of recreational opportunities. The huge base Drill Hall gymnasium/swimming pool complex was great, and the base Morale, Welfare and Recreation sponsored many athletic teams; John

Brouillette and I shot on the squadron's improbably successful pistol team. Out on the Chesapeake Bay, sailing, boating, fishing, and water sports were very popular. The great Bachelor Officers Quarters bar held well-attended Happy Hours every Friday and the Officers Club served good food and hosted many special events during the year. The base also had an excellent golf course. There were also a few good restaurants and pubs in the local community around Lexington Park and many events and activities there as well. There was no lack of fun times when we weren't working or flying.

Some personal notes for me. My father and mother both passed away within six months of each other during my tour. In addition, Tina and I separated, with the divorce finalized in 1980. Between her job with the Riggs Bank in Washington and my frequent travels, we had hardly seen each other, and she wanted to pursue her own career goals outside of Navy life. Yes, 1978 was a pretty high-stress year for me! On the other hand, in April 1979, I met and started dating Diane, the lady who would become my second wife a couple of years later.

Bill Harsanyi

After three years at Monterey, I walked away with a bachelor's degree in Oceanography and a master's in Telecommunications Management, making me right for TACAMO even more. Still, the Pacific refused to relinquish its hold on me. I went to Korea for two years, as part of U.S. Forces Korea headquarters section of the United Nations command, as Communications Officer and Communications Materials custodian.

Just after VQ-4 returned to 100 percent airborne coverage with the Bermuda Alert, I arrived in Patuxent River for my department head tour in 1975. There, I was first the Training Officer and worked with great sailors in refining the Replacement Training Division. I fleeted up to be the Operations Boss next and pulled some nice tickets in each job. With sea-shore duty rotation a little out of whack, I owed the payback assignment due for postgraduate school, but I pulled a plum afloat staff Communications Officer assignment in 1978 with Commander, Carrier Group Eight out of Norfolk, Virginia.

PART THREE

The ECX Comes to Life, 1980–1983

We interrupt the saga of the squadrons and their TACAMO commanding officers to introduce the next major change to the community: the birth of the E-6A airframe. Some of these tours are out of sequence with others by the same author, but we wished to consolidate the beginning of the E-6A in a single section. In the late 1970s, Boeing launched an independent research and development project to build the ECX, a Boeing 707 airframe with the new CFM-56 high-bypass turbofan, as a potential upgrade for the Air Force C-135 and E-3A fleets. The idea of replacing the aging EC-130 TACAMO aircraft was almost an afterthought, but they did studies and tests to determine that the ECX could, in fact, do the challenging TACAMO orbit and shopped the idea to both VQ-3 and VQ-4. The proposal fell on eager ears: the venerable EC-130s had taken a pounding over the years from constant maximum gross weight operations, with a communications suite that had grown enormously from the initial TACAMO III system deployed in 1968. They had been "ridden hard and put away wet" too many times. TACAMO "True Believers" in Washington were instrumental in turning the ECX into a program of record that would carry TACAMO to still higher levels of achievement.

CHAPTER 5

Starting the Program

Barry Coyle

I completed my tour in VQ-4 in July 1979 and, after some much-needed leave and a move to Alexandria, Virginia, reported to my first Pentagon assignment in the Chief of Naval Operations Staff, colloquially known as OPNAV. I was assigned to the Systems Analysis Division (OP-96), a billet coded for my primary subspecialty in Financial Management: Planning, payback for my master's degree in business administration.

OP-96 was responsible for program/project studies and analysis and Program, Objectives and Milestones planning, budgeting and scheduling for future programs. Our boss was Rear Admiral Lee Kollmorgen, a naval aviator from the attack community flying A-4 and A-7 aircraft. OP-96 kicked off each three-year budget cycle by first conducting studies and analyses, then preparing and presenting the annual Chief of Naval Operation's Program Analysis Memoranda, concentrating on new program starts and major changes to previously approved programs. OP-96 conducted both operational and cost-effectiveness analyses, organized into branches aligned with the major resource sponsors and acquisition agencies. I was assigned to the Command, Control, Communications and Intelligence cell within the General-Purpose Forces Branch, which primarily dealt with surface ship programs.

The General-Purpose Forces Branch Director was Captain Ted Baker, a brilliant guy and wonderful leader who would go on to become a vice admiral. My immediate boss in the Command, Control, Communications and Intelligence cell was a senior civilian named Paul Miller who had been in that position as long as anyone could remember, one of the Navy's most recognized and respected experts that specialized in field and Pentagon procedures. That summer, Paul faced training a whole new staff, since his new deputy, Commander Tom Gryzmalla, myself, and Lieutenant Pat McKim all reported in around the same time with no prior Pentagon or major staff experience (replacements for the three outgoing guys). The only holdover was Lieutenant (junior grade) Steve Honda, the administrative guy responsible for making slides for presentations, a low-level skill that would soon become the most important one in the entire cell. Paul assigned each of us a portfolio of projects and studies to be worked on for the Program Objectives and Milestones for Fiscal Year 1983 four years down the road. As the only aviator in the cell, I was assigned all the aircraft-related command and control projects, including TACAMO, aircraft carrier computers and data links. In addition, I got strategic communications, satellite communications and air navigation systems.

I immediately started studying up on my assigned programs and OPNAV and Pentagon procedures. The Program Objectives and Milestones for 1983 turned out to be an historic year for command, control, communications and intelligence programs, with many systems that are household words today getting their start then: the Global Positioning System; various next-generation satellite systems for ship, shore and air, and intelligence systems; and, of course, the E-6 aircraft. OP-941 became the OPNAV resource sponsor for TACAMO. That was an extremely interesting and busy two years!

Two things happened very early in my tour that made this first Pentagon tour even more interesting. One Monday morning, when I had only been on board about a month, Paul Miller called us all into his office. He told us that he far surpassed the minimum age and time in service requirements for retirement, and also had 60 days of unused leave, so he was going to retire and start on leave that same day. He then went to tell Captain Baker the news, had a very short turnover meeting with Tom, packed a box of personal items and left the office around lunch time, never to be seen again.

So now we were down to four, with Tom elevated to cell leader. He stayed just long enough to be laid low by a medical emergency. He never returned to OP-96, though he ultimately recovered. So now we were down to three, and none of us had gotten any kind of turnover from the two leads! Captain Baker appointed me as the cell leader. It took over a year to fill the deputy position and we never did get a replacement for Paul Miller.

So, there I was, a recently-promoted lieutenant commander filling a captain's billet, plus doing my original duties, a position I was to hold for almost a year and a half. Very interesting times, but it was the Navy: sometimes you just step up and deal with adversity. Our little group performed extremely well, learned a lot and got used to working alongside much more senior officers.

My TACAMO-related work in OP-96 included two major projects: Study Director for the Airborne VLF Replacement Study; and participation in the analysis and cost estimating to support procurement of the E-6A aircraft. The Airborne VLF Replacement Study, equivalent to today's Analysis of Alternatives process, was conducted by the Applied Physics Laboratory at Johns Hopkins University which had done extensive studies and analyses for TACAMO and strategic communications in the past. It was initiated in support of the new Ohio-class ballistic missile submarines. The *Ohio* was launched in 1979, its first operational patrol planned for 1981 in the Pacific. The Navy wanted to ensure its communications links with these new submarines were as capable as the ships themselves. The Airborne VLF Replacement Study had been underway for a couple of years, entering its final stages when I became the Staff Study Director. The study team had looked at various alternatives for providing communications to submerged submarines, which included an improved and expanded shore Very Low Frequency (VLF) network; Extremely Low Frequency transmissions from a fixed site in Wisconsin; blue-green laser links from satellites; and an improved and more robust TACAMO airborne VLF system. Each of these alternatives was analyzed for operational effectiveness, survivability and affordability. The Navy and the Office of the Secretary of Defense staff hoped a viable alternative to TACAMO would be found as that system, while it had proven very effective, was very expensive to operate. The aircraft losses, service life extensions, and communications suite upgrades had prevented the Navy from acquiring sufficient operating aircraft. Ultimately, however, the Airborne VLF Replacement Study eliminated all the other proposed systems and its final recommendation was to retain TACAMO airborne VLF with a more reliable aircraft and sufficient numbers to sustain the required mission. In this way, TACAMO obtained a strong endorsement to continue indefinitely and keep all of us "True Believers" employed a while longer!

While the OPNAV staff was conducting the Airborne VLF Replacement Study, the office of the Assistant Secretary of the Navy for Shipbuilding and Logistics and the NAVAIR TACAMO Program Office were looking at alternative aircraft to replace the EC-130 in the role. Boeing, at their own expense, had outfitted one of their early 707 test aircraft with huge CFM-56 fan jet engines to stir interest in replacing the engines in the huge Air Force inventory of C-135 airframes. As the EC-130 was nearing end of life, Boeing also flew extended orbit tests to demonstrate to everyone's satisfaction that a big swept-wing aircraft could match the EC-130 in this critical mission area. This Boeing proof-of-concept, initially known as ECX, caught the attention of the Navy. At the same time, Commander Floyd Painter, my previous commanding officer at VQ-4, had been assigned to OP-941D Strategic Communications after his command tour, leading the effort to develop a Mission Needs Statement to justify a replacement TACAMO aircraft, necessary to initiate new procurement programs. I provided him operational analyses and cost estimate information from the Airborne VLF Replacement Study. The ECX Mission Needs Statement was approved by the Secretary of the Navy and the Chief of Naval Operations about the same time as the Airborne VLF Replacement Study. Lockheed then proposed an alternative to the Boeing proposal based on their commercial L-100 (a stretched C-130). The task became a straight-forward performance and cost trade-off analysis between the two.

Although not without some controversy along the way, the Boeing proposal was the clear winner in that trade-off analysis. We next set about developing a life cycle estimate of sufficient quality to be used in budget planning. This estimating process was conducted by a team that included OPNAV and Naval Air Systems Command (NAVAIR) representatives. Since this was the first big four-engine jet ever procured by the Navy, NAVAIR had no estimating tools for it and reached out to the U.S. Air Force for data. One of the first challenges was to determine the total number of aircraft required. The Airborne VLF Replacement Study had determined that 14 aircraft would be required to support continuous airborne two-ocean operations from coastal bases, a figure that did not include attrition, training, and modification. I argued we needed to consider the history of the program and buy more than the minimum number for four reasons:

- TACAMO had lost two aircraft in mishaps;
- various modifications and aircraft reworks routinely kept two or more aircraft out of service;
- the community needed a dedicated test and evaluation aircraft, providing an additional pipeline aircraft when needed; and
- no matter how many aircraft we bought, they would be the last 707 airframes off that Boeing production line. If we guessed wrong, there would be no chance to buy more later.

Eventually that line of thought prevailed and the inventory objective was set at 16 aircraft: 14 operational, 1 test and evaluation bird, and 1 attrition/pipeline aircraft.

With the Airborne VLF Replacement Study complete and the ECX program largely set, the next challenge was to find a Navy funding source. All new programs were required to identify a Navy funding source and budget plan as part of the analysis. The only people in OPNAV strongly opposed to the ECX were the OP-05 Aviation staff. The acquisition cost estimate for the ECX was two billion in 1980 dollars—one hundred million dollars apiece for the airplanes, the rest for research, development, test and evaluation, initial spares and support equipment. The OP-05 folks vowed they would never give up that kind of money for a TACAMO aircraft, money desperately needed to buy F-14s, Phoenix missiles, E-2s and A-6s for more carrier air wings, and for continued development of the new F/A-18.

The search for funding then shifted to OP-941. Commander Painter and his boss, Captain Tim Wood, a submarine warfare officer and previous missile submarine commanding officer, identified a possible source of funding. The new Ohio-class submarines had originally been planned for 24 units. When the Navy buys a new class of ships, a budget line for each vessel is placed in the 20-year shipbuilding plan in the planned acquisition year. Then, when each year comes into view in the rolling Five Year Defense Plan, the Navy decides if it is going to procure that vessel in that year, delay funding or move the money to another purpose. Therefore, the Navy had a budget place-holder for 24 Ohio-class SSBNs, but the government had decided to build only 18 of them in order to remain within the strategic weapons and launchers guidelines of the Strategic Arms Limitation Talks. Therefore, the budget lines for the six unbuilt Ohio-class vessels and their Trident missiles, totaling $18 billion, were available for reprogramming to other purposes as Strategic Program 1 funds, "fenced" for use only on strategic programs. This would make reprogramming of the money to TACAMO, also a strategic program, easier. Captain Wood and Commander Painter led the negotiations among the OPNAV budget staffs, OP-02 (Submarines), and the Strategic Systems Program Office, securing agreement to use that funding for the ECX. This was the final piece making it possible to propose the ECX program in the Fiscal Year 1981 Program Analysis Memoranda.

From reading the description above, you may think that TACAMO and ECX were full-time jobs for me that first year, but it was really just a small part of my workload. The command-and-control Program Analysis Memoranda briefing was to be presented in November 1980. As that time approached, Steve, Pat and I began summarizing the analysis of our assigned projects and putting those summaries into the required briefing format, to be presented personally to the Chief of Naval Operations (CNO), Admiral Tom Hayward, in a room full of admirals who led the OPNAV Sponsor staffs, the budget and programming staffs, the Systems Commands, etc. Three or four-star representatives of the Navy fleet commanders also usually attended the Program Analysis Memoranda briefing, normally scheduled for three hours' duration.

Because of the seniority of the audience, only captains or very senior civilians presented the Program Analysis brief. Our plan was to have our branch director, Captain Baker, present the command-and-control brief, an extensive and complicated presentation that year. The brief had more than a few controversial pieces that would require the CNO's personal decisions, in addition to Captain Baker's own General-Purpose Forces Program Analysis brief. When we presented the first version to the captain, he was surprised by the technical detail of some of the analyses. He decided he was not going to be able to do a professional presentation of the command-and-control brief and asked me if I thought I could do it. I stupidly said, "Yes, sir, if they'll let me." He went immediately to Rear Admiral Kollmorgen to propose I present the brief. The admiral was skeptical, but tentatively approved it, subject to my performance in an upcoming "murder board" with him and several captains. They heard my brief, made changes to it with suggestions for improving the presentation, but in the end approved my presenting the final briefing to the CNO. There was then a second "murder board" of the final draft the day before presentation to the Chief of Naval Operations. This was with Rear Admiral Kollmorgen and several other flag officers. We incorporated their changes and prepared the slides for distribution as read-aheads that night.

The briefing was scheduled from 9 o'clock in the morning to noon the following day. When I delivered the final briefing to Admiral Kollmorgen, he said he would review it at home and that I was to come in at 6 o'clock the next day to go over any last-minute changes he might come up with. Here I thought we were done with changes! I dutifully returned at the appointed time the next morning, expecting nothing more than a few edits and improvements to my speaker notes. Instead, Admiral Kollmorgen had made changes to about half the slides in the 100-slide package, which took about 45 minutes to review with him. I told him that we didn't have time to make so many changes, and that the read-aheads were already out. He said he was sure my team could get it all done in time for the 9 o'clock briefing.

So, back to the office. I distributed the changed slides to Pat and Steve to update for their programs. When done, Pat went off to make the necessary copies, while Steve started making the revised slides from the admiral's mark-ups. Back then, we had primitive Wang word-processors, Harvard Graphics and no high-speed printing of overhead projector slides, just a slow thermo-plastic process. Some slides had to be constructed using little stickers or even be hand drawn. By show time, Steve's "low level skills" as a slide maker had come to the fore, as he had finished about half the slides before moving his art supplies down to the Admin office across from the CNO's briefing room. He continued to make the remaining slides as I began the brief. Pat was behind the briefing room screen, loading the rear-projection machine with the slides as I called for them, and receiving new ones as Steve finished them. All were perfectly done, completed well before they came up in the briefing. Whew!

After more than a year in the Pentagon, I was no longer a rookie when it came to briefing admirals, but those presentations were mostly to small groups in their offices or in briefing rooms with a few flag officers and many more junior folks present. I had even briefed the Chief of Naval Operations himself a few times in his office. However, I must admit to taking a big deep breath when I walked up to the podium that day. The room was filled only with admirals! The table was populated by three and four-star admirals, the two rows of chairs ringing the table occupied by one and two-stars, more admirals than I knew the Navy had! Admiral Hayward's Executive Assistant, a captain and the only other non-flag officer in the room besides me, sat in a folding chair way back in a corner to take notes. It didn't dawn on me until that moment that this was a big deal. I was briefing programs and projects costing more than 20 billion dollars, and these big guys would be making decisions based on the information I was about to present. Gulp!

The briefing was pretty well structured, all the Program Analysis presentations constructed the same way. For each program or issue, you first summarized the supporting analysis, discussed alternatives, presented a recommendation, and ended with a budget and funding slide. After each project was briefed, Admiral Hayward led a question and discussion period to make a decision, before moving on to the next topic. Briefers were known as "furniture," just part of the background, which made this a little easier for me. Nobody in the room asked me any questions, unless there was some detail that they didn't understand, so almost all the discussions were among the flag officers. It was nice to have those little breaks to help relieve the stress, heightened by the fact that I had never laid eyes on half the slides popping up on the screen. To make matters even worse, I was coming down with an ugly cold, a mild fever and slight sore throat, both of which got progressively worse during the briefing. With the stress and the fever, I was sweating like a marathon runner, swigging water and gobbling throat lozenges at every break.

With all those distractions, you might think our brief would have been a disaster, but our team met all those last-minute challenges, the briefing went smoothly, was well-received, and Admiral Hayward approved all our recommendations. The ECX program was only four slides in the three-hour brief, well-coordinated around all the relevant staffs with very little discussion. All the admirals agreed with proceeding with the ECX program and with the recommended funding source and profile. The CNO approved it and we moved on to the next item. That whole ECX piece took about 10 minutes and made my day.

And that is the story of how the ECX, soon to be the E-6A, was born. Interestingly, there were only a small number of "True Believers" involved in the initial ECX planning, although more would participate as the decision process continued. A group of hard-working and dedicated officers on several staffs got this program started and began a new era for TACAMO. Unfortunately, the CNO's decision at the Program Analysis briefing was not the final one. A new acquisition program of that size had to be approved by the Deputy Secretary of Defense. In addition, the Navy proposed the ECX in the Program Objectives and Milestones Fiscal Year 1983 as a high-priority unfunded project, believing that TACAMO was a joint program that should be funded with Secretary of Defense or Joint funding, not Navy money, the so-called "gold watch" budget strategy. For the next two years, while the ECX program worked through the 1983 budgeting process, the Navy staffs were subjected to a seemingly endless stream of requests for additional analysis, justifications and refined cost estimates. I worked on a few of those during my remaining months in OP-96, but most of the ECX final approval process fell on other individuals. NAVAIR had let a Request for Proposal to industry for their candidates for replacement of the EC-130 fleet, but only Boeing responded with their ECX. As a result, the Deputy Secretary of the Navy approved ECX as a sole-source procurement, meaning the NAVAIR Program Manager could award the program to Boeing without holding a formal competition, which probably shortened the procurement time by two years. He also directed the Navy to fund it using the originally identified Program 1 funding source.

After the 1980 Program Analysis briefing was done, Steve, Pat and I completed the required close-out tasks and reports then started in on our analyses to support the 1981 effort. In February 1981, two things happened that made me smile. First, one of our two cell leadership positions was filled with the arrival of Commander Dave Anderson. He had just completed a destroyer command tour, with previous major staff experience. He was an outstanding officer and also a smart guy who fit in well with the rest of us. He immediately took over cell leadership functions and I was happy to return to being a lieutenant commander analyst! Second, I received orders to report to VQ-3 for my third squadron tour, with a detaching date of June 1981, C-130 refresher training en route, and a reporting date of October 1. That reporting date came while VQ-3 was executing a change of homeport from Guam to NAS Barbers Point, Hawaii, scheduled for completion by September 30. The Bureau did not want to send newly-reporting officers to Guam, then pay for another move to Hawaii, so everyone going to VQ-3 in that timeframe got orders to report to Hawaii in October or later. I was eagerly anticipating getting back to the squadron.

Even though my tour in OP-96 was extremely busy and demanding, I remember it as one of my best. I learned a lot, it greatly contributed to my professional growth, and I got to make a significant contribution to the future of my own community. Pat McKim and I remain lifelong friends after working so closely together on that tour. He, too, became a captain. Steve Honda was the most successful of our little team. After his tour in OP-96, he transitioned to become a Public Affairs Officer, eventually rising to rear admiral and Chief of Naval Information. In fact, the extraordinary intelligence and talent of the officers in OP-96 are what I remember best. Our boss, Captain Baker, became a vice admiral. Almost all the officers I worked with in those two years achieved the rank of captain or above, half became flag officers, including two four-stars. Admiral Kollmorgen's relief, Rear Admiral Trost, would become CNO a few years later. You could not have asked for a better group of officers to serve with and learn from.

CHAPTER 6

A Rapid Acquisition

Ed Hampshire

Money was tight for the ECX procurement, and the Naval Air Systems Command (NAVAIR) Program Manager and many of his assistants had no TACAMO experience. Everything I proposed to make things better for the TACAMO squadrons was initially shot down, and it turned into a two year "slugfest" between the ECX Program Manager and myself to deliver the ECX as the best compromise for the money available. If only the program manager had TACAMO experience, he would have understood this "slugfest" shouldn't have been necessary to protect the new TACAMO fleet from repeating the mistakes of the past procurement of EC-130s. The program manager kept telling me that "better is the evil enemy of good enough," as we fought on every minute detail on each procurement specification. I ultimately threatened to write an official letter to the commander of NAVAIR saying that the ECX, by the current specification, would not offer any improvement over the EC-130 it was replacing and, in some cases, was not as good. At times, I felt like the lone person crying wolf. I fully expected my performance evaluation to reflect what a "pain in the rear" I felt I had become. Little did I know I would be sitting in that program manager's chair four years later making those decisions.

Vern Lochausen

Since almost all my work in my first VQ-3 tour as Special Projects Department was about resolving issues and preparing for the future, it just seemed right then to take shore duty orders to the TACAMO Program Office in Naval Air Systems Command, Crystal City, Virginia. Expecting to dig deeper into Herc issues and coming modifications, I was surprised to be given a pretty free agenda to be the fleet "trouble-shooter" for the new E-6 introduction. Instead of Herc meetings and conferences, I was suddenly immersed in E-6 design, production, logistics, training, and future upgrades. Officially, I was the E-6 Deputy Program Manager for Block Upgrades, a paper program to find ways to improve the cross-decked Herc mission avionics as soon as we could. An unexpected task was to defend the political decision to base the E-6 in Oklahoma. When Congressional delegations from Hawaii and Maryland called foul on this decision, I was tasked to take what VQ-3 Skipper Chuck Fitchet had called "the eight great lies about Tinker" and turn them into "the eight great reasons for Tinker." Captain Ernie Lewis educated me on how to research this and find the positives in the apparent negatives. This all culminated in drafting for him the responses to the Congressional and General Accounting Office questions. When the hearings started, I dutifully reported to Capitol Hill and observed the Navy leadership, and then Oklahoma Congressman Mickey Edwards, quote what we had written, dang near word for word!

PART FOUR

TACAMO Comes of Age, 1980–1985

TACAMO came of age in the 1980s after its designation as a warfare specialty in communications in 1979. TACAMO officers took major billets afloat on ships and carrier battle group staffs as communications officers, further familiarizing the fleet with the community's unique talents in that technical area. While the promotion of Bob Downey and Fil Baca to lieutenant commander had been an exceptional event, selection of junior officers to this critical rank quickly reached the normal range for other aviation squadrons. Second and third squadron tours were now the norm.

During this time, VQ-3 went from being the junior squadron to VQ-4 to an equal partner with the deployment of the Trident submarines in the Pacific in the early 1980s. In 1979, U.S. Pacific Command directed that VQ-3 was to double its fleet of aircraft and personnel, relocate to Hawaii, and stand up to 100 percent airborne coverage by 1983, all while transitioning into a new TACAMO communications suite!

Fil and Bob both made commander and screened to be our first TACAMO commanding officers: Baca commanding VQ-3 in 1983 and Downey VQ-4 in 1984. By odd coincidence, 1983 was the first year that Navy commands had the option of putting up the commanding officer's picture on their historical walls in color, rather than in black and white. By careful coordination between the squadrons, both chose to ensure the photos of Fil and Bob were the first in color, marking the beginning of TACAMO taking charge of its own destiny, though few today know that was no coincidence.

Fil and Bob opened the floodgates and there was never again a VP skipper of TACAMO.

CHAPTER 7

TACAMO Joins the Navy

Ed Hampshire

My detailer and I decided on the Naval Postgraduate School at Monterey for my master's degree as the next billet, based on my electrical engineering undergraduate degree and extensive maintenance and technical expertise. Could it be that the Navy believed in me enough now it was going to invest more time and money into my further education? Perhaps I really did have a future in the Navy after all. Maybe a tour in TACAMO wasn't a "kiss of death" as I had heard many times in the squadron. Besides myself, there were also several other officers from VQ-4 who had received orders to Monterey, and they were there when I arrived, including Lew McIntyre (yet again), Fil Baca, Dan Lashbrook, Denny Arneson, and Al Shuff. The Navy was certainly investing in so many TACAMO officers going to postgraduate school.

I thought back to my time spent as the Avionics Division Officer and saw the mess of poorly engineered, integrated, and documented mission systems in the EC-130. I therefore chose to go into the communications engineering curriculum, electronic engineering with a communications technology design emphasis. I hoped someday, with those qualifications, to be in a position to exert a positive influence on the design of TACAMO systems, making the lives of the sailors in the squadrons better and the systems more reliable. After all, I fully expected the TACAMO mission to be around long enough to make that contribution.

I graduated in June 1977 and my detailer assigned me to be Communications Officer on the USS *Forrestal*, one of three aircraft carriers he offered me. Well, no flying this tour, but at least I would be "rounding out" my naval career with a shipboard tour. There I could get underway ship-handling qualifications, skills recognized by the rest of the Navy before promotion boards. The Communications Officer is also a lieutenant commander department head job on a carrier. Apparently, the Navy still believed in me and my potential if it was sending me to this high-risk/high-payoff job and I would leave the ship with a very in-depth understanding and experience in naval communications. What better background could I hope for to enhance my desirability for a TACAMO-related job? This tour would be my "disassociated sea tour" that most pilots in the Navy usually received.

Andy Riddile

It was time in 1977 for study at the Naval Postgraduate School in Monterey, California. The TACAMO mission is a command-and-control mission, so it made sense I was selected for the inaugural Naval Postgraduate School course in command-and-control systems, given my expertise in the subject. I was now even more narrowly committing myself to a career not really understood by many. I found the command-and-control course exceptionally challenging in areas. I was a bit baffled at first when a professor was discussing Laplace transforms; I thought for a moment I had wandered into a French language class. My class of 16 officers and civilians pulled together and tackled the challenges of Naval Postgraduate School as a team, some remaining good friends to this day. Kermit Ayres followed me in the next class.

Shortly after I began this study, I learned I had been deep-selected to lieutenant commander. I was surprised not just at the early promotion, but also that the Navy had deep-selected someone in the outsider strategic air community, a community that had just promoted its first lieutenant commanders three years prior. Now, I was really committed. I left the school with a master's degree in Systems Technology (Command and Control). By this time, it was crystal-clear I was going to go for it in a small, little-appreciated aviation community with consequently little chance to make it into the most senior ranks of the Navy. However, in such a small, but strategically crucial, community, I could make a difference.

I received orders in 1979 to serve on the National Emergency Airborne Command Post, (NEACP, pronounced "Knee-Cap"), now the National Airborne Operations Center but still referred to by the press as "the gadget-packed doomsday jet" based at Offutt Air Force Base near Omaha, Nebraska. Army Colonel Travis Walker was my Battle Staff Team Chief, infantry all the way, a leader's leader, crystal-clear with what he wanted. Had he been at the Alamo, things would have been different. I was assigned as the Battle Staff Communications Officer and then as the Emergency Actions Officer for Operations Team One, one of three battle staffs of Joint Staff personnel.

There were occasions of excitement. On June 3, 1980, the Andrews Alert Facility klaxon sounded, wrenching the team members from whatever we were doing and putting us into our respective seats, strapped in, as the big white E-4B taxied toward the end of the runway. As I wiped the sleep from my eyes, I listened to a conference convened on a loudspeaker, giving indications of inbound Soviet intercontinental ballistic missiles. Shortly thereafter, the automated system revised its projection to an all-out attack with a massive number of missiles. As my Emergency Actions sergeant and I retrieved and unlocked the necessary documents, I forced thoughts of my family out of my mind. The materials were spread out in front of us and I advised Colonel Walker to launch the aircraft. He decided not to do so, later explaining there was no context for an attack besides the conference, which was not reporting a consistent attack pattern. U.S. relations with the Soviet Union at the time were no worse than usual and the number of attacking missiles seemed random. Soon, raw data from the satellites and early-warning radars ringing the country showed that no missiles had actually been launched. Later investigation showed a single integrated circuit, worth less than half a dollar, had failed at North American Air Defense Headquarters in Colorado, causing random numbers of attacking missiles to be displayed. The same thing happened again a few days later, although our response to that alert was jaded.

Then, on March 30, 1981, the klaxon sounded again. In minutes, the team members were in their seats on the aircraft with engines running when we learned President Reagan had been shot. Was this a decapitation attempt? Was this the first step in an attack on the nation? There were no Fast Reaction Procedure Cards for this specific kind of event. We kept the engines running, monitoring secure conferences among the military leadership. I was on the secure phone when General David Jones, Chairman of the Joint Chiefs of Staff, advised his commanders that there were no indications of an event greater than a lone-wolf assassination attempt, but that we should "keep our command-and-control heads up." That was us. It turned into a long night. The chain of custody for President Reagan's codes, kept in his coat pocket, was lost in the confusion, as the emergency room team at George Washington Hospital simply cut off his suit jacket and threw it into the corner of the room. The FBI later swept the operating room for potential evidence, finding the coat and, inside, a strange-looking card, necessitating its immediate replacement. The FBI works for the Justice Department, not the Defense Department. Yikes!

As Emergency Actions Officer, I was able to contribute in the areas of emergency actions and worldwide communications planning, and development of improved procedures. Given the mission to provide support to the president and to the chairman of the Joint Chiefs of Staff, these contributions had real meaning. This level of command sits at the top of the entire military strategic command-and-control structure. The assignment allowed me to learn all I could about the many things relevant to my growing area of expertise, except, of course, for all that happened at the White House. It turned out that gap in my experience would be filled in by a subsequent tour! Again, I was grateful for the support and interest I received from my colleagues and superiors.

Vern Lochausen

The University of Texas, with forty thousand students enrolled, versus the 4,800 at my alma mater Ole Miss, was a shock in some ways and liberating in others. No alerts, no "you're the last guy so you have to go" but also a total immersion in a real civilian community. The Naval Reserve Officers Training Corps (NROTC) commanding officer made it very clear, "You either make this tour count for your Navy career or make your plans to get out. Either way, you must maintain a professionalism that inspires these young people." Rogering that, I set out to transition to a management masters and entry into academia as a real professor with great leadership stories to tell, Bill Coyne vs. the Other Guy. Enter my next mentor, Dr. George Baker, U.S. Marine Corps retired. He took me under his wing and convinced me "not to burn the bridge back to the Navy." He set me up with a masters with a minor in community college management, taught by the nation's best professors in the Kellogg Community College Leadership Program. It was tailored to meet a Navy Education and Training Subspecialty while getting the masters that would set me up in academia. Motivating my company of midshipmen and Naval Enlisted Scientific Education Program cadets was not a part-time endeavor, so college courses were all late afternoon and evening. We created the best, most successful and most motivated company that was to produce several captains and colonels in the future. A community college, seeing my grade point average and Navy experience, made me an offer as assistant director of student services, at less salary than I was bringing home as a lieutenant. Come to find out, I was making as much as some of my professors with PhDs! George Baker was right about bridges, and the Navy extended one to me when TACAMO became a warfare specialty in 1979. He counseled me that even the worst skipper could serve as an example of how not to lead and that only one of the five under whom I had served met that criterion. Facing the prospect of returning to TACAMO full on, I approached my detailer: "I got my tickets punched here and I need a fleet ticket." He penciled me in for USS *Ranger*'s next Communications Officer, following the lead of Fil Baca, Bob Downey and Ed Hampshire. Later, his story changed: Permanent Change-of-Station money was short, TACAMO is building up and I was in demand to return to VQ-4. In the end, the money story was completely untrue; the detailer cut me orders to VQ-3 for the initial cadre at Barbers Point, Hawaii, as the squadron moved from Guam.

Lew McIntyre

From VQ-3, I went to Commander, Operational Test and Evaluation Force as Airborne Systems Operational Test Director, with primary focus on TACAMO: TACAMO Improvement Program Phase Two final approval; Electromagnetic Pulse Hardening; and the Enhanced Verdin Operational Evaluations. Chief Radioman Don Decker, one of my VQ-3 communications supervisors, was my able assistant, and became a lifelong friend. During this time, I worked closely with my former skipper from VQ-3, Hugh "Barney" Barnhill, now the Naval Air Systems Command (NAVAIR) deputy program manager for TACAMO. He was rolling out the new model Hercs, to expand VQ-3 assets to support 100 percent, and the ECX during his tenure became more than just a gleam in the marketing eye of Boeing; it became the E-6A Mercury, with CFM-56 engines and wings extensively modified to support orbit; not as good as the Herc, but good enough, and with air-to-air refueling capability, greatly extended range and better on-station times. Air refueling gave us a very long in-flight capability as long as we did not run out of tankers. Together, we worked up a test strategy to guide the acquisition.

We also conducted the first operational evaluation of the Electromagnetic Pulse Hardening program. This program was a combination of shielding, filtering and limiting to protect the electronics inside the aircraft from the effects of high-altitude nuclear detonations, which had the potential to damage or upset electronic equipment over a wide area. We tested the aircraft at the Air Force Weapons Laboratory at Kirtland Air Force Base in New Mexico. Part of this program was hardness assurance and maintenance surveillance to periodically retest all aircraft to ensure hardness is maintained, despite corrosion, wear and tear, and component changes. The EC-130 program was inherited by the E-6 and is now considered "the Gold Standard" for aircraft electromagnetic pulse hardening. Interestingly, I flew what was to be my last flight in the EC-130 for the program in the same airframe I had flown my very first TACAMO flight, Bureau Number 151891, with Rich Adamo, my squadron mate from VQ-3, as Airborne Communications Officer (ACO).

During this time, the first of the "True Believers" began bubbling to the top: Fil Baca screened for command, followed by Bob Downey and

A diagram revealing EC-130's TACAMO IVB layout circa 1975. (Collins Aerospace)

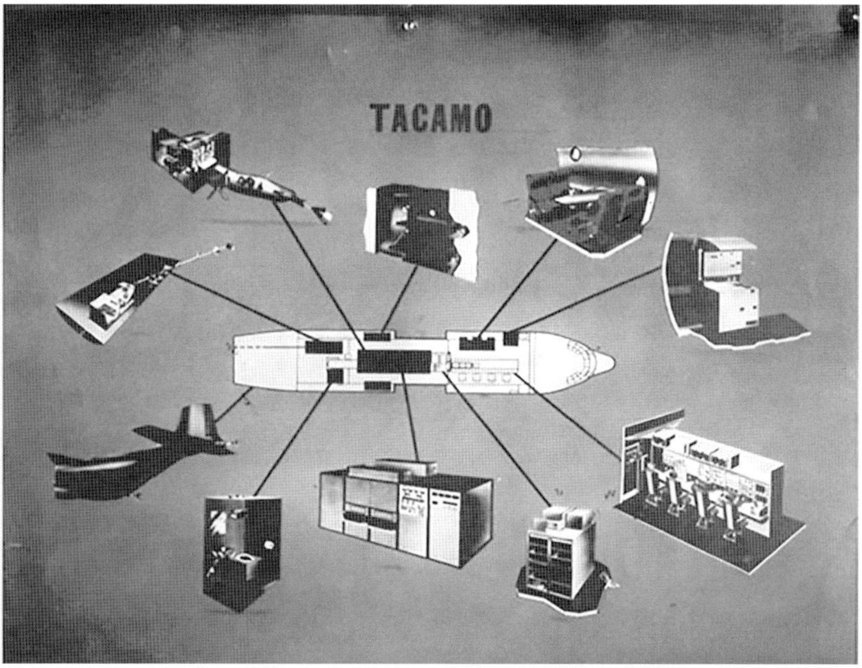

The various components of TACAMO IVB and their location within the EC-130. (Collins Aerospace)

An unusual sight for VQ-3 in the 1970s—four birds together! (Barry Coyle)

A less unusual sight—#4 engine stopped and its prop feathered! (Barry Coyle)

VQ-3 hangar entrance, 1971. (Barry Coyle)

Commander Bill Loeffler, VQ-3 CO, 1971. (Barry Coyle)

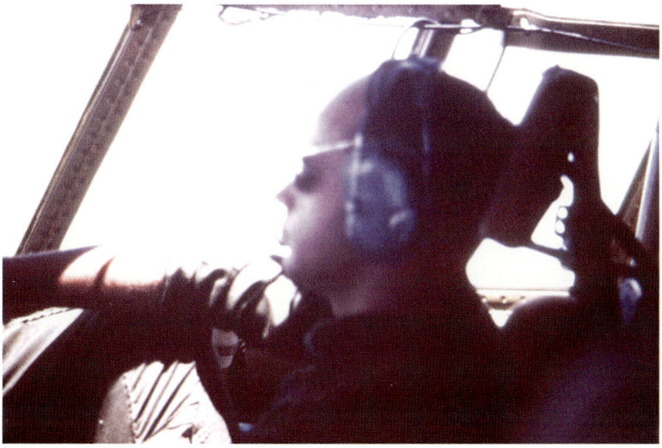

Bill Loeffler's trusty third pilot, Lieutenant (junior grad) Barry Coyle. (Barry Coyle)

Executive Officer Commander R. Dunmire and CO Commander K. Krause, VQ-3, 1972. (Barry Coyle)

EC-130G 151890 en route to Maryland's Eastern Shore, port wing ablaze, January 1972. (Ken deGraffenreid)

'890 in Bessie Gore's cornfield near Salisbury, Maryland, following its successful, and expertly done, forced landing. (Ken deGraffenreid)

'890 damage being inspected by VQ-4 Safety Officer Lieutenant Ken deGraffenreid, January 1972. (Ken deGraffenreid)

VQ-4 "Fin Flash" circa 1972. (Ken deGraffenreid)

Lew McIntyre marrying Karen, Skipper Dave Thompson best man. (Lew McIntyre)

The kiss and the Arch of Swords, Agaña, Guam. (Lew McIntyre)

Bureau Number '891 on the trestle at Albuquerque for EMP testing, 1982. (Official U.S. Air Force photograph)

TACAMO Improvement Program, Phase II Comm Central, with TACAMO Message Processing System in foreground. (Official U.S. Navy photograph)

Lew McIntyre signing something important for VQ-3, 1978. (Lew McIntyre)

New Herc '348, VQ-4, circa 1977. (Mike Davidson)

Three-engine ferry flight escorted by Mike Clemens. (Mike Davidson)

VQ-4's tenth anniversary, 1978. (Mike Davidson)

Commander Brian Anderson farewells "True Believer" Mike Davidson. (Mike Davidson)

VQ-4 Crew Eleven, NAS Bermuda, 1978. (Mike Davidson)

VQ-3 KC-130F logistic support bird, Barbers Point, Hawaii, circa 1981. (Barry Coyle)

EC-130Q off Barbers Point, Hawaii, circa 1985. (Official U.S. Navy photograph)

"True Believers." Commander Barry Coyle relieves Commander Bill Harsanyi, VQ-3, November 1985. (Barry Coyle)

Alert launch Barbers Point, Hawaii, circa 1985. (Barry Coyle)

Herc on ice somewhere in the Northern Hemisphere. (Mike Davidson)

Commander Coyle with COMPATWINGSPAC Rear Admiral P. D. Smith, 1986. (Barry Coyle)

"True Believers" Commander Chuck Fitchet relieves Commander Barry Coyle, VQ-3, 1986. (Barry Coyle)

E-6A rollout, December 1986. (Barry Coyle)

E-6A first flight, 1987. (Official U.S. Navy photograph)

The big CFM-56 engine of the E-6A. (Barry Coyle)

"TACAMO DET WEST," circa1976. Left to right: Dan Lashbrook, Denny Arneson, Al Shuff, Lew McIntyre, Fil Baca, and Ed Hampshire. (Lewis McIntyre)

E-6A interior arrangement. It was a substantially bigger airframe than the EC-130. (Boeing Company)

E-6A communications central circa 1990. (Official U.S. Navy photograph)

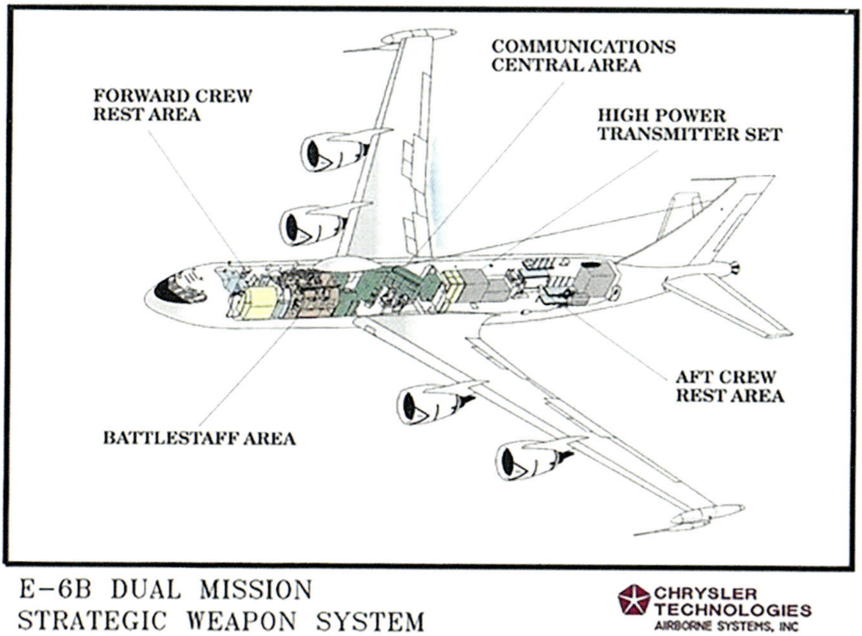

An annotated diagram of the E-6B's interior arrangement. Compare this to the earlier diagram of the EC-130 for a bigger layout, with a seat for the ACO, no longer sitting on the ACO box!. (Chrysler Technologies Airborne Systems Inc, now part of Raytheon)

Nora Wingfield (center right) and VQ-4 shipmates. (Ed Hampshire)

TACAMO commanding officers and commodores. Left to right: CDR Bob Young (VQ-3); CDR Tom Trotter (VQ-3, SCW-1); CDR Vern Lochausen (VQ-3, SCW-1); CDR Mike Davidson (VQ-3); CAPT Chuck Fitchet (VQ-3); CAPT Barry Coyle (VQ-3); CDR Andy Riddile (VQ-4, SCW-1); CAPT Ed Hampshire (VQ-4, PMA-271); CDR P. A. Moore (VQ-4; CDR Paul Jackson (VQ-4). In civilian clothes, CDR (ret) Jim Bailey (VQ-3); CAPT (Ret) Bob Neiderstadt (VQ-3). (Barry Coyle)

Ed Hampshire. All had taken carrier tours, which seemed to be a logical progression: to broaden experience in TACAMO with fleet experience that a selection board, composed of non-TACAMO senior officers, could comprehend. It was here that I made two critical misjudgments that sidelined my progress as a "True Believer," at least for a while.

My first was to turn down the opportunity to apply for Aviation Engineering Duty Officer. I had always been highly regarded as an engineering type and, with a master's in avionics engineering from Monterey, and my Test and Evaluation Force and squadron experience, I should have had no problems being selected. My problem with putting my name before the selection board was that, at that time, I had to do it before being promoted to commander and, if selected, I would not be eligible for command screen for VQ-3 and VQ-4. For me, this was the gold ring, and I could not choose to give up that dream for aviation engineering duty.

The second misjudgment was to turn down both Fil Baca's and Bob Downey's solicitation for me to be Maintenance or Operations Department Head under them. Working with Fil, in particular, would have been a dynamite job, especially in Ops; three years prior, I had planned out the roadmap he would be following, standing up to 100 percent coverage and moving to Barbers Point. I opted, instead, to follow their career pattern of a carrier tour, getting a billet as Communications Officer for Commander, Carrier Group One.

The carrier group was a grueling but extremely satisfying tour. I was based out of San Diego, Karen's hometown, enabling us to connect closely with her family, at least when I was there, in a very special way. I served on three carriers, the *Carl Vinson* and *Midway* briefly in my 1983 deployment, and the *Constellation* in my 1984–1985 workup and deployment. I was responsible for the battle group's entire tactical network of communications, and I found TACAMO veterans ensconced in many key positions in naval communications: Bruce Cloud, Bill Coyne's predecessor, commanded Naval Communications Station Stockton; Wes May commanded Naval Communications Area Master Station Western Pacific on Guam, with retired Master Chief Radioman Dunn from VQ-3 as his Area Operations Officer; and Lieutenant

Commanders Norm Tindall and Legare Davis were communications officers for Carrier Groups Five and Seven. We all found our TACAMO experience put us uniquely in touch with the specialized field of Navy tactical communications.

I worked under two great leaders, Rear Admirals Paul McCartney and "Bud" Edney, and a super chief of staff, Captain Sam Ward, oddly enough a submariner, but hands down, the greatest manager I have ever served under. They all made this a most rewarding tour.

I made commander while on the staff, which was a big moment, but that was followed by the big disappointment: I failed to command screen. My contemporaries Chuck Fitchet, Andy Riddile, and Kermit Ayres made it; I did not. I had followed the carrier route, but for this selection board, for the first time, all three TACAMO candidates, except me, had three particularly challenging squadron tours.

Everyone who has failed to screen or to be promoted has experienced this disappointment, but you reach a point where you can sit and sulk or map out an alternate course for your life. Like Moses, I had a loss of faith in TACAMO in that one choice of sea duty. I was allowed to see the Promised Land of command, but not to enter in.

Mike Davidson

The Bureau of Naval Personnel was not the tour I expected—it was much more. First, I was in the Officer Performance Division, directly responsible for processing all Relief for Cause requests on naval officers. I'd never heard of this process before, so I read through the office historical files, the fire hose treatment. Most cases were from the surface Navy. Substandard aviators lost their wings and the Bureau would have to transfer them elsewhere. The submarine community could likewise determine an officer was "not qualified for duty involving submarines" and get a replacement. There were no such means by which the surface Navy could disqualify their officers, so Relief for Cause was developed. This allowed them to remove individuals who could not perform or got into serious trouble with the Uniform Code of Military Justice or law enforcement.

My supervisor was a former destroyer skipper who had the patience to teach me the intricacies of shipboard life. He found a large cross-section picture of a destroyer and took me to school on various aspects of ships that were new to me. The surface ships' Fleet Rehabilitation and Modernization service life extensions and overhauls were long overdue after arduous on-station operations in Vietnam. New squadron commodores showed an amazing patience with their skippers on these ships but had none at all for those whose ships ran afoul of the Board for Inspection and Survey. The Board evaluates a ship's readiness to conduct combat operations at sea, about every five years, through an extensive system of checks on installed equipment. It was like the Administrative and Material inspections we experienced in VQ-4, but with less admin and more material. We had special files on these ships' captains and their chief engineering officers and analyzed the data for trends to explain the increasing number of Reliefs for Cause.

I was approaching the age of 30 with lots of experience in the Herc but no currency. I had started in the T-28 Trojan proficiency flying program at Naval Air Facility Andrews, but the program was then shut down. I had applications out to two airlines for whom I would be happy to fly, including United Airlines. They called me for an interview during my last year at the Bureau, but then suddenly cancelled it, advising me they were laying off over 700 pilots. Since I had no airline prospects and was taking on a new spouse and stepson, I accepted a commission in the regular Navy, with a two-year service obligation. My new detailer and I had lunch one day and he asked me what I really wanted to do with my life now that I was regular Navy. I answered, "Have a great Navy career!" He laughed and asked me if I had ever thought about duty in Greenland, thus beginning a lifelong friendship.

What I really wanted to do was to get to a flying outfit. My detailer fought off pressure from an admiral in the western Pacific to get C-130 pilots out to Guam to fly logistics missions. He slated me back to VQ-4 instead. I was happy with this, since I had previously turned down an offer to go to Naval Postgraduate School for a master's degree, as well as an offer to change designator to the Training and Administration of the Reserve where I would have been assured of flying DC-9s.

Fil Baca

It seemed there was new life for the community and a defining career path for TACAMO. I was privileged to carry its mantra, sent back to Naval Postgraduate School again, this time with squadron mates Lew McIntyre, Denny Arneson, Al Shuff, and Ed Hampshire, all lieutenants, this time for telecommunications management. All of us married folks took turns hosting bachelor Lew for dinners and parties. Lew opted for a second tour in TACAMO, and Ed Hampshire and I opted for tours as carrier communications officers, he on the USS *Forrestal* and I on the USS *Independence*. In 1979, TACAMO succeeded in becoming a warfare specialty, a result of the insistence by us and many others to return to the community. After that tour, I was sent to Kirtland Air Force Base Defense Nuclear Agency in Albuquerque to get the joint ticket punched as the Chief of the Joint Nuclear Coordination Center. I missed my department head tour, but my detailer was convinced the carrier tour would qualify as a disassociated department head tour.

Lew McIntyre, who had been with me in VQ-4 and Monterey, came out to Kirtland Air Force Base to conduct the Electromagnetic Pulse Hardening test program for the EC-130. Lew gave me a fantastic tour of the huge all-wood "trestle" where he had an EC-130 "laboratory" perched hundreds of feet above a canyon, ready to be bombarded with many tests. We had many "flying TACAMO-style happy hours" at my house back in those days to keep Southwest TACAMO alive! When we'd go to Happy Hour, people would often inquire how the Navy got to New Mexico. Our pleasant refrain was that we couldn't talk about it and could only say that "We came in our submarines down the Rio Grande!"

CHAPTER 8

From One Island Paradise to Another

Barry Coyle

Diane and I married in March 1981. Her son Chauncey, from a previous marriage, became my stepson in late June. Maybe they would become "True Believers," too! Most Navy moves are hectic, stressful, and not much fun, but not this one. I checked out of OP-96 in early June and our new little family packed up and set out on our first Navy adventure, spending time with family that we wouldn't be seeing for a while and visiting as many National Parks and scenic sites as we could down the Shenandoah and Blue Ridge Parkways, and the Daniel Boone National Forest, en route to Little Rock in mid-July.

I got a nice surprise for my C-130 refresher training as the Air Force paired me up with an Air Force major named Howie, who had completed two previous tours in Hercs as an instructor pilot and evaluator, with orders to be the Training Wing Standardization/Evaluation Officer at Little Rock. He and I became the first students for a young captain fresh out of instructor training. Howie and I had about 8,000 hours between us and many years of instructor experience, so we spent as much time training our instructor as vice-versa—as I'm sure was intended by that pairing, which, as one might expect, was trouble-free and went by rapidly. Even better than the flying match-up, Howie and his family were big outdoor people too, so we spent most weekends camping, canoeing, tubing, hiking, fishing, and generally exploring the wonderful Arkansas parks system, a great summer for both flying and recreation.

After completion of training, after some leave for family farewells, we flew to Hawaii, staying at the Hale Koa on Waikiki Beach for about 10 days while securing local housing. We found a nice townhouse in Makakilo, just up the hill from Barbers Point. We didn't know it then, but that would be our home for the next six years. And then it was back to work!

VQ-3's official homeport change from Guam to Barbers Point was October 1, 1981, the day I checked in, but the last pieces of the transition were still in progress. Our new home was Hangar 110, large enough to hold two EC-130's totally enclosed, with workspace for the big squadron VQ-3 was soon to become. This building had been unused for several years prior to our arrival and required considerable clean-up, fix-up, paint-up, most of which was accomplished by squadron personnel. When I checked in, VQ-3 had two EC-130Q and two KC-130F aircraft, the second F model to assist with moving equipment and personnel from Guam to Hawaii, and about 200 personnel. Over the next two years, the squadron would grow to seven EC-130Qs, one KC-130F and 600 personnel. At the same time, the squadron was increasing the number of mission flights to achieve 100 percent airborne coverage in the Pacific by October 1, 1983. The next two years would prove to be very busy!

VQ-3's operational commander remained Commander-in-Chief, U.S. Pacific Forces (CINCPAC), headquartered at Camp Smith, Hawaii. Administratively, we were assigned to the Commander, Patrol Wings Pacific Fleet at NAS Moffett Field, California, with our immediate administrative boss Commander Patrol Wing Two on board the naval air station. Patrol Wing Two consisted of five VP (patrol) squadrons and VPU-2, all flying P-3 Orions, and VQ-3, so we were a little bit of the odd man out. The VP community was tremendously supportive and helpful throughout VQ-3's build-up phase and subsequently with sustained operations and E-6 transition planning.

With the TACAMO warfare specialty now four years old, we early "True Believers" now found ourselves in a "be careful what you wish for" situation. We had worked hard to build this community, rising through the ranks, but we were now senior enough that we had to lead what we had created! It was our job now as department heads, and very soon to be executive officers and commanding officers, to provide the leadership, mentoring and professional development to the more junior personnel to keep the community strong, successful and growing. In VQ-3, the major department head and assistant positions were filled by officers with one or two prior TACAMO tours: I was assigned as head of the newly-formed Training Department; Bill Wilt was in Ops; Frank Kockler in Admin; and Vern Lochausen in Comm. We also had a fine group of TACAMO-experienced lieutenants on their second tours filling many assistant department head and division officer positions. This growing cadre of "True Believers" would prove successful in grooming a new generation of officers and enlisted personnel who would tackle the challenges of the future. VQ-4 was similarly blessed with experienced "True Believers." The community had also placed experienced TACAMO officers on the major staffs of Commander-in-Chief, U.S. Atlantic Forces (CINCLANT), the Secretary of the Navy, OP-941, Office of the Secretary of Defense and Naval Air Systems Command (NAVAIR) so there were more and more knowledgeable officers supporting the community and providing analysis and informed recommendations to senior leaders.

Commanding officers during this period were Commanders Jim Bailey, Joe "Ragpicker" Gerard, and our first home-grown TACAMO commanding and executive officers, Fil Baca and Bill Harsanyi. Commander Bailey presided over the successful and accident-free relocation of VQ-3 to Hawaii. Joe Gerard was an outstanding, if hard-nosed, Exec, and a great commanding officer. As Exec, his primary project was refurbishment of the hangar and barracks, which he approached with his normal fanatical attention to detail. Part of his long-held leadership philosophy was that there were no small things; he sweated every task equally, demanding full attention to detail and completion with excellence and speed. Supervising an augmented First Lieutenant Division and many working parties, he quickly had both Hangar 110 and our assigned barracks transformed from neglected old buildings into places where we were proud to work and show off to our many visitors. As Commanding Officer, he led the squadron through an incredibly difficult and fast-paced period of training and build-up toward 100 percent airborne operations. He was very intelligent, focused on the mission, and driven to excel and exceed, but he was also very even-handed, had an enthusiastic sense of humor, and many characteristics that made him an effective and popular commanding officer. Commander Gerard also had a special distinction as the last VP Officer to command VQ-3. His Exec, Commander Fidel "Fil" Baca was the very first TACAMO Warfare Specialty officer to command a TACAMO squadron, to be followed a few months later by Commander Bob Downey in VQ-4, completing the transition from VP officers to TACAMO "True Believers" in command. Commander Bill Harsanyi was Fil's Exec.

Interestingly, during the run-up to Commander Gerard's change of command, there was no mention at all that his tour was the end of an era for VP and the beginning of a new day for TACAMO. Maybe they thought we were going to fail, but we didn't; following Commanders Baca and Downey, there has never been a non-TACAMO commanding officer of either squadron. Fil was a very hard-nosed and aggressive executive officer who had us guessing what kind of commanding officer he would be. When he took command in June 1983, he turned out to be superb, smart, even-handed, tough when he needed to be, and a good leader and mentor to squadron personnel. Fil led the completion of the squadron build-up and initiation of 100 percent airborne operations in the Pacific.

Throughout my two consecutive tours in VQ-3 at Barbers Point from 1981 to 1987, as we built up from 200 to nearly 600 people, the detailers provided us with extraordinarily talented and professional officers, chiefs and enlisted personnel, a true blessing. Most had prior TACAMO tours, but some were serving disassociated tours from other multi-engine communities, many of whom quickly qualified as instructors in this new community. The TACAMO "True Believers" did their job well, training and leading squadron personnel to develop the next generation of "True Believers" who would go on to lead the community's transition to the new E-6A aircraft in a few years. Of the men who served with me during these years, many went on to be squadron and wing commanders: Lochausen (squadron and wing), Moore, Duvall, Hobbs, Keilty (squadron and wing), Diggs, Cush, Flynn, Sereno, Strance, Gallamore (squadron and E-6 Program Manager for NAVAIR), and many more. It was pretty easy for the squadron to excel with talent like this at all levels. More "True Believers" were being developed at the same time in VQ-4 under the leadership of Bob Downey and Eddie Hampshire.

No discussion of professional development in VQ-3 during these years would be complete without covering the incredible contributions of female officers to VQ-3's success, and the squadron's role in expanding female participation throughout the Navy. The first women entered naval aviation training with the group graduating in 1974. In 1976, the Naval Academy and the Naval Reserve Officers Training Corps (NROTC) Scholarship program were opened to women, with the first graduates in the Class of 1980. In the late 1970s, with considerable "encouragement" from Congress, all the Services began to expand the number of units where increasing numbers of women could serve. Somehow, the brain trust in Washington determined that TACAMO—the very tip of the spear in the event of nuclear war—was a "non-combat" community and therefore suitable for the assignment of women under the laws of the time.

When I arrived in VQ-3 in late 1981 we already had two female pilots, Wendi Bryan Carpenter and Janine Igou, both about halfway through their first squadron tour. Cyndi Koehler Burgunder and Robin Braun arrived shortly after I did, both outstanding pilots and officers who made their mark on the squadron. Wendi and Robin both left active duty after their initial obligated service but stayed in the Naval Reserve to become flag officers, Wendi a rear admiral and Robin a vice admiral and Chief of Naval Reserve. Janine became a training squadron commanding officer and captain in a distinguished regular Navy career. Beginning in 1982, we began receiving female officers from the Naval Academy Classes of 1980 and 1981: Nancy Fitzgerald, Barb Righter, Cheryl Sullivan, Sue Davies, and Peggy Klein. We also received women from other commissioning sources including Lizette Stuber and Jane Treadway, the daughter of our Maintenance Officer. Eventually our wardroom of over 100 officers included 20 women. VQ-4 had similar numbers, but the only one of those whom I knew was Nora Wingfield, later Nora Wingfield Tyson. Many of these women became "True Believers" as well and went on to distinguished Navy careers. Sue Davies, Jane Treadway, Peggy Klein, and Nora Tyson became squadron commanding officers and captains. Our

Peggy Klein, and Nora Tyson from VQ-4, were ultimately to be selected for flag rank. Nora became the first woman to command a carrier battle group and retired in 2017 as a vice admiral commanding the Third Fleet, truly a woman of incredible first accomplishments.

We had a wardroom of remarkable men and women throughout my two tours in Hawaii. Most of the first tour officers who chose not to make the Navy a career were just as good as the ones who became "True Believers," so the talent was pretty spectacular. The professional development ladders in ground jobs and flight crews hadn't changed, but now, as department heads and senior instructor pilots, it was our job to lead, mentor, guide, and instruct the junior officers. We also had to work together to select the right people for the right jobs during their rotations through departments. Judging by the success of the squadron and the number of "True Believers" developed, we must have done a pretty good job!

Enlisted personnel in the squadron were also extraordinary, working as hard and showing the same dedication as the officers. We had an especially strong Chiefs Mess, with many experienced TACAMO chiefs providing outstanding leadership throughout the build-up period. Because I spent so much time flying and in other training roles, I came to know many of the flight engineers well. Flight engineer instructors like Larry Barks, Gary Breeden, Dan Shore, Dorsey Martin, Ralph Chaffin, and others made invaluable contributions to safely training flight engineers and pilots.

As Training Department Head, it was my job to oversee development of the aircrew training plans and coordinate all training evolutions with the Operations, Maintenance, Naval Aviation Training and Operating Procedures Standardization (NATOPS), and Communications Departments to ensure we could mount the required flights and integrate flight and ground training for the enlisted aircrew personnel. In addition to all the required training flights, VQ-3 was also tasked with flying operational missions, the number of which grew as we received more aircraft and qualified more crews. Most mission flights in the early months of this build-up were flown locally in order to maximize the training opportunities, but we also flew some deployment operations to train crews in flying remote operations and give people a chance for travel.

We kept the second F-model for about six months after VQ-3 moved to Hawaii. Using the F-models, simulators at El Toro, and the mission birds as needed, we kept up with all the cockpit crew training requirements. During 1982, two EC-130Qs were transferred to us from VQ-4 and, with four mission birds, we were able to pick up the pace of full crew training, meeting all our goals through 1982. A lot of flying was involved and we instructors spent a lot of time in airplanes or simulators, accomplished without any aircraft mishaps. In fact, the entire evolution went pretty much according to plan, although a lot of work by all hands was required to pull it off.

In November 1982, Commander Bill Wilt left the squadron and I moved over to be Operations Officer, with Gary Hobbs replacing me in Training. We continued to execute and refine the training and operational plans while gradually increasing the number of mission flights. In February 1983, we received the first of three new construction EC-130Qs, the other two arriving in June and October. I had the pleasure of being the Aircraft Commander on the team that picked up that first new airplane in February. The aircraft had been delivered to E-Systems (later Rockwell-Collins) at Love Field in Dallas, Texas, for installation of the communications suite, reel systems, and final fit-out before delivery to the Navy. Picking up a new airplane is a complex process that required careful planning. They couldn't have picked a worse place for this aircraft modification work than Love Field. A compact, crowded airport with a 6,000-foot runway in the middle of downtown Dallas was not the ideal place to be flying a new, unknown, heavy EC-130. Take-offs and landings there, surrounded by tall buildings, were not for the faint of heart! With Commander Gerard on the trip as commanding officer and ACO/Mission Commander, and Gary Hobbs and Jack Pohl as my co-pilots, it was a very interesting trip, but it went off without any problems. We completed all the required test flights and delivered the aircraft to Barbers Point without incident. That was the one and only time in my career I was fortunate enough to be able to pick up a brand-new airplane at a factory; a great experience. Delivery of the next two aircraft also went well and on schedule.

When VQ-3 received its sixth mission aircraft in June 1983, we had 10 trained aircrews with the remainder of the training and build-up program on track. Our attention in Operations shifted to achieving 100 percent airborne, implementing a schedule similar to that used in VQ-4. With the outstanding assistance of Patrol Wings Pacific, we had set up an alert detachment at Naval Air Station Moffett Field, California. This site consisted of a double-wide trailer for the alert crew with sleeping quarters, lockers, showers, kitchen, recreation room, and ready room. There was also a second trailer to house the maintenance and support detachment, both walking distance from the aircraft parking pad. We discovered alert launches could be accomplished very quickly. We also converted a large space in our hangar at Barbers Point into a standby alert facility, to be used in case the weather, primarily fog, precluded alert aircraft operations at Moffett Field, or the alert aircraft went down. We used the standby alert on a regular basis over the next few years, a good bit of fortuitous planning. We now had sufficient aircraft, crews and alert sites to perform 100 percent airborne operations, completing our first week on August 1, 1983, two months ahead of the original plan, under Fil Baca as Commanding Officer and Bill Harsanyi as Exec. It was especially satisfying to finally achieve that two-ocean 100 percent airborne coverage with two TACAMO guys in charge! The "True Believers" had finally arrived.

The brief description does not really give the complete picture of how incredibly challenging VQ-3's successful build-up was: an all-hands effort requiring dedication, long working and flying hours, and just plain hard work to solve all the problems and execute the complex training, operational and maintenance plans. VQ-3 was awarded the Navy Unit Commendation for its performance during this period, ensuring every squadron member received appropriate recognition for his or her contribution.

As in my previous squadron tours, VQ-3 and Barbers Point provided numerous recreational activities for Navy people and their families. There were the usual sports teams, running clubs, gyms, pools, but also beaches, boat and surfboard rentals. Whatever wasn't available at Barbers Point was often available at the many other military installations on Oahu. VQ-3 held squadron parties and wardroom events which were always well attended in a squadron that maintained high morale and cohesiveness during my entire time there.

Of course, Barbers Point was just a few miles from Honolulu and all the big city attractions available there, including all the touristy stuff around Waikiki Beach. Travel to the other Hawaiian islands was easy and inexpensive so there were many opportunities for off duty stress-relieving activities.

One thing about living in Hawaii: all our friends and family suddenly wanted to visit us! Diane's parents and sister visited a couple of times and we both had various friends and family members visit at least once. This gave us a chance to become excellent tour guides, visit many places on Oahu and get out to the other islands. We managed to visit the "Big Island" of Hawaii, Maui, and Kauai, all more than once. There were also great international travel opportunities available and Diane and I managed to fit in two nice vacations while out there, one to Japan, the second to Bangkok and Hong Kong.

Diane and I enjoyed our six years on Oahu. Two of our children were born there, Michael in May 1982 and Catherine in March 1985. With Chauncey in school and two young ones to care for, Diane was just as busy as I was! Of course, we also had to fit in all of Chauncey's school, sports, and scouting activities. Sometimes I wonder how we fit it all in! With all the long hours and travel of VQ-3 personnel, the spouses, without a doubt, carried the load of running their families. The Officer and Enlisted Spouses Clubs were very strong in VQ-3 and those clubs helped their members take care of families and supported one another in stressful times. Diane made several lifelong friends during this period. I could go on about life in Hawaii, but I think you get the picture. Great, beautiful place to live for a few years; recreational opportunities that contributed to high squadron morale. No doubt the Hawaii location contributed to more than a few TACAMO folks becoming, or remaining, "True Believers."

Vern Lochausen

With the knowledge that TACAMO was now a warfare specialty that wanted me back for VQ-3's standup in its new location at Barbers Point, I determined to be the best that I could be, by making the squadron the best it could be. Attending training at Pax for the new mission systems, I was assigned the midnight to 8am class. Staying after class, I entered the VQ-4 squadron spaces and introduced myself as former VQ-4 and soon to be VQ-3. I made no bones about my mission: learn everything about how the "Shadows" were operating, copy their procedures and processes and export them to VQ-3. It was going really well, junior officer to junior officer, until my future executive officer, Joe Gerard, caught me and gave me orders, "I like what you are doing. Here's a list of what I want you to get also." Fulfilling that directive earned me a spot as a junior department head in his regime. As Special Projects Department Head, I owed Joe a pile of deliverables once we got to Barbers. It never stopped. He appointed me the lead on hangar renovation, design team for the new hangar for the ECX airframe now becoming a program of record as the E-6, maintenance vans upgrade for VQ-3, and the "VQ-3 One Hundred Percent Airborne, Eighteen crews with Alert" Plan of Actions and Milestones. That was 67 action items, many assigned to my senior "real" department heads. I tracked mine and theirs, briefed every two weeks, maintained a message and document history, and ghost-wrote his monthly reports to the Navy and Unified Command seniors. Those reports included the status of a $2.5 million rehab of Hangar 110 at Barbers, an avionics repair facility, crew training sources, aircraft delivery, and selection of an alert site on the West Coast. Clearly, other departments and junior officers did the hard-core work, but the skipper had me setting the goals and tracking completion status, not making me too popular with my peers. With a very small staff of two plus myself, we covered the logistics conferences, the operational conferences, and maintained a continual dialogue for him with the VP wing, Naval Air Forces, Pacific (AIRPAC) staff and the TACAMO program manager at NAVAIR. When I left that tour, Joe awarded me the "most flight hours on United" award, for all those trips, and several other kudos. In all that work, I had become a TACAMO expert, schooled by chiefs on maintenance, ops, supply, and messaging. In the end, by October 1983, VQ-3 was manned up, all new EC-130Qs on the line, flying continuous airborne alert backed up by an alert at Moffett Field, and a standby alert at Barbers. Never, since standing up in 1968, had the squadron so operated, and the lessons learned from VQ-4 were making it easier for crews and better all around. The new birds were a big part of it. The first new one, 161223, never seemed to break. Maintenance Control had a pool going to forecast her first Not Mission Capable missed mission. She sometimes flew over 200 hours in a single month.

Joe's mantra was "VQ-3 is not the good old boys from Guam anymore, it is the best damn TACAMO squadron." With brand-new Hercs arriving and the fruits of all those action items, we were flush with everything we needed. Joe was a VP guy and he taught me how to play that game and handle seniors. He and I briefed every staff between the local VP wing and Pacific Fleet Headquarters, with frequent trips to San Diego to brief AIRPAC. When we briefed Rear Admiral Crawford Easterling, then the Pacific Fleet Ops Director, on the plans of action, milestones and status for 100 percent coverage, he stopped the briefing and asked "Joe … with only eight aircraft, why do you need so dang many crews?" Joe walked through the chart again and tallied all the missions, alerts, standbys, etc. The admiral still wasn't convinced, saying "I got that. What are the rest of those people doing?"

Joe fired back "Admiral, somebody has to run the freaking squadron!" Joe Gerard Lesson #1: If the shark bites, bite back. Later, Easterling, now a vice admiral in charge at AIRPAC, stopped Joe's briefing of the plan of action to his staff: "I want everyone on this staff to understand the most important thing to happen in this force in the next year is the standup of VQ-3. Now carry on, Joe." So it was. VQ-3 got what it needed and didn't have to live on a shoestring, including having two KC-130F aircrew trainers for quite a while.

From this VQ-3 tour, I never looked back and never again looked outside TACAMO.

Under Joe Gerard, my mandate was clear: "Look at every issue in TACAMO that needs improvement and see that VQ-3 doesn't have that issue. Make it the best." Little did I know then that he was competing head-to-head with his counterpart Chuck Osier, then VQ-4 skipper. This became crystal-clear when Joe and I took a crew and a brand new Herc from Barbers to Pax in mid-winter. We briefed the "Shadow" wardroom and exchanged issues and solutions with them and their Chiefs Mess.

It was a good exchange, but just before we departed late one night, Joe loaded the "Shadow" flag from the wardroom into our aircraft just before taxiing. He made Osier come get it, thereby ensuring a two-way exchange. From then to what I observe today, it is Game On: "Ironman" Squadron competing with the "Shadows," for the betterment of both.

The first VQ-3 tour, though not a major department head one, was still golden. The impact my contributions made getting the squadron on step for 100 percent airborne coverage were recognized. A number of the old VQ-4 crew came to join us in making VQ-3 a full-up round: Mark Herkert came along with John Brouillette, Mike Clemens, Buddy Baker, Jim Klepper, Ken Hibbler, and, as mentioned, my VT-29 instructors Bill Wilt and Norm Tindall. Tough to compete with all that talent that was senior to me. The first TACAMO-grown skipper, Fil Baca, checked in to relieve Joe Gerard and I was soon shipped off to the Naval War College for a year to come back and pay my dues as a real department head. While I was there, the Marine Barracks in Beirut, Lebanon, was destroyed by a radical Islamic suicide terrorist who crashed through the barricades in a truck loaded with explosives. Over 200 Marines were killed and Americans were suddenly thinking that terrorists might be a problem. Then President Reagan made strategic nuclear deterrence his number one priority in his 1984 budget. We studied the implications of that, one being full Navy support of the new ECX replacement aircraft for the EC-130 Hercules.

In late 1984, I returned to VQ-3 for my department head tour. I was the Communications Officer at the very time that traitors John Walker and Jonathon Pollard had been caught, their impact being the total replacement of much of our coding and crypto devices, a major and rapidly enacted change in our operations. Innovative communicators and radiomen, like Lieutenant Bill Marlette and Master Chief Radioman Kenny Cates, created a clock system that facilitated the changes and we made it through that period without too many problems.

Moving on to be the Ops Boss, I was faced with the loss of all the new model Hercs whose reliability had so facilitated VQ-3's transition to 100 percent coverage. They were to be traded to VQ-4 for the older G/Q series, in preparation for us to be the first squadron to receive the new E-6As. The perils of being first! The G/Q-model age and reliability issues soon complicated a stable flight schedule supporting continuous airborne operations. At one point, we were down to our last option to make the next mission: we sent a flight engineer to Marine Corps Air Station El Toro on a holiday weekend to rob a part from a Marine KC-130. I had the CINCPAC Duty Officer, a Navy captain, working with me, along with Fleet Marine Forces Pacific Headquarters, but the Marines fought us until the very last minute. The flight engineer later reported that he took the part off a Marine Herc with four bare engine firewalls, not likely to fly for months. So much for our Force Activity Designator One priority. Having to use it that day showed me just how hard it was to maintain the airborne coverage over the Pacific with just eight pretty tired birds after 20 years of flying. Still, the folks conducting the mission in VQ-3 were many old hands from my first VQ-4 tour and some retreads from my first VQ-3 tour. Both had the "eye of the tiger" and the experience to get the job done. The hard work they turned in, both in operations and maintenance, led to a rewarding tour for me as the Operations Boss.

CHAPTER 9

Continuing One Hundred Percent

Andy Riddile

In 1981, I was reassigned to VQ-4 for my department head tour. In 1979, the Chief of Naval Operations had established the Airborne Strategic/Electronic Warfare Communities (VQ-3 & 4/VQ-1 & 2) as Aviation Officer Communities. Now a warfare specialty would allow TACAMO aviation officers to compete for operational command of those squadrons. The quality of officers gradually but conspicuously increased. By the time I checked back into VQ-4, the professionalism of the wardroom officers had increased considerably over what I had experienced in previous squadron tours. This gradual increase in professionalism was largely due to the persistent efforts of certain commanding officers. During the earlier years, before TACAMO was designated a warfare specialty, the very best officers were discouraged from returning to the community, because, without this designation, they would have little chance to eventually emerge as squadron commanding officers. This naturally capped the overall professional capabilities of the community wardrooms. Extraordinarily, my commanding officers during this particular tour, Commanders Hilton, Osier, and Fletcher, seemed to dedicate themselves to making the point publicly that the small TACAMO community had received short shrift from the Navy since its inception. They constantly made it known when the Navy failed to provide required support.

During this tour, an unusual and highly sensitive All Officers Meeting was conducted by the Naval Investigative Service with the objective of instructing officers that the Human Intelligence threat against squadron aircrews was real and proven, especially outside the United States. Also, during this tour, a sailor assigned to the base photo lab was arrested for espionage or something close to it. Further, it was suspected he had access to classified materials involving TACAMO operations. These incidents tended to underscore the importance to the enemy of the TACAMO mission. Again, noted.

Back then, it was uncommon for Naval Flight Officers (NFO) to serve as squadron Maintenance Officer under the assumption that NFOs did not generally know the airframe as well as pilots. Chuck Osier saw the "something in me" and assigned me as squadron Maintenance Officer, which was one of the most challenging and rewarding assignments I ever had, seven aircraft and over 400 sailors. We set about to define and revamp key trouble-prone programs, setting comprehensive goals, and regularly measuring progress toward these goals, motivating leadership and performance. We achieved pacesetter status with extraordinarily high inspection marks from higher authority.

Toward the end of this tour, Chuck Osier sent me to Norfolk for a few weeks to assist his Wing Commander, Tactical Support Wing One, with a particularly difficult project. I frequently found myself working in the commodore's office and once he asked me to take a seat at his desk to read some materials. As I took his seat, I lightheartedly commented, "Well, this is about as close to wing commander as I'll ever get." He quickly disagreed with the remark, encouraging me to "keep doing what you're doing."

During this tour, I found myself fairly demanding of my colleagues and subordinates, especially in terms of professionalism. Our mission was one of the most important to U.S. national security and, by God, we were going to do it to the very best of our ability. VQ-4 operations and maintenance, and all other support elements, were achieving new heights in professional performance.

Ed Hampshire

After I completed my tour on USS *Forrestal*, I received orders back to VQ-4 as a pilot. Yes, TACAMO was still around and this was going to be my squadron department head tour. The Bureau of Personnel had just designated TACAMO as a warfare specialty prior to my reporting for duty at VQ-4 and would be screening commanding officers from within our new community. So far, my gamble of sticking with TACAMO had paid off and now I just needed to make myself the "best qualified" officer to screen for command. I knew I was either on my way to doing this or I was in serious trouble when the commanding officer of VQ-4 contacted me at the Air Force C-130 school to tell me I was going to be the Maintenance Officer and to expect an order modification to Aviation Maintenance Officer School. The current Maintenance Officer was going to be relieved and I was to take over about as soon as I reported aboard. That sounded like a pretty bad situation. I was somewhat apprehensive about my new job, but I eventually spent two years as the Maintenance Department Head, I think that's about 20 dog years, and I still hate phones to this day!

Before the end of those two years, word came that a new aircraft was being procured to replace our old and worn-out EC-130s. NAVAIR (Naval Air Systems Command) called the VQ-4 commanding officer, Commander Frank Hilton, asking if the squadron had any good candidates to be the Navy's new chief engineer for this ECX procurement. I was immediately "sold down the river" by the commanding officer and received orders for a three-year tour as the new ECX Class Desk, the chief engineer, at NAVAIR at Crystal City in the Washington, D.C., area. Be careful what you wish for! I was finally in a position to use my engineering education and TACAMO experience to influence and fix those problems, problems when I was the Avionics Division Officer, problems still plaguing me as the Maintenance Department Head. The new aircraft procurement was now proof that my faith in the future of TACAMO had not been misplaced.

Mike Davidson

Little Rock C-130 refresher training gave me time to think about my future life. I had considered a naval career to be a fallback position if I didn't have positive leads for an airline career. I remarried after Little

Rock and checked back into VQ-4 to the comments of "That's not the wife he had when he left here." I dealt with it.

I quickly requalified in the EC-130, including an instructor pilot designation. I owed the Navy a little more time for accepting a regular commission and I would still be in my early 30s, still a competitive age for the airlines, so I turned in my resignation effective at the end of my obligated service. I was in line for a crew assignment when I turned it in, surprising Skipper Tom Joyner and Exec Frank Hilton. They had both presumed I was career-oriented and an assistant department head this tour.

I was sidetracked from holding my own crew and assigned as Lieutenant Dave Gray's second pilot on the infamous Crew Eight. I was on that fateful deployment when our flight engineer, Chief Gus Agresto, changed two engines in Rota, Spain, on one stop, and then changed one of those again at our next stop in Lajes. The last replacement engine had to be ferried in from Pax River on the squadron's KC-130 training bird. I spent more time at Lajes than I ever thought possible. After a successful check flight, the squadron simply said to bring the bird home after we had sufficient crew rest.

My family sat down and discussed my job situation. They were waiting in line at the gas pumps before sunrise and keeping the cars filled while putting up with the gas station employees. I had no real airline job prospects due to skyrocketing fuel prices, although the reserve VP (patrol) squadron at Pax River was interested and would pull some strings to get me in. I had a private meeting with Commander Hilton and Skipper Joyner about pulling my resignation request. They both agreed to put me back on track for a naval career and Joyner said I wouldn't be penalized on my fitness reports under his signature. A short time later, I was included with the plethora of lieutenants selected for lieutenant commander. I remember the day when we were frocked to our new rank. We had not discussed or rehearsed the "post" command after the frocking. We turned in three or four different directions, giving the squadron the biggest entertainment it had seen in years.

I went to work with the Ops boss, Lieutenant Commander Chuck "Spiderman" Fitchet, as his assistant, and life went on. Our worst two days in Operations were the day we thought we had a missing airplane. We kicked everyone out of the Operations Control Center and brought Skipper Joyner and the Executive Officer, Frank Hilton, down to be in on the search. It was ironic that the Commander Naval Forces, Atlantic Vice Admiral Gus Kinnear, was flying up to present us the Battle Efficiency Award, or Battle "E", that very afternoon. We called every base we visited, asking if one of our birds was there, a negative response from all of them. One Air Force base said they didn't see any Navy aircraft on their log, but the base ops coordinator, on duty when it should have landed, had gone home to bed. We asked them to wake him up and check. In the meantime, I called the base's police department and asked if they were guarding one of those strange Navy C-130s and got our first affirmative answer. We soon discovered the aircraft and crew had diverted there for maintenance, but the word didn't get back to us in a timely manner. Early the next morning, the same crew's mission commander called me and asked for Skipper Joyner's home phone number. I wasn't privy to the subject until the skipper called me to advise that three of the mission commander's crewmembers had been shot, one critically, the night before. When it rains, it pours. Our prospective executive officer, Commander Chuck Osier, had recently reported on board and he was dispatched to their location to get the real version of what happened and to provide support to the crew.

After leaving VQ-4, my next tour took me to Commander-in-Chief, U.S. Forces, Atlantic (CINCLANT) to serve as the TACAMO-Airborne Command Post Coordinator, for my first joint duty assignment. After the CINCLANT tour, I returned to VQ-4 for my department head tour. Our commanding officer was Captain-select Paul Fletcher, the last VP skipper to command a TACAMO squadron. His Exec was Commander Bob Downey, VQ-4's first TACAMO-bred command-screened officer. Captain Fletcher was a superb leader and strategist. After my first assignment as the head of the Replacement Training Department, I became the squadron Maintenance Officer. One of our tasks was to transfer the "old Qs" to VQ-3 Hawaii. Everyone thought these tired Hercs would be there briefly until the E-6As arrived at VQ-3. Little did they know! One of our bright, industrious young sailors took out several nice, clean soundproofing panels in the back end and replaced them with damaged, ratty ones before the aircraft left. Hey, it was going somewhere else, we could use the cleaner panels here, right? Wrong. VQ-3 raised a stink about these panels and rightly so. I took the next transferring bird out to Hawaii and did the necessary *mea culpas* with Skipper Barry Coyle and their Maintenance Officer, the late Commander Ty Tyler.

Little did I know I would be dealing with those ratty old EC-130Qs for a lot longer in the future than I expected!

CHAPTER 10

"True Believers" Take Command

Fil Baca: VQ-3 Commanding Officer 1983–1984

While in Albuquerque, I was promoted to commander. My former boss while I was the communicator on the "Indy," Admiral Jim Service, called me at home and told me he had been selected to take over Battle Force, Sixth Fleet in the Mediterranean Sea, and asked if I would go with him to be his Communications Officer. I requested his permission to defer until after the results of my Aviation Command Selection Board results were announced, and that, yes, I would go with him anywhere if I were not selected for command. He understood and the job would be open for me whatever the results.

Fortune struck again and I was selected for aviation command and slated for VQ-3 on Guam. I flew out to the island to look it over and visited the squadron. The junior officers welcomed their future skipper, but my bride was adamant she wouldn't go to Guam, and not for the first time. So, the Navy moved VQ-3 to Hawaii! I just knew they'd see it her way again!

I asked the detailer for some refresher training at VQ-4. My arrival was cordial but insincere and hostile, with the skipper, from the VP (patrol) community, intimating he had tried to de-screen me from command because of my TACAMO-only background! I discussed this with my detailer, who was very supportive, retorting that this could not happen, that I had been selected by a competent selection board.

Arriving in Hawaii in 1982, three months before the change of command, I was not allowed in the squadron spaces and "stashed" at Commander-in-Chief Pacific Fleet Headquarters in Honolulu until a few days before my change of command. Heretofore, this command had been owned by VP as an "alternate command" reserved for the VP community; the commanding officer, and all former skippers, had come from the VP community, VQ-3 reported to a VP wing, the naval air station was commanded by a former VP skipper, and the VP wing reported to Patrol Wings Pacific at Naval Air Station Moffett Field, California. They were unwilling to let an "outsider" take this precious assignment from their rolls! My tour as executive officer began in 1982 and was accordingly difficult.

Squadron spaces were very nice, newly renovated and very spacious. The new enlisted barracks were built specifically for the arrival of VQ-3 from Guam and its expansion to 600 enlisted personnel. The fresh paint and the smell of newness was everywhere. Our "Gedunk" offered ice cream, candy, popcorn, sodas, and other "pogey bait." Squadron posters and patches were available. Spaces were kept proudly clean with shiny floors and a look of obvious pride. The chief petty officers had their own Chiefs Mess. However, squadron morale was pretty low, something I set my sights on for a correction, if I survived my executive officer tour. I did, and assumed command in 1983, the very first TACAMO-bred commanding officer. Most of the VP commanding officers wore unique khaki tailor-made uniforms, which were just stunning, and I wanted some. One told me they came from the tailor shop at Cubi Point. I ordered some and then could be "in uniform" when I attended the commodore's weekly commanding officers' meetings.

I ended the self-appointed experts of "can't do" who refused any innovation because of real or imagined authority or prohibition. I announced to the department heads that "can't do" was a banned phrase, excluded from our vocabulary and then was caught by it myself. One afternoon at a mandatory Happy Hour, Tom Trotter, who later become a TACAMO commodore when we stood up our own wing a decade later, asked me if he could get a crew together and take our C-130 training bird to Cubi Point to get tailor-made uniforms for all the officers. I replied, "No, we can't do that because CINCPAC has limited or prohibited any of our assets to go beyond 180 degrees west." Tom had caught me, maybe trapped me, because I had violated my own dictum of "can't do!" I instantly apologized to him and asked him to find a way, it was a superb idea, and I asked to participate. Tom and Vern Lochausen, who would also become commodore, were VQ-3's Special Project Officers. While they didn't agree on some things, they always seemed to formulate the absolute best of the best of solutions for all special projects!

They found the way; virtually every officer had tailor-made khakis which fit perfectly! They loved their uniforms and really took pride in deservedly strutting with a "cock of the walk" demeanor. Some of us ordered tailor-made dress blues with crimson or gold lining which made for a lot of buzz wherever they went. Some even went for the tailor-made formal dress uniforms with different, unique linings.

One welcome challenge came from this: the enlisted component wanted to get their uniforms tailor-made also, not only their blues and whites but their dungarees as well! We gladly obliged! This was during the demise of "the Zumwalt era" of long hair and beards and we were trying to accelerate its end. VQ-3 became the "Peacocks of the Pacific." Visitors and strangers alike would ask, "Who are these people exuding such pride in uniforms?" It became easy to identify a TACAMO officer or enlisted person.

Officers were inspected on Wednesdays, and the department heads would do the same, with their division officers, with their divisions. It was always fun 'n zest!

On another significant occasion, I received a "Personal For" from Commander, Naval Air Forces Pacific in San Diego, Vice Admiral Easterling, stating he was coming out to "visit" TACAMOPAC. I think someone, either on his staff or Patrol Wing One's, got wind of the visit and informed our commodore. His chief of staff called me and told me to "stand by for heavy rolls" because the commodore was livid! He put me on hold for what seemed an eternity, and then the commodore came on with a tirade of, "What the hell was I doing bypassing the whole chain of command to communicate with the three-star commander and not even observe genteel Navy protocol?" I tried to explain I had no idea of this. He just continued his vitriol and slammed down the phone on me. I believed the squadron deserved the best and I was ready. The chief of staff called again and said the boss wanted to talk to me. I didn't want to talk to him. The commodore came on and said he knew why the admiral was coming to visit. Admiral Easterling had a reputation for being extreme, stern, righteous and fiercely loyal, not only to his superiors, but also to subordinates. He had even fired a carrier skipper and now he was coming to fire me! The commodore felt that perhaps he should have fired me sooner and, because he hadn't been invited to the party, he reaffirmed words to the effect that "It wasn't his fault what would occur next." I collected my things to take home and prepared.

The department heads and I met to discuss the next day's strategy. We expected the admiral and his aide and perhaps a couple of his staff officers. Our strategy would be welcoming, honest, open and proud. VQ-3 was very special and they were just excited to show themselves. There was no special "field day" and no special preparations to prepare for a crucifying inspection. How many folks get the privilege of a three-star admiral visit? It was easy: TACAMOPAC was always ready and willing.

The admiral arrived just as we were having normal Wednesday quarters and, to my surprise, he had several staff cars accompanying him, loaded with nine captains and one commander! They went through the entire squadron spaces, talking to almost everyone. Unbeknownst to me, and a surprise indeed to the admiral's staff, everyone wore their tailor-made dungarees and khakis.

The admiral and his staff were incredulous. This was the best of the best. After his staff had completed their "interrogations" of a great bunch of proud people excited to show off their squadron, uniforms, workspaces and planes, they gathered in my office, along with Bill Harsanyi, the Executive Officer, Barry Coyle, the Operations Officer (both to become future commanding officers), and Al Treadway, the Maintenance Officer. The large office was adorned quite well with comfortable furniture and lithographs and a view of the TACAMOPAC tarmac parking lot, but it suddenly seemed too small. The admiral and his staff were served coffee and donuts, and it was quiet until the admiral asked, "How are the women doing in the squadron?" VQ-3 was then the only operational squadron that accepted women as pilots and NFOs.

"Great!" I said. "They are industrious, wear their uniforms with pride and outperform virtually any other officers and sailors around." It became eerily quiet as the admiral slowly took another sip of coffee and said, "You obviously didn't hear me, I asked you how the women are doing?"

You could have heard a pin drop. A friend who had been on his staff had warned me the admiral was irascible, cantankerous and enjoyed being very difficult. I looked at the admiral and his staff for some hint of clarification or help but saw only blank faces. This was unreasonable and unwarranted, but if he was really here to fire me, I'd make it easy and get it over with. I blurted out: "Admiral, the women in TACAMOPAC are SIERRA HOTEL!" That was a Navy phonetic for superlative, expletives deleted! Now it was really quiet, some of his staff looking at me as if I was toast! Again, the agonizing ritual of taking a slow sip of his coffee. then looking up and turning to his staff to remark, "I think that's a pretty good answer, boys, don't you?" They couldn't have been more eager to answer in giddy agreement.

From that moment on, VQ-3 could do no wrong. Many of the "problems" women were going to create turned into a professional competition and, while there was a small component of hard-core gender malcontents, the great majority of the squadron was strongly supportive of the women and of each other.

Pilot training became a problem. The squadron had one aircraft used primarily for pilot training, and the Bureau of Personnel was detailing pilots faster than they could qualify in progression to aircraft commander in the required time. Phone calls didn't work, despite promises to the contrary. The system was rigged to meet aircraft commander qualifications in a specified time, based on other models which were not applicable to unique TACAMO requirements. Repeated letters to the Bureau reporting why a pilot did not make aircraft commander in the allotted time finally got their attention after a good briefing to folks who could understand the problem. These efforts resulted in a slowdown of pilot arrivals and a speed up of qualifications.

Maintenance was a challenge. Different era/model C-130/EC-130s and modernizing platforms caused shortages in many spare parts. Some spares were not available at all, especially in the unique, new EC-130Q communications suites. There was only one of certain equipment per aircraft; no spares! Even so, at the weekly commodore's commanding officers meetings, VQ-3 had the highest maintenance capability of any other squadron!

Operations, Communications, Safety, Administration and Training were challenging for all the reasons the other departments were, and they all excelled as the best.

The VP wing had a "Golden Orion Award" destined for the squadron with the highest overall retention rate. However, VQ-3 was classified as a non-deployable squadron and thus denied competition, despite having the highest retention rates of any command on that base and that wing. The squadron was finally permitted to compete, but in our own singular category, for the "Golden Hercules" for retention. At my change of command, the command had achieved 100 percent retention for first term, second term and career! Admiral S. R. Foley, Commander-in-Chief, Pacific Fleet, personally awarded VQ-3 the Navy Unit Commendation.

The squadron would receive its complement of new EC-130Qs close to delivery schedule and the department heads wanted to take VQ-3 TACAMOPAC to 100 percent airborne coverage. Training, maintenance, parts delivery, and all the necessary dots were connected. The plan was "murder boarded" and taken to the wing to push for approval. Naval Air Forces, Pacific (AIRPAC) got wind of this and wanted a brief. The commodore required extensive briefings prior to flying to San Diego with squadron representatives to brief them. Admiral Easterling had piercing questions and concerns which our reps allayed. One hundred percent continuous airborne coverage, 24/7, as our sister squadron VQ-4 had been doing for 10 years, began two months ahead of schedule thanks to Barry Coyle, Vern Lochausen, Tom Trotter, Al Treadway, and Gary Hobbs (key to the success)!

I was privileged to have the greatest bunch of leaders who gave me absolute support and loyalty, no matter the difficulties, and welcomed any challenge they created externally or internally! I was blessed to be in the right time in the right place for these "SIERRA HOTEL Tigers" desirous of success.

Officers, chiefs, and enlisted would bring fresh ideas of what could be and they had the super desire to make that success! They all wanted to do what they could to promote themselves and every one of their shipmates at the same time! It was a time of positive reinforcement, "can do" spirit and the best of the best.

I knew less than anybody! All the rest carried me and we all had fun and zest! We were getting new EC-130Qs and, in that era before computerization, we didn't have an Individual Material Readiness List to use when ordering spare parts. We had two warrant officers painstakingly build such a list, allowing VQ-3 to operate and order repair/replacement parts.

The officer complement was eager to support and do for me and to this day I don't know why. I think the enlisted complement loved me! I felt like I was the director placed in a higher spot than I should be and supported by a greater bunch of people than I deserved.

Somehow, I survived and inherited an eager bunch of Tigers wanting to prove their mettle and moxie and make VQ-3 excel. I was amazed at the gold mine I inherited. The commanding officer's office was nicely adorned in a refurbished hangar and even had its own head and shower. The sweet smell of success, staunch desire to accomplish and real "can do spirit" abounded and morale squadron-wide exploded. The naysayers lost and TACAMO won. VQ-3 and TACAMO had become the best of the best. Having been around the Navy for more than half a century, and still involved now, with four daughters married to the Navy and one son in the Navy, I feel and live "Navy Pride," thanks in particular to the people of TACAMOPAC.

My time as commanding officer was challenging and precarious, and at times I just wanted to get it over with, but I had such a bunch of super loyal supporters who made the squadron a super success. I've mentioned a couple of names above and I'm compelled to acknowledge others who gave me their absolute best, and I know they were some of the very best in the U.S. Navy. From the VQ-3 wardroom during my tenure would ultimately come 10 VQ skippers: Bill Harsanyi, Barry Coyle, Chuck Fitchet, Mike Davidson, Joe Sereno, Peggy Klein, Sue Davies, Jay Gallamore, Jack Pohl, and Chris Schnedar; six who went to command other communities, Gary Hobbs, Jeanie Igou (Clemens), Don Fox, John Phillips, Dave Buckey, and Joe Flynn; six TACAMO commodores, Captains Vern Lochausen, Tom Trotter, John Keilty, Joe Sereno, Peggy Klein, Dan Seesholtz; and three flag officers, Vice Admiral Robin Braun, Rear Admiral Peggy Klein, and Rear Admiral Wendi Carpenter. Many other loyal folks who proceeded up the line developed the unique TACAMO spirit. Captain Jay Gallamore went on to become the Program Manager for TACAMO at the Naval Air Systems Command, as did Ed Hampshire. Others remained loyal to the community after retirement: "Buffalo" Bill Crowell and, of course, Lew McIntyre and Kris Strance.

This is an impressive accomplishment for a community that, 10 years prior, had never produced a lieutenant commander!

I went on to the CNO OP-941D where I oversaw the establishment of requirements and funding for the E-6 airframe that would replace the EC-130, TACAMO's ultimate relocation to its new home in Tinker Air Force Base, Oklahoma, and the standing up of its own wing, Strategic

Communications Wing One. TACAMO was no longer the stepchild of VP, but, yes, it still meant "Take Charge and Move Out."

Bob Downey: VQ-4 Commanding Officer 1984–1985

During my tour at Tinker Air Force Base from 1981 to 1983, I qualified as mission crew commander in the Airborne Warning and Control System, E-3A, and brought in a lot of tactical data link experience gleaned through my tour on the *Midway*. There were a lot of interoperability issues between the E-3A and the Navy battle groups when the aircraft deployed to support them. I established a database of key parameters, encouraged frequent exchanges between Navy E-2 Hawkeye crews and the E-3 crews, and demanded no-notice interoperability.

Lew McIntyre was a major help in this. He passed through Tinker to visit me, en route to San Diego and Carrier Group One, and had already anticipated E-3 interoperability issues; this powerful radar platform had gained a bad reputation with the fleet. Lew invited my E-3 crews to the

USS *Constellation* for at sea cross-training, and I reciprocated by inviting his combat teams to fly E-3 training missions. He learned that message data from the battle group was not getting to the aircrews, en route for anywhere from several days to a week from Tinker to rendezvous with Indian Ocean battle groups. As a result, they missed communications plan changes and changes in location that left them often in the wrong place, at the wrong time, and on the wrong frequency. Lew recommended procedures which TACAMO used that allowed the aircrews to get their message traffic at any base operations, without the sender having foreknowledge of their itinerary.

I also flew with the E-3 to Keflavik, Iceland, a familiar base skippered by a former VQ-4 commanding officer, Captain Wes May. I flew several missions to Kadena in Japan, also a familiar spot, and the Middle East, Riyadh and Bahrain. I was overjoyed when Fil Baca and I became the first "True Believers" screened for command. Fil was to take VQ-3 in 1983 and I was to take VQ-4 the following year. The first two lieutenants to make lieutenant commander, both after being passed over once, were now to become the first homegrown commanding officers. It was my sincerest desire to make my executive and commanding officer tours successful, to blaze that trail for others to follow. Pat was glad to be back to the TACAMO family and I was Exec to a super commanding officer, Paul Fletcher, who guided me through the challenges of command. He was to be the last P-3 Orion skipper to command VQ-3 or VQ-4, so he was the end of an era, though we were as yet uncertain what was to follow.

Our big challenge was to keep the tired first-generation EC-130Gs and Qs flying, as VQ-3 had gotten most of the new production aircraft, preparing to stand up to 100 percent airborne coverage. We fielded the first major upgrade to the TACAMO communications suite since TACAMO IVB 10 years earlier, the TACAMO Improvement Program, Phase II. This upgrade included a state-of-the-art satellite communications system, improved data distribution, and a computer console on which to send, receive, store, and forward data message traffic. Goodbye to punched paper tape and clattering teletypes! We also received the first aircraft hardened against the effects of nuclear electromagnetic pulse, but these new systems involved a lot of training, maintenance headaches, logistics issues, and, of course, we had multiple versions of aircraft and crews that could fly one type but not the other.

On the other hand, we had by now 15 years of experience with high-tempo operations, a well-established alert detachment in Bermuda, and mature communications. We had enormous corporate knowledge, with Andy Riddile, fresh from the National Emergency Airborne Command Post, as the Maintenance Officer, followed by Mike Davidson, and Chuck Fitchet as Operations Officer. What a team of professionals!

And my junior officers, what can I say? The greatest had to be our women and what a team we had! In the mid-80s, there were only six squadrons accepting female pilots and Naval Flight Officers (NFOs): VR-24 and VRC-50 transport squadrons; VXN-8 and VXE-6 development and Antarctic squadrons; and VQ-3 and 4. And the TACAMO squadrons were the only ones offering them a designation as a warfare specialist, despite the fact they were excluded from combat assignments. As a result, both squadrons became extremely sought-after billets for female aviators. Our female junior officers called themselves "The Nurse Corps": Nora Wingfield, Shelley Pennington, Dana Dotten, Mary Brigden, Linda Crowe, Robin Erichsen, Lizette Stuber, Cindy Mason, Ruth Silvia and Jane O'Dea. These women excelled at all aspects of flying and squadron life. Nora Wingfield Tyson went on to blaze a trail for women, taking command of VQ-4, the USS *Bataan* (LHD-5) as her "deep draft" command, then flag rank and command of Carrier Strike Group Two, and ultimately to vice admiral, assigned as Commander, U.S. Third Fleet, the first woman to ever hold those billets.

In September 1984 came my change of command, with Ed Hampshire as my executive officer. My photograph was posted on the now quite long line of past commanding officers of VQ-4, including Don Kellerman and Bruce Cloud, under whom I had served on my first TACAMO tour in the early 1970s, but mine was in color! For the first time, the previous year, the Navy had allowed color photographs, but the junior officers in VQ-3 had finagled the VQ-4 officers to ensure my picture, not Paul Fletcher's, was to be the first posted in living color. To this day, the TACAMO skippers of VQ-3 and VQ-4 are in color, while our VP predecessors are in black and white.

With Ed Hampshire to keep my irascible spirit from getting us both in trouble, it was a truly rewarding tour. We won the Commander Tactical Support Wing One commodore's trophy for the most improved squadron in readiness and maintenance statistics, personnel training, aircrew proficiency, and significantly improved quality of VQ-4's strategically important mission. We received an "Excellent" on the Wing Administration/Material Inspection with the Executive Department receiving an "Outstanding." We won the Battle "E" Award, while achieving a milestone 150,000 accident-free flight hours, recognized by *Approach Magazine*, in an article titled "Who Are These Guys?" We maintained a mission capable rate of 90.7 percent from February to November 1985 and an overall average of 84 percent for the year. Finally, we received the vote of confidence from our enlisted troops who chose to re-enlist, earning us the Bronze Anchor for retention.

We didn't miss the chance to have fun during my command tour. We held a dining out, always a good opportunity for the junior officers to legally "roast" the leadership, and produced the VQ-4 Cruise Book to capture everyone's memories for all time. We won the Division A Softball Championship for Naval Air Station Patuxent River and supported the first ever VR-1 TACAMO Detachment and VQ-3/VQ-4 Reunion, uniting those early pioneers and plankowners with the newest generation of TACAMO fliers.

But all good things must end. I received orders to Naval Telecommunications Command and, in December, read those orders to my most trusted relief, Ed Hampshire. I could not have left the squadron in more capable hands.

CHAPTER II

Preparing for the E-6

The breakneck changes of the 1980s continued at an accelerating pace. The main driver for this tempo was the imminent deployment of the E-6 in the late 1980s which required a carefully choreographed transition from the turboprop EC-130, an airframe common throughout the Navy inventory, to a heavy four-engine jet unique to TACAMO. However, as with all well-laid plans, there came a glitch. Structural failures late in flight testing delayed the E-6 deployment by a year, throwing those plans in to disarray.

During this time, the TACAMO "True Believers" found themselves at the highest levels of our nation's policy and planning centers, even at the White House itself.

Bill Harsanyi: VQ-3 Commanding Officer 1984–1985

Carrier Group Eight wasn't West Virginia, but it was as close to home as I had been in years, Sharon Kaye and I both being natives of that fine state. My duties on the staff were challenging enough, being the Emergency Actions Officer, Tactical Action Officer and the Battle Group Watch Officer. It should have been a pretty calm time in the Mediterranean Sea but, no, the Russians went into Afghanistan, the Iranian government fell, and terrorists took the American Embassy in Tehran! We sailed the *Nimitz* around the Cape of Good Hope and into the Indian Ocean and set up the first "Gonzo Station" while the air wing supported the

Iranian hostage rescue attempt, Operation *Eagle Claw*, remaining at sea for almost 150 consecutive days.

Finally, in late 1980, I went to shore duty, thankfully in Norfolk, still not far from home, in an assignment at Commander, Naval Air Force Atlantic (AIRLANT). They figured out ahead of time that I was to be staff communications officer, in charge of the AIRLANT communications center. I was also to be the TACAMO Liaison Officer, working the issues VQ-4 faced in those days.

And they had a few issues! The last of the VP (patrol squadron) skippers were dealing with the latest TACAMO Improvement Programs. VQ-3 was moving to Barbers, getting new Hercs, and doubling in size to stand up to 100 percent airborne coverage in the Pacific. Skipper Chuck Osier was running a friendly competition with Skipper Joe Gerard at VQ-3 and both squadrons were looking at alternative alert sites.

While Fil Baca had the honor of being the first TACAMO-grown skipper, I had the honor of being the second, assuming command of VQ-3 behind Fil at Barbers Point in 1984, just a month ahead of Bob Downey assuming command of VQ-4 at Patuxent River.

Talk about a dream team! Barry Coyle as my Ops Officer, Norm Tindall in Admin, and Al Treadway in Maintenance, all of them, except Al, TACAMO "retreads" who knew this business and made it happen. Al was TACAMO's first Limited Duty Officer assigned as Maintenance Officer, a program started in the VP community to ensure large squadrons had professional maintainers in charge on the hangar deck. Al made his department the best in the wing. My Operations Schedules Officer was none other than Lieutenant Robin Braun, later to become a vice admiral and Chief of Naval Reserves.

Fil had been the skipper when VQ-3 stood up 100 per cent airborne coverage, capitalizing on the fine work done under Joe Gerard's executive and command tours and a dynamite host of talented retreads who had previous VQ-3 and VQ-4 tours at Guam and Patuxent River. My role was to smooth out the operation, refine it and make it hum. And hum it did! During my command tour, the squadron was awarded the Meritorious Unit Commendation, its second Battle "E," as well as Naval Air Forces, Pacific (AIRPAC) and Patrol Wings Pacific maintenance and retention awards. Well-deserved recognition for an entire squadron of outstanding performers.

The squadron faced a number of challenges during my tour. Operationally, we had achieved 100 percent airborne status in August 1983 with just six EC-130Q aircraft. In October, we took possession of our final new EC-130 and, with seven mission aircraft, we were able to expand squadron operations and fly more missions on deployment. In the mid to late 1980s, Cold War tensions with the Soviet Union rose to the highest levels ever. Both sides were deploying new generations of strategic nuclear weapons—intercontinental ballistic missiles, bombers and SSBNs (ICBM-equipped nuclear-powered submarines). President Reagan had authorized the "Star Wars" space-based surveillance and weapons systems. The Soviet Union was mired in its awful Afghanistan war and was not pleased that their Afghan and *mujahidin* foes were being equipped with American weapons. Much of our operational planning, especially at higher levels with U.S. Pacific Command Forces, had the feel of real war planning.

Within the squadron, we started planning for the community's transition to the newly funded E-6A aircraft under construction at

Boeing. The E-6 was planned to be fielded first in the Pacific, so Naval Air Systems Command (NAVAIR) implemented a complex transition plan that required all the oldest EC-130s from VQ-4 to be transferred to VQ-3, replaced by that squadron's newest Hercs, just recently provided for the squadron's stand-up to 100 percent coverage. This inter-squadron transfer process took more than a year. Some aircraft were transferred following extended maintenance periods, but others were direct exchanges between the squadrons. As we got the older aircraft, our previously outstanding maintenance availability began to fall off, partly because of the older aircraft, but also because the Navy supply system had to adjust to the new locations of the TACAMO aircraft. In addition to the transfers, NAVAIR implemented the TACAMO Improvement Program modification to the aircraft. This mod installed satellite communications capability—radios and controls inside, antennas on the fuselage and in wingtip pods, and the associated wiring. This mod took two months per aircraft. A few were accomplished in major maintenance, but most required aircraft to be withdrawn from the squadrons. We continued to deal with all of these aircraft availability problems throughout my tour and into subsequent years.

Two personnel programs also presented challenges for us in these years. First, President Reagan declared a War on Drugs in the military. The Secretary of Defense quickly implemented a zero tolerance for drug abuse policy in the Defense Department, and the Chief of Naval Operations followed with the "Not in My Navy" campaign, which included both scheduled and random drug testing, along with new regulations that gave commanding officers the needed tools to enforce the policies. Essentially, these new regulations required us to discharge or court-martial all drug abusers, even first-time offenders. The screenings, investigations, and masts created by these anti-drug programs created a huge administrative burden. I spent my whole Navy career using positive leadership and mentoring techniques, working hard to turn around troubled sailors and officers to help them reach their full potential. These "no second chance" programs stuck in my craw more than a little bit, but, of course, we had to do it, and the anti-drug programs succeeded. Within the next two years, the Navy had cleared the decks of all of its worst drug offenders and troublemakers, tremendously improving the quality and productivity of the entire force in the process, but it was no fun doing it at the ship and squadron level.

Our second personnel challenge was more fun. This was the task to fully integrate a large number of female officers and sailors into the squadron. As Congress and Defense continued to expand the roles and opportunities for women in the armed forces, the TACAMO squadrons were the first warfare specialty community chosen to take on larger number numbers of women. A few female pilots were already serving in VQ-3, but now, with the first women graduating from the Naval Academy and Naval Reserve Officers Training Corps (NROTC) colleges now completing flight training, the Bureau wanted to send many more women to career-building assignments; TACAMO provided them the opportunity. Eventually, the squadron would be 20 percent women, both officer and enlisted. We had around 20 female aircrew officers, both pilots and Naval Flight Officers (NFOs). Our performance in this area was being closely watched by the Bureau and our VP brethren in the wing. No doubt they knew they'd be next, if we succeeded; we did, in impressive fashion, too. I think our smooth integration of large numbers of women was due to two factors. First was the extraordinary performance of the women themselves. With few exceptions, the women who reported to VQ-3 were smart, dedicated, hard-working and skilled in their aircrew positions. Most had been college athletes and could hold their own with the men in physical training. As these officers worked their way up the ladders in ground and flight duties, they earned the respect and admiration of the entire squadron. I truly believe the performance of the squadron overall improved due to the presence of these high-quality leaders. The second reason we succeeded was that we were just too busy to have any petty conflicts distract us from our mission. The entire squadron leadership team, myself, the Exec, department heads and Chiefs Mess, adopted and enforced the attitude that every officer and sailor who reported aboard VQ-3, regardless of race, gender, or religion, had a job to do and had to do it with dedication and excellence. There could be no discrimination or harassment, no slacking, if we were going to continue to be successful as a squadron. That attitude took hold throughout VQ-3 and greatly contributed to the success of our women. VQ-3 in those years became a leadership development crucible for both male and female officers. Many of our officers went on themselves to become squadron commanding officers, wing commanders and successful senior officers, some even admirals. So much for TACAMO being a dead-end backwater! I think we accomplished our goals and set a standard for the entire Navy to follow.

At the end of my tour in VQ-3 in November 1985, I was assigned to duty in OPNAV (OP 940) where I would continue to support the community as the E-6 program worked its way through the Pentagon decision process.

Barry Coyle: VQ-3 Commanding Officer 1985–1987

In July 1983, I was promoted to commander and frocked, although I would not be formally promoted until the following June. Later that year, I was selected for command and slated to be Bill Harsanyi's Exec. Needless to say, I was very happy about this upcoming assignment, but the VP community did not allow three commanders to serve in a squadron at the same time. So, after some negotiations with my detailer, in February 1984 I was assigned to the staff of Commander, Patrol Wing Two where I would work and also attend a number of schools to prepare me for command, to report back to VQ-3 in July 1984, one month prior to Fil Baca's planned August change of command.

I settled into routine staff work at Patrol Wing Two as the first TACAMO Liaison Officer and attended commanding officer leadership and legal training locally. In April, I was off to Monterey for Command Aviation Safety, the commanding officer Aviation Supply Course in Athens, Georgia, then up to Washington for visits to the detailers, OP-941, and the NAVAIR Program Office to get the latest updates on ongoing activities and E-6 progress. I spent a couple of days at VQ-4, trading info with Bob Downey and Ed Hampshire and getting updated on their squadron operations, then back to VQ-3 as the prospective executive officer. I spent a few weeks working side-by-side with Bill in the Exec's office. Then it was show time!

Bill became Commanding Officer, and I his Exec, in August 1984. I had worked for Bill previously in VQ-4 and on various things subsequently. We had an outstanding professional relationship and it was my great honor and pleasure to serve as his Exec. Through the end of my tour in February 1987, VQ-3 had two primary missions that drove our daily lives. First, we had to continue to fly 100 percent airborne coverage. Second, we became increasingly involved in planning for the community's transition to the E-6A.

After first attaining 100 percent airborne in 1983, we gradually increased the length of deployments and the number of available deployment sites as crews became more proficient and the tasking became heavier. In addition to mission flying, we continuously trained replacement crews as people rotated in and out. As commanding officer, Bill led the operations, training, communications, Naval Aviation Training and Operating Procedures Standardization (NATOPS)/Safety, and maintenance departments. As Exec, I oversaw administrative and support functions—correspondence, personnel matters, hangar, barracks and vehicle maintenance, and security. Bill and I shared a similar leadership philosophy, both of us strongly believing in delegation, pushing task accomplishment and leadership down to the lowest level. We had so much talent at every level that success was pretty much ensured by just handing out assignments and setting priorities, then getting out of the way to let people work. VQ-3 continued to excel under Bill's command, winning a Meritorious Unit Commendation, a third consecutive Battle "E," wing and fleet maintenance and retention awards.

The squadron's success in these years did not come easily, requiring hard work from all hands, especially in the Maintenance Department. Meeting the demanding flight schedule became a challenge. VQ-3 had received the seven newest EC-130Qs from 1981 through 1983 to support the build-up to 100 percent airborne. In 1984, this flow reversed to support fielding the E-6A first to VQ-3 in 1989. Only the first two E-6As, those going to operational test, would get new communications suites. All others required communications suites removed from an EC-130 to be installed in an E-6A, so, to get an E-6A, an EC-130 had to be turned in. The EC-130 fleet would be retired from oldest to newest, thus the plan called for the oldest aircraft to go to VQ-3 prior to the E-6A transition, a process that took well over a year to complete. There were more than a few months when we were down to six mission aircraft. Older aircraft are more difficult to maintain than new ones and the supply chain took a long time to catch up to older EC-130G/Q logistics, needing a different set of spares and parts. In addition to more and longer maintenance events, we faced longer delays getting needed parts throughout my tour. In spite of the challenges, VQ-3's maintenance professionals kept the aircraft flying and gradually improved our mission-capable rates to match the best squadrons in the wing.

That aircraft inventory/maintenance situation was probably the biggest challenge Bill and I faced during our command tours, demanding constant attention to flight schedules and operations, as well as the monitoring of key maintenance evolutions, but we managed to maintain unbroken 100 percent airborne coverage and meet all of our other commitments, all accomplished without any aircraft accidents or incidents.

In early 1985, NAVAIR designated VQ-3 as the Fleet Introduction Team for the E-6A to represent the NAVAIR Program Office at the squadron and Barbers Point, the receiving naval air station, to conduct local analyses, and to make recommendations to the Program Office regarding facilities, support equipment, and operational considerations. To pay proper attention to this important additional duty, Bill reorganized the Special Projects Department, staffing it with some of the squadron's best and brightest, officers and enlisted, people with sharp minds and plenty of TACAMO experience, but young enough to be able to serve future tours in the E-6A. Mike Duvall was the first Special Projects Department Head with Dale Hurt as his assistant. We staffed the department with an enlisted aircrew member from each crew position, and a couple of ground maintenance people, and set them to work.

It might seem a little early to be getting into detailed planning for fielding the E-6A, but the procurement plan demanded it. The first aircraft was scheduled for roll-out in late 1986 with delivery to the Navy for test in early 1987, the second following a few months later. The first operational aircraft was scheduled for delivery to VQ-3 in early 1989. Since it took a couple of years to get funding for military construction projects, plus the actual construction time, 1985 was by no means too early for planning a 1989 arrival. In 1985, the Navy's plan was for VQ-3 and 4 to continue operations from Barbers Point and Patuxent River. When we received detailed aircraft specifications and performance figures from Boeing and NAVAIR, we quickly realized a lot of work was going to be required at Barbers Point to support the E-6A. The 8,000-foot runways were not long enough for heavy E-6A operations and at least one would have to be extended. The runways, taxiways and ramps were not strong enough to support continuous operations of these planes, which weighed more than twice as much as an EC-130. A new hangar was required and the fuel farm needed expansion. And more. We sent all these analyses and recommendations to the Program Office through Naval Air Station Barbers Point so cost estimates and formal projects could be initiated.

The Special Projects Department also began to look for bases for an alert site for E-6A operations. Patrol Wings Pacific had decided Naval Air Station Moffett Field would not be suitable as the E-6A alert site, primarily because of the noise, but also because field upgrades similar to those at Barbers Point would be required, not cost effective to support one or two aircraft. We started researching other potential bases, focusing on Air Force bases that were already prepared to handle large four-engine jet aircraft.

When I assumed command in November 1985, we were still working hard on this Barbers Point bed-down plan. I assigned my Exec, Chuck Fitchet, to lead the Alert Site project to split up the work; he would have the chance to complete that effort during his command tour. In December 1985 and January 1986, Chuck joined formal Site Survey Teams looking for potential alert sites, eventually choosing Travis Air Force Base. Then, suddenly, there came a huge change to the plan. In February 1986, the Air Force, apparently in response to Navy inquiries about using its bases as alert sites, offered a long list of suitable bases around the country and suggested they would welcome the Navy E-6A program at both alert sites and main operating bases. This set off some quick analysis in NAVAIR, Chief of Naval Operations Staff and the Navy decided it would be both cost-effective and operationally advantageous to co-locate both TACAMO squadrons at a single airfield in the middle of the country. With the new basing concept decided, we set out to determine which bases to use.

In April 1986, I was assigned to another Site Survey Team, visiting six Air Force bases in the central U.S., selected by a group of Navy and Air Force staff officers in Washington. This trip would take me out of the squadron for six weeks early in my command tour, and I protested mightily, but Commander-in-Chief, U.S. Pacific Forces (CINCPAC), Admiral Hardesty, personally directed me to go because he wanted a knowledgeable operational representative on the team. We visited Little Rock, Whiteman, Blytheville, Ellsworth, Dyess and Offutt Air Force Bases, spending a few days at each base, touring facilities and going through a detailed checklist with base personnel. We then went to AIRPAC in San Diego and developed our final report. The survey team unanimously recommended Little Rock Air Force Base as the best choice among those fields surveyed. About a month after the Site Survey Report was submitted, Secretary of the Navy John Lehman sent me a "Personal For" message asking for my assessment as the current commanding officer of the operational advantages of coastal basing vs.

mid-U.S. basing. It was the position of CINCPAC that coastal basing provided the best operational locations for the TACAMO mission, a position I strongly supported, so I replied to Secretary Lehman with that position: operationally, coastal basing was preferred. Around August 1986, we learned that Secretary Lehman had approved Tinker Air Force Base in Oklahoma as the final mid-U.S. base for co-location of VQ-3 and 4. We were a little surprised since Tinker had not been one of the bases offered by the Air Force and had not been formally surveyed. This decision set off a political battle that lasted several years and delayed the final funding and construction of TACAMO facilities there until 1990. Congressional delegations from Hawaii, Maryland, Arkansas and Oklahoma battled each other and the Navy over the basing decision, holding up funding and demanding repeated analyses and justifications for Tinker. Eventually the Tinker decision prevailed, but that was long after my tour was over.

Meanwhile, our Special Projects team shifted their focus to planning for relocation to Tinker and establishing a West Coast alert site at Travis. In November 1986, I participated in a site survey of Tinker, and we obtained the detailed knowledge required to put together a meaningful facilities and bed-down plan. Development of this plan continued through the end of my command tour.

While reviewing some preliminary hangar and site plans for Tinker in late August 1986, it became obvious to me the Navy's plan was to just drop two Navy squadrons, with commander skippers, on Tinker Air Force Base and let them fend for themselves. Thinking of my own situation as odd-man-out in a Navy patrol wing, I was pretty sure two stand-alone Navy squadrons on an Air Force base would not be a good situation. I actually sketched out my initial ideas for a TACAMO wing on an airport bar napkin while waiting for my flight back from the 1986 AIRPAC Commanders Conference. Then, with the help of Chuck Fitchett, Mike Duvall, Dale Hurt, Vern Lochausen, and others, we refined and submitted a proposal to create a Strategic Communications Wing which would be headquartered at Tinker with the VQ squadrons to provide on-site senior Navy leadership. In developing this wing concept, we considered five factors:

- provide an organizational structure similar to that of an Air Force wing;
- expand command opportunities for TACAMO officers;
- reduce the size of the squadrons to more manageable organizations;
- consolidate all TACAMO training functions under control of the wing; and
- retain some of the existing chain of command structure to encourage support within higher-echelon Navy commands.

With these elements in mind, I submitted a proposal for Strategic Communications Wing One that included:

- A wing headquarters, with appropriate staff and facilities, with a TACAMO captain as wing commander. The wing would report administratively to AIRPAC through Commander, Patrol Wings Pacific.
- Two operational squadrons (VQ-3 and VQ-4), reduced in size and tasked just with the operation of the aircraft. These squadrons would report operationally to CINCPAC and CINCLANT, respectively, and administratively to the TACAMO wing.
- A training squadron also commanded by a TACAMO commander. This squadron would consolidate all TACAMO training: simulators; navigation training; aircrew training; and specialized maintenance training within the TACAMO chain of command, with all training facilities located at Tinker. This eventually stood up as VQ-7, "The Roughnecks."
- A maintenance squadron that would be assigned all the operational E-6 aircraft and conduct all scheduled and major maintenance, mirroring Air Force organizations as the best method to manage a limited inventory of aircraft. Of all the ideas on that napkin, only this one failed to materialize.

I believed this proposed organization would achieve all the desired management goals while expanding TACAMO command opportunities by two commander billets and one captain command.

I fully expected my VP chain of command to disapprove this proposal but, in fact, they heartily embraced it. I guess they were happy to get rid of us! Commander, Patrol Wing Two endorsed the proposed organization in just a few days and forwarded it to Commander, Patrol Wings Pacific. I traveled to California to brief it to both Patrol Wings Pacific and AIRPAC, where it was favorably endorsed and quickly forwarded to CNO and the Bureau of Personnel via AIRLANT for final approval. Within a few months, the wing concept received final approval, but in a modified form as recommended by various parties during the normal review process. The initial Strategic Communications Wing organization that was approved included a Wing Headquarters, VQ-3, VQ-4 and a Naval Training Support Unit, a significant accomplishment for the maturing TACAMO community.

Another important E-6A project initiated during my command tour was a personnel exchange program with the U.S. Air Force. The E-6 was the first large, four-engine jet procured by the Navy. Therefore, the Navy had no pilots qualified to fly it, or to train other Navy pilots in this model aircraft. Working with the Air Force, we developed an exchange program that would take six TACAMO pilots who had completed their first squadron tours and train them to fly the Air Force KC-135 aircraft at Ellsworth Air Force Base. Following this initial training, the TACAMO pilots would be assigned to KC-135 squadrons for three years to gain experience and qualifications as aircraft commanders and instructor pilots. Following these Air Force tours, they would return to TACAMO squadrons to become the initial cadre of E-6 instructors. In exchange, the Air Force got pilot billets in the TACAMO squadrons. VQ-3 and VQ-4 each selected three lieutenant pilots from a group of first-tour volunteers; Lou Ciochetto, Randy King and Jay Gallamore were the three VQ-3 selectees. Todd Tracy was one of the VQ-4 pilots; he and Jay would both go on to be TACAMO commanding officers and Jay would also become the E-6 Program manager at NAVAIR. This was a successful program that supported the safe and orderly training of initial E-6 flight crews.

My last big E-6 event was, as the VQ-3 representative, attending the roll-out ceremony for the very first E-6A in December 1986, taking along a half a dozen junior officers so they could get a glimpse of the future. This event was held with great fanfare and ceremony at the Boeing plant in Renton, Washington, near Seattle. A couple of weeks before the ceremony, the Navy and Boeing announced the E-6A was going to be named "TACAMO IV." I thought this was an inappropriate name and wrote a personal letter to Secretary of the Navy Lehman recommending approval of a better name from four candidate choices. He chose "Hermes," the Greek messenger of the Gods, announced at the roll-out ceremony, which later was "Latinized" to "Mercury." It really was a boost to squadron personnel to see this first big airplane completed and sitting on the ramp, providing a sense of urgency to our planning efforts that heretofore had seemed a little abstract. The roll-out was attended by a large crowd of Boeing and Navy personnel and dignitaries, congressmen and admirals. The event was well-covered by local media; I got a TV interview and my picture on the front page of the Seattle paper.

All the E-6 planning work was very interesting and I am glad I had the opportunity to make some significant contributions to starting up this next generation of TACAMO aircraft and bases. Still, the E-6 work and associated travel were a distraction from my primary job, to lead one of the Navy's largest squadrons. Fortunately, I was blessed with a great Exec, fantastic department heads (Ty Tyler, P. A. Moore, Vern Lochausen, Rich Gehri, John Brouillette, etc.) outstanding junior officers, and the best Chiefs Mess a commanding officer could hope for. The squadron continued to meet all operational, training and maintenance commitments and goals, and perform at an extraordinary level of excellence whether I was fully engaged or not. During my command tour, VQ-3 won another Meritorious Unit Commendation, our fourth consecutive Battle "E" and wing and type commander maintenance and retention awards. That's all credit to the leadership and hard work of all hands.

In August, I became the 1986 Pacific Fleet recipient of the Vice Admiral James Bond Stockdale Award for Inspirational Leadership. This award was sponsored by Vice Admiral Stockdale and is presented annually to one ship, submarine, or squadron commanding officer in the Atlantic and Pacific Fleets. It is significant because candidates must be nominated by another commanding officer serving at the same time, a peer award widely considered a "commanding officer of the year" recognition. The Atlantic Fleet winner in 1986 was a destroyer skipper, so I was the only aviator that year. I am also the only commanding officer of TACAMO, or any other land-based multi-engine squadron, to ever win the Stockdale Award. Although given as a personal award, I always considered this a unit award. Nobody would have known who I was, if it hadn't been for the spectacular performance of the men and women of VQ-3. I was quite surprised to have been chosen for this award that year. It was the height of the Cold War and ships and squadrons everywhere were engaged in confrontations of various intensity with Soviet units. In addition, we had ships and squadrons in actual combat. An F-14 Tomcat squadron had shot down two MiGs over Libya and several A-6 Intruder and A-7 Corsair II squadrons were engaged in close air support operations in that year's Middle East battle in Lebanon. There were clearly some skippers who had seen more action than I.

My Stockdale Award comes with two amusing stories. Both are in the vein of "no good deed goes unpunished" that help to keep you humble. The Stockdale Awards were announced by message in August 1986 while I was attending the annual AIRPAC Commanders Conference at NAS North Island, California. The conference included every available commanding officer, from admirals to commanders, who reported to AIRPAC. Since I was an AIRPAC squadron skipper and the only naval aviator selected that year, what better place to publicly announce the latest Stockdale Award winner, right? Well, Vice Admiral "Snake" Service, who was then the commander of AIRPAC and a great supporter of TACAMO, refused to make that announcement. He was a fighter pilot, having flown F-8 Crusaders and F-4 Phantoms in Vietnam, and was just as flabbergasted as I that a multi-engine land-based pilot won this award. He couldn't bring himself to acknowledge it publicly, though he did shake my hand and mutter congratulations at a reception near the end of the conference. Second, I was ordered to go to Washington in September for a ceremony where the CNO, Admiral Trost, would present the awards to both recipients. I tried to beg off from that trip to no avail. So off I went to the Pentagon, expecting to get a nice certificate and some photos. It was a very nice and mercifully short ceremony, but the actual Stockdale Award is no certificate. It is a beautiful 10 by 14-inch solid brass plaque mounted to an inch-thick wood backing, with a wooden display base eight inches deep, weighing 25 pounds. I shipped it back so I didn't have to struggle with it on the 6,000-mile trip home.

I was interviewed for both local Hawaii and national news clips and the Navy news service came to Hawaii to do a whole feature piece on VQ-3 which aired on national TV in the fall. I got my 15 minutes of fame, despite the hiccups described above. Even better, this award resulted in my opportunity to personally meet Admiral Stockdale, whom I greatly admired. By 1986, he had retired from the Navy and was working as a senior fellow at the Hoover Institution, a conservative foreign policy think-tank located at Stanford University. The admiral invited me to visit him there, a short distance from Moffett Field where I was a frequent visitor. I spent most of the day talking with him and he invited me to a very enlightening lunch with several of his colleagues. This meeting set off a regular correspondence between us that lasted several years and I continued to meet with him and his wonderful wife Sybil several more times over the next few years.

After that very busy August and September, Diane and I took some much-needed leave for a very nice trip to Taipei, Bangkok and Hong Kong, then it was back to work. Squadron operations and E-6 planning continued as previously described. Very busy but also routine by then. After the E-6 roll-out in December, the holidays were upon us, then in January, it was time to prepare for my change of command, scheduled for late February. In mid-January, Mike Davidson, Chuck's prospective executive officer, reported aboard and we were able to start turning over the commanding officer and exec's jobs as well as completing all the required change of command inspections and reports.

My change of command went as scheduled on February 20, 1987, a nice outdoor ceremony on a beautiful Hawaii day. I didn't know it then, but that would be my last full-time involvement with TACAMO after 17 years of almost continuous service in the community.

Ed Hampshire: VQ-4 Commanding Officer 1985–1986

Halfway through my three-year tour as the ECX Class Desk, I found out I had screened for aviation command and would be going back to VQ-4 as the prospective commanding officer. I would be leaving the NAVAIR Class Desk job about a year early and reporting to VQ-4 in 1984 as the prospective executive officer under Bob Downey after some schools en route. My belief in TACAMO and its future had indeed paid off as I had just been offered the best job in the Navy for an aviator, the squadron commanding officer. I took command from Bob in 1985.

As I returned to VQ-4, I was confident the talent in the squadron at that time was such that it would be able to excel in our operational mission and administrative functions if used properly. This optimistic view came from my years of serving with the majority of the people in the leadership positions in the squadron. They just needed to be pointed in the right direction and set free to do their jobs in the best way they knew how. I viewed one of my primary jobs was to help develop the capabilities of the officer corps of the squadron so our future in this new warfare community would be secure. As I had the opportunity to talk to these people during billet changes or just walking around the squadron, I would always emphasize that I didn't need to tell them how to do their jobs, because I had already done their jobs and I didn't need to do them again. I viewed my primary job to be ensuring they all had the tools, resources, and work environment to execute their jobs as effectively and efficiently as possible. In short, I worked for them, if they just told me what they needed to do their jobs. I also provided the buffer between them and the world outside the squadron of conflicting demands and distractions.

Of equal priority to everyone having what they needed was ensuring the enlisted quarters of the squadron had the best possible living conditions. The VQ-4 Bachelor Enlisted Quarters (BEQ) received the Naval Air Station "Room of the Month" for six consecutive months in a row with seven for the year. The VQ-4 management of their BEQ rooms served as a model for the entire naval air station.

When I returned to VQ-4 for my command tour, I found the squadron administrative control, formerly under the Commander, Naval Air Force, U.S. Atlantic Fleet, had been transferred to Commander, Tactical Support Wing One in 1975. Although often supportive over the intervening 10 years, the wing turned out to be a hindrance to our operations and was a major distraction from having a most enjoyable command tour. At the change of command when I became the commanding officer, the wing commander came to my office after the ceremony and told me "the squadron was over-manned and over-funded prima donnas," an exception to the austere funding and personnel climate the rest of the Navy was experiencing. Several times I had to go to our operational commander, the Commander-in-Chief of the U.S. Atlantic Forces, to keep the wing commander from taking some of our operational funding or manpower to help his other squadrons. I think this made my life much harder and created a somewhat hostile relationship with the wing.

Some of the squadron's accomplishments, despite this headwind, included an "outstanding" on VQ-4's Administrative and Material Inspection by the wing, 100 percent participation in advancement exams, the highest retention rates in the wing, an increase to over 90 percent mission capable rate for the aircraft, and over 15 years and over one hundred and sixty thousand hours of accident-free flying. VQ-4 was also the Commander, Naval Air Force, U.S. Atlantic Fleet nominee for the Secretary of Defense Phoenix Maintenance Excellence Award.

I take very little credit for any of these accomplishments by VQ-4. It was and always will be the men and women of the squadron that earned these statistics. I just tried to provide the proper environment for them to excel and succeed.

Andy Riddile: VQ-4 Commanding Officer 1986–1987

Then, it came. I found myself pacing in a wood-paneled reception room in the East Wing of the White House. Only during the following interview by the White House Military Office Deputy Director, General Matt Caulfield, and my future boss, Jack Mills, did I begin to understand why I was there. They needed someone, who, as a Presidential Emergency Plans Officer, understood strategic command and control. I joined a very small, highly classified group charged with ensuring the uninterrupted functioning of the presidency. I served as Chairman of the Contingency Planning for the Presidency Command and Control Committee, establishing the framework for top-quality, well-planned and coordinated presidential command and control systems. I also had the opportunity to serve as the first Director of the President's Emergency Operations Center after successful design, construction and operation of the first tactical command center in the White House. Along with the president's helicopter pilot and the president's pilot, I also served as spokesman for the acquisition and improvement of all presidential aircraft. All of this formed the final piece of the puzzle and I was assigned to improve it. Because this was at the highest level of our nation's strategic command and control structure, the understanding I received, and the consequent significance of the improvements achieved, making a difference actually became easy. Some of those improvements still serve the uninterrupted functioning of the presidency 32 years later.

It was becoming increasingly important to me professionally to influence the detailing of officers assigned to replace me. To ensure the continued success of all that I had put into place or had begun to put into place in the White House, I was able to get Kermit Ayres, a very highly regarded TACAMO officer, assigned as my relief. He was a pro and proved to be so many times. For the past three decades, there has been at least one TACAMO officer serving in the White House Military Office ever since! These TACAMO officers have served in positions ranging from President's Emergency Operations Center Watch Officer to the White House Military Office Deputy Director, a very senior position recently filled by TACAMO's Don Diggs, previously filled by General Caulfield and, subsequently, by General Chuck Krulak, who later served as Commandant of the Marine Corps.

Once again, I was called to leave my assignment early. This time, the Navy had selected me for command of VQ-4. I was honored first to support Captain Eddie Hampshire as his executive officer in 1985. Ed was the second "home-grown" TACAMO commanding officer. He was exceptionally knowledgeable in the TACAMO mission and thoroughly committed to it, a pioneer in the testing of EC-130 aircraft. Ed and

I enjoyed a very constructive professional and personal relationship. He essentially trusted me with a free rein, enabling me to begin early my planning for command of the squadron when it was my turn. Ed and I became good friends.

Although I delighted in my tour as Executive Officer, I was ready when it came time for change of command in 1986. I had plans for a highly methodical institution of professional performance improvement. I also instituted a professional development program for the wardroom that, among other things, brought in outside luminaries to emphasize to the officers the prominence of the TACAMO mission in national security. Two of the more interesting luminaries were none other than President Reagan's Senior Director of Intelligence Programs on the National Security Council Staff, Ken deGraffenreid, and the famous author, Tom Clancy. Ken, a fellow "True Believer," had previously served in VQ-4. Tom was a local insurance agent and popular author of *Red Storm Rising* and *The Hunt for Red October*. During my command, the squadron received the 1987 Commander-in-Chief, U.S. Atlantic Fleet (CINCLANTFLT) Golden Anchor Award, the 1987 Chief of Naval Operations Safety "S," the 1987 Commander Naval Air Forces, Atlantic Battle "E," and nomination by CINCLANTFLT for the coveted 1987 Department of Defense Phoenix Award for maintenance excellence. VQ-4 also won the Meritorious Unit Commendation in 1987. The squadron had pulled together in an extraordinary way, achieving new heights in every aspect of performance. None of this could have been achieved had I not once again "arranged" for my closest Navy buddy, Kermit Ayres, to serve as my executive officer and then as my relief. What a privilege to have him backing me up. He remains my closest buddy today.

This is a good point to acknowledge how much the hundreds of enlisted sailors, men and women, throughout my career influenced me, both professionally and personally. Their incredibly professional performance contributed enormously to the success of my career. Two chief petty officers were particularly special: Master Chief Avionics Technician Wayne Tyson and Master Chief Yeoman Mike Roach. These gentlemen were the epitome of good naval leadership and guided me through many tough challenges. They were my counselors, my guides, my advisors, and my supporters. I trusted them unreservedly. Master Chief Tyson was my Command Master Chief at VQ-4, and he, too, remains a good friend. Master Chief Roach was Kermit Ayres's Command Master Chief at VQ-4. Alas, he has since passed away. Many others had a directly positive effect on me, and I remember each of them by name, but there are far too many to list here.

Mark Herkert

Following VQ-4, my path took me away from TACAMO and flying for about seven years. I took a tour as a recruiting officer in Omaha, Nebraska. Recruiting was not an easy duty. It was not only very hard on me personally due to the time away from home, but also, and perhaps more so, on my family. My greatest joy during this tour was the birth of our daughter, Ashley. Fortunately, Shirley found employment at the Offutt Air Force Base hospital. After about a year into the tour, we had almost made the decision to leave the service. However, following a great motivational talk by my skipper and long discussions with Shirley, I decided to stay on active duty. I will always remain very appreciative of the sailors who are our recruiters. Recruiting is undoubtedly one of the hardest jobs in the U.S. Navy.

My next set of orders were to the USS *Coral Sea* out of Alameda as Operations Administrative Officer. So much for returning to TACAMO for my next sea duty and the pleasures of flying! Instead, we headed west to the San Francisco Bay Area. I guess that is why they are called orders. Shirley, Bryce, Ashley, and I packed up, moved to California, and bought a house in Hayward, only to find out the *Coral Sea* would be executing a home port change to Norfolk following one last period in Alameda. Fortunately, Shirley was able to find a job at a local hospital. Not easy on her, raising two kids and working while I was underway. I joined the ship in Sasebo, Japan, and completed the end of a cruise. The following year saw us in a yard period followed by workups with the air wing. My job was very busy underway, coordinating operations with other ships in company and with air operations. Following workups, we made a "round-the-world" cruise including transiting the Suez Canal and ending in the Norfolk Naval Shipyard in Virginia.

We were fortunate my next duty station was the Naval Postgraduate School in Monterey. The family could remain in our house in Hayward, Shirley retained her job at the hospital, while I studied all week and spent the weekends with family. I really enjoyed getting to know my family again. I also enjoyed postgraduate school, the educators and the opportunity to earn a master's degree.

When I finally did get back to TACAMO, I was to remain there for the rest of my working career; first on active duty and then as a defense contractor. I got orders to VQ-3, now relocated to Barbers Point, Hawaii.

West Coast flying was very different from what I had experienced flying out of Patuxent River. Most of our stops were in the western U.S., with a few in Canada. There were fewer locations and thus things became fairly routine. We stood alert at Naval Air Station Moffett Field in trailers that rocked with the wind.

Our operating schedule was the same as what I had flown in VQ-4, 100 percent airborne coverage, but the make-up of the squadron's personnel had significantly changed. The squadron was almost half female, both officer and enlisted.

The number of lieutenant commanders in the squadron was significantly higher. Ten years earlier, during my first tour in VQ-4, only the department heads were lieutenant commanders, none of whom had any prior TACAMO experience, and many of whom had been "passed over" for promotion to commander and for command screening; the Training Department Head was a first tour lieutenant. Junior officers could get as much responsibility as they wanted, due to the paucity of lieutenant commanders and the fact that many of those in the middle grade were "marking time" to mandatory retirement at 20 years.

A decade later, there were more departments, all filled by lieutenant commanders on their second or even third tour in TACAMO. Lieutenant commanders also filled all assistant department billets, previously reserved for second-tour lieutenants, and some even served as division officers, hoping against hope for a competitive assignment. The competition deprived many first and second tour junior officers of decent career development billets, leading to an exodus of some really great junior officers. I was fortunate enough to be assigned as Maintenance Officer in this competitive environment.

Hawaii was such a great place to be stationed! We lived in Mililani, and, through Boy Scouts and other neighborhood activities, got to know many locals and experience the Hawaiian culture.

My skippers during my department head tour were Commanders Barry Coyle, Chuck Fitchet and Mike Davidson. While I had been away, TACAMO had become a warfare specialty and all were TACAMO experienced, each with three squadron tours before their command tour. The difference was tremendous in that I felt these skippers thoroughly understood and really believed in the mission. As with the ship and VQ-4 tour, my fondest memories are of the sailors who believed in and executed the mission.

While serving as the VQ-3 Maintenance Department Head, I was approached by Commander Mike Duvall about serving as the Officer-in-Charge of the introduction team for the new E-6A aircraft. Shirley and I decided another tour in Hawaii sounded like a good idea for the kids and us, so I signed on. The Fleet Introduction Team was assigned to Commander, Patrol Wing Two, and I had the great opportunity to work for Captains Oliver and Ryan. Although of the P-3 community, they greatly supported TACAMO, VQ-3 and the Fleet Introduction Team. We had many program perturbations with slow aircraft delivery, lack of finalized aircraft technical publications, and late to non-existent training equipment and courses. Patrol Wing Two was there supporting us the entire way. As the Navy was getting ready to take delivery of its first E-6A, the decision was made to move the two squadrons to Tinker Air Force Base. The Fleet Introduction Team was assigned the responsibility of working with Tinker and the Corps of Engineers to design the new facilities.

Lew McIntyre

After my carrier tour, I chose to continue my strategic communications experience and got orders to the Battle Staff of the National Emergency

Airborne Command Post (NEACP), the E-4B 747 airframe, based in Offutt Air Force Base, Nebraska, now known as the National Airborne Operations Center.

I was deployed with Carrier Group One on the USS *Constellation* midway through our Indian Ocean deployment when my orders came in early June, to report in July. Admiral Bud Edney and his chief of staff, Captain Sam Ward, pulled every string to delay the reporting date, to no avail. "Join Staff priority." What had I got myself into?

I did a very quick turnover with my relief, took the C-2 aircraft to Diego Garcia and an Air Force C-141 to Mogadishu, for refueling, well before Somalia collapsed into chaos, then Nairobi, Sigonella, Torrejon and Dover; like a TACAMO deployment on steroids. In the meanwhile, my wife Karen, never shy about getting things done, came to be well known to Admiral Easterling and his staff, using the "JCS priority" to expedite the movers. I came back to find the house packed up, except for my ham antenna, which she left for me to take down. Then it was off to Nebraska. I rolled into Bellevue around mid-July and contacted my sponsor, Commander Jim Blomquist, about when and where I should check in. "Oh, no need to check in tomorrow, the team is on crew rest." When I asked about the following day, he told me they would be on crew rest for a week. Their deployments must be really arduous!

As it turned out, I had to go to Air Force flight physiology in Ellsworth Air Force Base, Montana, before I could fly. I made my first flight in mid-August. I served under U.S. Army Colonel John Dooley, a truly unforgettable character.

I was on watch on the NEACP when the *Vincennes* shot down the Iranian airliner. We had been following their armed confrontation with Iranian speedboats with a great deal of interest as the operational reports flowed in, livening up an otherwise boring midwatch. Then came their alert that an Iranian F-14 was en route to their location, not responding to calls, then the shootdown, then a few minutes later, a report from Commander, Mideast Force that an Iranian airliner was missing near their location. Not five minutes later, Captain Rogers of the *Vincennes* sent a message saying he had taken all measures necessary to preserve his ship and his crew, and he, and he alone, was responsible for all events.

He could not have known for sure what happened at that point, but he did not wait to assume responsibility for it. I was never so proud to be a naval officer as that day.

One day, we landed at some location to find ourselves parked next to a familiar Hercules with two orange drogues. I went over to visit the crew, just beginning to deplane after a mission. I asked to see the mission commander, who turned out to be Lieutenant Bill Okoniewski, someone with whom I was to have a close professional relationship as he rose to captain over the next 20 years. He gave me and my battle staff team members a tour of the bird and asked for a tour of ours. This was normally something almost impossible to get. Nevertheless, I asked Colonel Dooley if the TACAMO crew could get a quick tour, since they were, after all, on a companion command and control platform. To my great surprise, Colonel Dooley, who had not once but several times refused Air Force base commanders tours of the aircraft without a need-to-know, enthusiastically welcomed Bill and his crew, set them in the briefing room with a big "Welcome, Lieutenant Okoniewski and Crew" on the briefing board, and personally gave them a NEACP mission brief, with his staff at their disposal for questions. They then got about an hour's tour of the aircraft.

At the Joint Strategic Target Planning Staff, I was head of the Command and Control Wargames Analysis team. A lot of interesting stories there, but I can't tell you any.

I was coming up on 20 years' service. The Berlin Wall had come down, Soviet generals were being invited to tours of our strategic command and control centers and strategic forces. It seemed the Cold War was over, and we had won. I looked about at my fellow commanders who had no future but to wait out the clock. I didn't play golf, so it seemed like a good time to try my hand at civilian life. I had a master's in aeronautical engineering, but I felt my credentials were much more on the management side. So, before leaving active duty, I wrote up a scholarly-sounding article for *Communications Quarterly*, "Error Correction in Data Transmission" on Hamming codes, appropriately enough in a ham radio magazine, and taught a course as an adjunct professor at Bellevue Community College on telecommunications and computer programming. That was a truly enjoyable experience.

I came away from those two tours with a profound appreciation of TACAMO and, at long last, its recognition in the role of strategic communications in ending the Cold War. I completed my final Navy 1.5 mile run in a respectable 10:45, paced by TACAMO Lieutenant Tom "Rocket" Maser, later to be TACAMO CO and then the Wing Chief Staff Officer. I detached from active duty on July 31, 1990, expecting to see a generation of peace at last.

The next day, Saddam Hussein invaded Kuwait.

CHAPTER 12

The E-6A Arrives ... But Not on Time!

During the late 1980s, the key challenge was preparing for the arrival of the E-6A. This required a carefully orchestrated training pipeline, phasing out the Hercules flight crew from VQ-3 and bringing in aircrew trained only in the E-6A. But the airplane did not cooperate during flight testing. Rudder reversals caused loss of part of the tail, not once, but twice, just to show that this was not a one-time event. This threw a year's delay into the transition; the first-generation EC-130Gs and Qs, rotated to VQ-3 to swap out the oldest birds first, having been "ridden hard and put away wet" many times over in the past 20 years, now had to be nursed through yet another year.

Mike Davidson: VQ-3 Commanding Officer 1987–1988

After my department head tour, I relieved Captain Fil Baca at the OPNAV TACAMO sponsor desk. I wasn't even comfortable in the job when the news came in; I had screened for operational squadron command of either VQ-3 or VQ-4. The other officer who screened was in a NATO Defense school in Italy and wouldn't be available until the following spring. Since VQ-3 needed a new Exec on board in four months, I received orders to that squadron.

My 30 months at VQ-3 from 1986 to 1988 were both awesome and challenging due to several things. My commanding officer and former

Ops Boss from VQ-4, Chuck "Spiderman" Fitchet, was as understanding and patient as a boss could be, considering the headaches we had.

First, the Navy and several U.S. Congressmen got into a shoving match over just where the squadrons and Pacific alert detachment would be based. Senator Ted Stevens of Alaska said there was plenty of room at Eielson Air Force Base in Anchorage for all the aircraft and squadrons. The California congressmen said we could temporarily homeport at Travis until the Tinker facilities were finished. Senator Dan Inouye of Hawaii said the squadron would be leaving Hawaii over his dead body. Scores of sailors lined up at the office to see about pulling their Page 13s which they signed for E-6A training. Captain Ed Hampshire, the Program Manager at Naval Air Systems Command (NAVAIR), held firm. We went to Oklahoma City to centralize all parts of this mission and to take advantage of the repair and overhaul facilities common to both the Air Force's E-3 Airborne Warning and Control System aircraft and the E-6A at Tinker Air Force Base.

Second, part of the tail assembly and rudder separated from the first E-6A to be delivered to VQ-3. This happened on a final check flight over Moses Lake in Washington State. When the flight was repeated with new components, it happened again. That threw the whole delivery and EC-130/E-6A personnel transfer schedules off-kilter, cascading downward to put a whole gaggle of other things in disarray.

Through all this, upgrades to the ramp surface and squadron hangar endlessly disrupted our daily routine and created potential for major damage to aircraft engines from debris.

The people were simply the best and kept us flying safely through their heart and dedication. A skipper could have not asked for more.

We maintained 100 percent 24/7 coverage and did it safely the whole time. Commander Vern Lochausen came in as my Exec and was ready for command the second he walked in the door. He was the right man at the right place and time.

Vern Lochausen: VQ-3 Commanding Officer 1988–1989

When the time came for Aviation Command Screen in 1984, I took a few days off to go fishing in the Shenandoah Mountains, just by myself. I wanted to think about what a select for me would mean and what a "failed to select" could tell me about my career performance and future. When I returned to work, Skipper Fil Baca, in his usual humorous manner asked me what my future plans were and I said, "It depends." Before I could say more, he said, "You'd better be packing for Hawaii there, new skipper. Congratulations!"

News like that should be all good. To me it was. To my 13-year-old daughter, it was devastating. She ran upstairs to her room crying when she heard the news that evening, but on we went. My brain wanted it all to be just right. I went into the planning mode. Details were important. I visited the Pilot Exchange Program "boys" at the 2nd Airborne Command and Control Squadron at Rapid City, South Dakota, and Lew Ciochetto, the Senior Officer Present Afloat. Yes, "Afloat" in South Dakota; the Navy is nothing without its traditions! He was flying the EC-135, preparing to become one of the initial cadre of E-6 Mercury pilots to lead my squadron in introducing the jet to TACAMO operations. The squadron commander, an Air Force lieutenant colonel, was riding the Navy pilots for not conforming to the Air Force flight suit regulations, patches and such. Therefore, I arrived to visit him in my new, hot E-6 blue flight suit, Aviation Working Greens fore and aft cover, and my old Herc leather flight jacket. After his initial greeting and handshake, he said "Now I understand why I can't get your pilots to conform to regulations."

My reply would become a mantra for me then and years later. "Colonel, we are the Navy, and uniform regulations for the Air Force don't apply to Navy pilots. As long as my pilots fly according to your Dash One and make their missions, I don't think what patches they wear, and in what position on the flight suit they wear them, really should matter." The conversation got better when I asked him the biggest issues I should expect, transitioning Herc crews to the Merc. He left the flight suit issue behind and laid out some very good tips, including angle of bank with big engines hanging off the wing, and air refueling proficiency. He was right on the mark. The concern of angle of bank and the concomitant risk of dragging an engine pod on landing remains today.

Priority Number One: introduce the jet to fleet operations and do so safely. En route to Hawaii, I visited Naval Air Forces, Pacific (AIRPAC) Staff at Coronado. I asked the captains who led the readiness and safety departments for any advice on bringing the jet out, transitioning a squadron from straight-wing turboprops to heavy, swept-wing jets. The AIRPAC Chief of Staff captured it for me: "Best thing to do, Vern? Don't screw this up." Therefore, I planned even harder; details are important. What did we need to do in Safety, Operations, Maintenance, Communications, Training, Admin, and Security to make this transition complete safely and on time?

I found that some of the worst people I had encountered in the Navy, the junior officers, the department heads, and the skippers who weren't so good, were very useful to me as examples of how not to handle things. I walked in with an agenda. Mike Davidson, the Exec and upcoming Commanding Officer, allowed me to influence things for the future, as he expected to hand me the yoke of VQ-3 leadership in the middle of the transition from EC-130 to E-6A. He approved plans and guided me as his eager executive officer. Symbolic of our partnership was the photo of us on the roof of the hangar, with our Hercs on the ramp below, as we held a banner for the 20th anniversary of VQ-3 in July 1988.

By that time, it was evident Mike would be able to pick up the first E-6 but not stay for introduction to operations. The jet wasn't cooperating with the plan. The tail failures delayed everything! Everything was delayed by this event, threatening the whole program at the last moment, and leaving no alternatives to the aging Hercs. EC-130 crews' departures were delayed and their tours extended to "Prudent Limit of Endurance," while the E-6 Merc crews, with no EC-130 training, had no airplanes to fly, despite being ready to go. They initiated "flight suit Friday" to keep up their morale and remind themselves they were still flight crew. A group of junior officers were selected to continue EC-130 operations, carrying out the mission until the E-6 could be delivered to pick up the load. Naturally, this group developed an "Old TACAMO Just Got PLE'd" patch which sold like hotcakes.

Skipper Mike Davidson flew to Seattle and, with the E-6 Navy test pilots, delivered the E-6 to us at VQ-3. A photo alongside Diamond Head was taken through coordination with our Barbers Point neighbor squadron VC-1. We made the jet's arrival a memorable event for the skipper, forming side boys from the boarding ladder to the hangar ladder leading to his office. However, with the tail losses still under investigation, fleet pilots were not permitted to fly the jet and it was used on the deck to train crews as much as was possible. NAVAIR named it the Highly Mobile Ground Trainer. The Merc and Herc were parked diagonally nose to nose for my outgoing change of command, complete with a huge welcoming *lei* for the Merc and a green Hawaii gecko image painted below the flight deck windows, a reference to the ability of that lizard, and the jet, to lose its tail and regrow a new one. I relieved Mike in 1988 and took command of the squadron and the transition.

With a clearance to fly the jet with a speed restriction, VQ-3 crews flew to Seattle to begin delivering jets to Barbers. The crews quickly qualified, having waited patiently for so long to do so, and by October 1989 the first operational Mercury mission was completed.

Meanwhile, NAVAIR reworked the Herc drawdown schedule. The Herc crews began to deliver them to strip out for cross-deck of the mission suite to Mercs. Most wound up in the Aircraft Maintenance and Regeneration Center, "The Boneyard", at Davis-Monthan Air Force Base, Arizona. Those Hercs that were destined there were special. I took a page from the Eighth Air Force bombers of World War II, allowing crews to paint nose art on each one before their last deployment and subsequent delivery to the Boneyard. Being junior officers, they took full advantage and the art was not limited to just the aircraft nose. Those crews maintained a record for professionalism and their morale perked up with this freedom.

The Maintenance Master Chief asked me if somehow his maintenance crews could paint a Herc. Bureau Number 156173 had been returned to VQ-3 after strip-out to become a TC-130Q flight deck crew training and proficiency aircraft. My log book shows more hours in '173 than any other Herc and she had become very special to me. As she approached the time to depart for retirement at the Boneyard, I agreed to let the maintainers have at it. And did they ever! One young metalsmith spent several night check shifts painting a surfer on a wave on her vertical tail, no small feat. Later, in my greatest loss as the commanding officer, he took his own life over a "Dear John" letter. I decided then to go along on '173's last flight. As each Herc departed, I wrote a departure message and sent it out to all TACAMO units, and I met the crews, as they prepared to depart, and watched them leave.

Merc junior officers wanted a patch too. One enterprising officer developed a design that, after consultation with Merc crews, Boeing volunteered to provide them for each crew position, to be awarded once a person qualified. Boeing also shared a design for thousand-hour pins and provided those as well to the squadron. Concerns about foreign object damage dampened the acceptance of the pins, but the patches were coveted and proudly worn. A junior officer who had come to us from the A-6 Intruder community developed an inverted triangle patch with just E-6 on it.

The Herc departures brought me full circle in my career. These were my friends, my partners, the very birds that had given me a career. I did not want to see them go and wondered then if I would ever see them again. As much as this made me sad, the arrival of the Mercs and thrill felt by all hands in flying and maintaining them was the fulfillment of my career, or so it felt then. I had stayed the course, believed in TACAMO, and it had rewarded me by allowing me to be in the middle of the new age of TACAMO. What could be better than this?

Ed Hampshire: TACAMO Program Manager 1989–1993

Two years after my command tour in VQ-4, I again returned to the TACAMO community in 1988, screened and selected to be a Major Program Manager of a program with over a billion dollars in procurement. This would be a major shore command position but, more importantly for me, it meant I would be going back to support the community in which I had spent my career. I was going to be the Program Manager for the Airborne Strategic Communications Program Office, called PMA-271. All my years in the Navy trying to make myself the most qualified for this job, and be able to influence and correct the errors of the past TACAMO systems that I experienced, had finally paid off. I was elated! I was now responsible for the leadership, acquisition and delivery of all Navy airborne strategic systems, two joint Navy/Air Force programs and one French Foreign Military Sales program. I managed six separate programs with over a two-billion-dollar budget.

I arrived at this job with more in-depth knowledge of the E-6A aircraft than anyone before, since I had been the Navy's Chief Engineer for the ECX initial procurement specification, contract award, and design reviews. I also carried with me a deep understanding of the TACAMO operational environment and missions due to my three tours in a TACAMO squadron. I had an established personal relationship with many of the key players in the Office of the Secretary of Defense, Joint Chiefs of Staff, and offices of the Chief of Naval Operations that would make this job easier to execute. In short, I personally knew the people that gave us our missions and provided us the budget to do it. NAVAIR was very glad to have me check on board as the new Program Manager due to my Class Desk experience, my operational knowledge, and especially with my personal contacts within the Defense Department.

When I assumed command of the program office in 1987, the first E-6A was soon to be delivered to VQ-3, delayed by a year by the tail failure. The new facilities were under construction at Tinker Air Force

Base, and the EC-130s had to be extended in operational mission service with VQ-3 for an undetermined timeframe with their mix of qualified E-6 and EC-130 crews. Major challenges were definitely ahead in addition to a "normal" fleet introduction of a new aircraft. We were also preparing to move both squadrons to the new facilities at Tinker and stand-up Strategic Communications Wing One as the newly established TACAMO wing with Andy Riddile as the first commodore.

One thing I was determined to do as Program Manager was to actually fly some operational missions in the E-6A with VQ-3. I personally delivered two birds to VQ-3 and listened to what the aircrews and the squadron had to say about the aircraft and their training. I flew about 50 hours' pilot time in the E-6 on actual missions to make sure I got the feel of the aircraft and how best to use the aircraft operationally. I was even able to do one air refueling and several landings. I also spent time talking to and observing the communications crew on how their part of the missions had improved with the E-6A, soliciting their concerns and recommended improvements. I was thus better able to understand any problems the squadron might bring up to me and I also knew the priority on any fixes or enhancements with the limited funds available. I feel I really had my fingers on the pulse of making the transition from EC-130s to E-6s as smooth as possible. I don't believe any aircraft procurement had a shorter line of communication between the end customer and the person responsible for procuring the aircraft than the E-6A did; I'm proud of that.

One thing I fought for as the ECX Class Desk was an auto-orbit capability, though it was rejected at the time. As Program Manager, I now had influence to get this auto-orbit capability restarted, though via a back channel to Boeing so it looked like it was their idea and didn't cost the Navy any development money. I personally gave the study report information from Cornell Aeronautical Lab's instrumented drogue study, prepared by Dr. Lawton, to Norm Bialek at Boeing for their use; I had flown these test flights in my early TACAMO days. This study proposed an auto-orbit capability that eventually was put in the E-6 to stabilize the wire in orbit and, with that, signal strength. This became a Boeing-proposed change to the E-6A and was incorporated after the initial E-6A production.

Towards the end of my tour as the Program Manager in 1992, we had set up the program to consolidate the Navy TACAMO and Air Force Airborne Command Post missions into the E-6A; that would then become the E-6B. At this point in time, it was very obvious to everyone that TACAMO was no longer an "interim" system for a survivable communications link to our missile submarines, but the essential link to all of our nation's strategic forces. TACAMO had certainly arrived and was here for the foreseeable future.

This book is about the stories of the naval officers who stuck it out with TACAMO through the tough and good times in the life of the TACAMO squadrons. We are labeled the "True Believers" because of our faith that the TACAMO mission was a very important one that would endure into the future. It would be an injustice to not also mention at least two other people who were civil servants that had significant continuing contributions to TACAMO. They too were "True Believers" and staked their careers on TACAMO. They were both essential to my success at NAVAIR.

The first was my Deputy Program Manager in PMA-271, Jay McCormick. He started as an electrical engineer with TACAMO II very early on when the project was managed by the Naval Electronics Systems Command. He moved to NAVAIR with the TACAMO project management, and eventually became the Deputy PMA-271. His historical knowledge was significant and many times he kept TACAMO development from repeating prior mistakes.

The second person was also an electrical engineer, Mickey DiPasquo from the Naval Air Development Center, where TACAMO had its very beginnings in the EC-121. She started in the TACAMO field with the ECX procurement specifications development, helping me immensely as the ECX Class Desk. She continued to be intimately involved with TACAMO for the rest of her career with the Navy. She even made at least one full deployment with a VQ-4 aircrew in an EC-130, sitting in every position in the aircraft to learn what that position did and what design issues needed fixes or improvements. She used that information to guide design and aircraft integration solutions for all of the TACAMO projects with which she was subsequently involved. At one point she was even the PMA-271 interim E-6 project manager. She was also solely responsible for the design and integration of the Airborne Command Post Modification into the E-6A.

The final summary is easy for me. My decisions to remain in TACAMO were really just small ones made along the way one at a time. There was never any big soul-searching decision made to stick with TACAMO. My career took the path it did, just because I couldn't believe that TACAMO would actually go away, so I kept coming back. TACAMO made my 26-year ride in the Navy a great and rewarding personal experience! I have no regrets!

PART FIVE

The Wing Stands Up, 1990–1995

The relocation of VQ-3 and VQ-4 to Tinker Air Force Base also demanded a Navy organization to represent the squadrons at the flag level on that base. Thus, TACAMO stepped out of the last residual shadow of the Navy patrol and transport communities under which it had so long been an often-unacknowledged stepchild. Strategic Communications Wing One stood up in 1992 as the sole representative of the TACAMO mission, dedicated to just that mission and no other.

CHAPTER 13

The Inception

Vern Lochausen

In the middle of my command tour in 1989, it was evident that one day the squadrons would be relocated to Tinker Air Force Base to take advantage of the depot maintenance the Air Force performed there on the E-3, another derivative of the Boeing 707 airframe. We had made the case in Joint Staff meetings that the E-6 alone could provide coast-to-coast connections if it had an appropriate operating area. That, and a number of other factors, led to the decision to move from the coastal locations. Mike Duvall was at Naval Air Forces, Pacific (AIRPAC) trying to manage all the TACAMO issues, along with the Navy support for the Antarctic Program, which also used C-130s. AIRPAC Vice Admiral Jack Fetterman had visited VQ-3 and we gave him some briefings on our transition at AIRPAC. I was to relieve Mike Duvall at AIRPAC as my post-command tour and, suddenly, front and center on my desk, was Tinker Air Force Base, with its construction projects, negotiations with the base, and the relocations. Mike had a huge notebook of all the main and ancillary issues, and I took that over and converted it to accordion files as each issue began to cook.

Living in Coronado was a dream, but the hours and the travel were not. Every month it was off to Tinker and, in the right season, in Denver for the Antarctic programs. The admiral gave me tons of freedom and direct liaison with the Secretary of Defense, the Joint Staff, and Pacific Fleet Headquarters. *Desert Storm* went down while I was in that job, leaving me with the memory of the ships leaving San Diego for the Middle East, local community and radio stations covering the event.

Two trusted friends and TACAMO officers had joined in the effort, Norm Tindall and Mark Herkert forming the initial party at Tinker, Norm for the relationship building, and Mark for the construction supervision and initial Navy detachment leadership. Kermit Ayres and I worked up the papers on community issues, especially when the Cold War was declared over and we all stopped flying 100 percent airborne. Our white papers got the final number of jets and crews while others worked the wing staff structure.

My first trip to Tinker Air Force Base was potentially a hostile event, but I had AIRPAC's backing and direction to "go in there and form a relationship." Mark and I had studied bad joint basing examples, to learn again how not to do it, and determined the Navy needed to pay their way at Tinker. That worked! With very few exceptions, we "rented" from the Air Force at Tinker and provided funding via a signed agreement. Andy Riddile was selected as the first Commodore and Norm as his Chief Staff Officer. I escorted Andy to meet the Air Logistics Commander, Major General Joe Spires, in the general's office.

Back then, the base staff were all about six feet tall or more. The general was not. As he shook hands with Andy, also stature-challenged, he said, "Welcome Andy, finally a leader of normal height." Norm and Andy and the small Navy detachment staff planned and executed the wing standup, following the template Mark and others had laid out. Vice President Dan Quale was the keynote speaker along with Vice Admiral Jerry O. Tuttle, the very officer who was charged in the early 1960s as a lieutenant with creating TACAMO, giving it its name from scribbled notes on his tasking memo. The very next year, Norm retired and I was designated as his replacement. On the home front, moving from Coronado, in my eldest daughter's junior year in high school, to some place called Oklahoma did not play well, worse than the orders I had received while in Fairfax, Virginia, to move back to Hawaii for my commanding officer tour.

We did the moving to Oklahoma as we had done the relocation from Guam to Hawaii, in stages. First, I went out ahead, living alone for several months before bringing them out. The locals nabbed me immediately and I found myself in a very friendly lunch meeting with the Choctaw Chamber of Commerce at the Old Germany Restaurant, convincing me to buy and build a home there. So many advantages: a small town, no traffic, no crime, and an easy commute to the wing. All the Oklahoma City civic and business leaders welcomed the Navy in a very big way. I copied the Tomcat Operational Advisory Group structure to create one for TACAMO, getting all the commands involved in our presence in Tinker to see it and support it. Andy's D.C. connections ensured its success and top cover.

We created a structure of key supporting TACAMO officers assigned to a variety of staffs in our chain of command, leading to a very well-defined "community message" which we created with help from those officers and Andy, and later, from Kermit Ayres. This greatly aided my selection as commodore, and I followed Kermit. I had led the building of a staff, reorganizing the TACAMO squadrons under the wing, and supporting the U.S. Strategic Command, the unified joint command which replaced the all-Air Force Strategic Air Command. The U.S. Strategic Command had become our operational boss, replacing the Atlantic and Pacific commanders. We moved the Boeing 707 trainers to Tinker and we even sold AIRPAC on the need for two Beechcraft C-12s. It didn't hurt that the former assistant AIRPAC comptroller agreed to come to the wing as our first comptroller. He knew how to obtain, fence, and manage the funds we needed, and he and I had the right contact on the AIRPAC staff to see that TACAMO's needs were met.

Mark Herkert

I led the E-6A Fleet Introduction Team for VQ-3 from 1988 to 1990. Our major task was planning for the bed-down of the E-6 at Barbers Point and Patuxent River. The E-6 weighed twice what the old Herc did, requiring greatly enhanced infrastructure. At Barbers Point we used over a hundred cement trucks of concrete to shore up taxiways and ramps. We also constructed facilities within VQ-3's hangar to house the Boeing Contractor Logistics Support, housing spare parts and ground support equipment.

After completion of initial aircraft delivery, and the decision made to relocate to Tinker, I and most of my team flew to Tulsa to assist the Army Corps of Engineers with the design of the facilities, a really nice experience. We remained there until construction started, then we permanently relocated to Tinker as the newly created Strategic Communication Support Unit to oversee construction, work with the base to prepare to bed down the two squadrons and to stand up the new Navy units at Tinker. These new units included Strategic Communications Wing One itself, as well as the Naval Aviation Maintenance Training Group, the Naval Strategic Communications Support Unit and the Navy Personnel Support Detachment. We worked with Norm Tindall, already on site as the TACAMO Liaison Officer representing AIRPAC to the Air Force organizations at Tinker. Our offices were in a trailer, mercifully no longer in existence, near what is now the southern Base Exchange mini-mart. Our team included a civilian secretary, Lisa Gawith, Senior Chief Burkhouse, two first class petty officers who would subsequently make chief, Aviation Electronic Technicians Ben Corson and Aviation Metalsmith Greg Garcia, and a second-class petty officer, Aviation Storekeeper Monica Kraft. While Commander Norm Tindall worked with community leaders and the squadrons to pave the way for the sailors' move to Oklahoma, the Fleet Introduction Team concentrated on overseeing construction and working the details of support from Tinker.

It was a wonderful thing to see the future TACAMO facilities rise out of the ground and take shape. The Army Corps of Engineers and Guernsey & Company built an amazing set of facilities for us. And it was very interesting bringing the Navy culture onto an Air Force base.

The local population could not have been more welcoming. We often say Oklahoma City is a Navy town due to the great reception we received. Individuals who deserve significant mention are Rear Admirals Kirkpatrick, Ackerman, and Slavonic, and especially Major General Joe Spires. Their efforts to welcome TACAMO sailors to Oklahoma created a bond that exists to this day. Rear Admiral A. R. Mannes, Commander, Patrol Wings Pacific, and his staff, to whom I reported, provided great support as we stood up the Navy at Tinker and prepared for the standup of Strategic Communications Wing One.

Following standup of the Wing, I became part of the Commodore's staff.

CHAPTER 14

Strategic Communications Wing One

Andy Riddile: Commodore 1992–1994

National Security Decision Directive, "United States Nuclear Weapons Command and Control," was published on August 21, 1987, the handiwork of "True Believer" Ken deGraffenreid and Ollie North. It established a U.S. Nuclear Command and Control System Support Staff charged with conducting unified Federal Government planning to coordinate National Command and Control research, development, acquisition, and integration of an architecture for effective and responsive strategic command and control. I was assigned as the Chief of the Architecture Branch. One of my contributions here was the identification and analysis of various deficiencies in the U.S. National Command and Control capability. We were able to implement improved plans and procedures. This was another highly specialized unit which could benefit from my now highly specialized expertise.

Once more, I was to leave my assignment early. This time, I was to serve as Senior Military Advisor to the Vice President of the United States. I have always suspected that Ken deGraffenreid had a prominent hand in these orders. After all, he was friends with my new boss, the vice president's National Security Advisor, Cary Lord. Here, my expertise in strategic command and control was going to take somewhat of a break. I represented the vice president on numerous interagency policy coordinating committees covering a wide range of issues including counter-narcotics operations, emergency actions procedures, command and control connectivity, current intelligence support, and counter-terrorism operations. I found myself neck-deep in the 1991 Persian Gulf War. Although I did serve the vice president in a classified command and control role, I also found myself in a coordination role with the White House Military Office and in charge of all the military personnel assigned to vice presidential support. I was also responsible for keeping the vice president fully informed and effectively engaged in policy issues associated with political, military, and economic affairs throughout Latin America, spending significant time conducting advance work in South America. It was a heady assignment which was again called short.

By 1991, the Navy and Congress had made the decision to relocate all TACAMO squadrons and support organizations to centrally located Tinker Air Force Base. The decision was both operational and political. The nature of the decision didn't matter much to me, as I listened to my detailer tell me over the phone that I had been selected as the first commander of Strategic Communications Wing One and Task Force

124. Utterly surprised. Now folks were going to call me "commodore." When I arrived at the Navy wing for the first time, I found on Tinker one two-star Air Force general, two one-star generals, and 57 full-bird colonels. Knowing the Air Force is no more enamored with strategic warfare than is the Navy, and in anticipation of the archetypal "butt-sniffing," I decided to make the actual commissioning ceremony of the wing not only very public, but also as memorable as possible, to drive a stake in the ground. So, I brought in every important person conceivable, starting with Vice President Quayle as guest of honor, and including the TACAMO "inventor," Vice Admiral Jerry O. Tuttle, Oklahoma's Governor Walters, Senator Boren, Representative Mickey Edwards, General Spiers, generals and admirals in my chains of command and other senior admirals, generals, and civilians, both in government and in the community. In front of an American flag, larger than the one in the movie *Patton*, stood Air Force Two prominently parked on the ramp, with a large cadre of local and national news camera operators. The adventure was launched on May 29, 1992. My mom, dad, and kids sat in the front row.

Some of my favorite memories include nurturing relationships with the Air Force leadership and with the welcoming community. Assembling "Team Tinker" included a smooth integration of forces. With the help of Rear Admiral Ralph Tindal, we made it clear that, as a task force commander, I reported operationally directly to the four-star Commander-in-Chief, U.S. Strategic Command, along with the other task force commanders, most of whom sported three stars. We continued to place superior TACAMO officers at key billets at all headquarters and, interestingly, we acquired a survivable, road-mobile capability for force endurability; Naval Air Systems Command (NAVAIR) soon wondered how they suddenly owned a whole mess of trucks.

The initial squadron commanding officers, Bob Young and Paul Jackson, the officer-in-charge Mark Peterson, and the officers and sailors assigned to us, performed far beyond expectation, even knowing just how good they all were. John Keilty, Mike McDermott, Kris Strance, and Dave Hawkins followed them. As another representative example, Commander Don Diggs served as the new wing's first operations officer.

An expert in TACAMO operations, Don nevertheless found it no small challenge first to integrate Pacific and Atlantic Fleet operations and then assimilate these combined operations into the greater force structure of U.S. Strategic Command. He did it successfully and his work stands today, largely unchanged a quarter century later. Don later served as VQ-4's commanding officer and then in very senior positions in the Office of the Secretary Defense and in the White House Military Office. We dealt with disparate operations, airframe transitions, community reorganization, chain of command restructuring, reduced manpower, multiple homeport changes, additional JCS tasking, and civilian community liaison. Consummate professionals, such as Norm Tindall, Mark Herkert, and Chief of Staff Vern Lochausen, later himself to command the wing, expertly laid the groundwork. I was blessed again with superior leadership in the persons of Rear Admirals Tony Maness, John Ryan, and, again, Ralph Tindal, an enormously rewarding tour. Having established the Navy's newest air wing, in the center of the country on an Air Force base, we set the standard for commands establishing inter-service programs. Finally, guess who relieved me: Kermit Ayres, yet another "True Believer," who seemed to be always following me.

I knew my chance for selection to rear admiral was minimal as my Navy resumé was too highly specialized. Indeed, my flag selection board did not put me on the promotion list the first time. Despite protests from my operational boss, Admiral Hank Chiles, that I was still likely for promotion, I requested retirement, serving my last tour as a Federal Executive Fellow in Washington, D.C., at RAND Corporation.

After 23 years, TACAMO had become the embodiment of professionalism. My service was blessed with the symbols of the Presidential Service Badge, the Vice-Presidential Service Badge, the Office of the Secretary of Defense Identification Badge, the Organization of the Joint Chiefs of Staff Identification Badge, the U.S. Strategic Command Identification Badge, and the Command at Sea Insignia. I remain deeply grateful for the opportunity I had to serve with the officers, the chief petty officers, and the men and women of TACAMO. It was time to move on to serve in different ways.

Vern Lochausen: Commodore 1996–1998

When I became the commodore, I realized I had reached the end of a journey that started back in VQ-3 in my second tour when I was Special Projects, when I forged a special relationship with NAVAIR. Each successive tour built on the experience of the last, leading me to a wider circle of contacts in higher and higher headquarters.

- First step: VQ-3 Special Projects where the ECX replacement for the Herc and a hangar for it at Barbers were on my plate.
- Second step: to NAVAIR where I was in the middle of the E-6 buy, build and test, and the whole decision to base at Tinker.
- Third step: to VQ-3 as the first E-6 commanding officer, starting with all Hercs and ending with all Mercs.
- Fourth step: E-6 commanding officer to E-6 quasi-community leader in setting up for Tinker and the wing.
- Fifth step: to AIRPAC then to Tinker as the deputy, and finally, three years later, I'm the commodore.

We excelled in many areas. It was all new, the jets, the facilities, the support structure, the community, the organization. We built new buildings and two new enlisted quarters. We won the Omaha Trophy, the Strategic Command operational excellence award. When presenting it, General Gene Habiger, USAF, U.S. Strategic Command's commander, told me we had "out-SAC'd the former SAC units" in meeting our mission requirements and going beyond in global exercises. Strategic Air Command (SAC) had been the gold standard for big operational exercises and force mobility. To beat them in the eyes of Strategic Command, which was originally SAC Headquarters, was a really big deal.

During that last tour, Mike Duvall, now Executive Officer of VXE-6, the Antarctic support squadron, made good on a favor I had offered him when at AIRPAC. We sent a stripped-out former TACAMO Herc to his squadron as an additional logistics support asset, which he arranged to have fail its service life inspection at Tinker. It became our permanent static display. The Oklahoma City Air Guard, the wing maintainers, Rockwell, and lots of volunteers came together and it was restored, cosmetically at least, to TACAMO configuration. I learned that my log book contained the connection I missed. VQ-4 Crew Ten took that bird on my first deployment in the 1970s, and I was the Airborne Communications Officer (ACO). I found the crew picture from Bermuda from the start of that trip. For the Herc dedication, in my change of command week, Delta Captain and former Crew Ten aircraft commander Frank Caruso came and spoke, he in Delta blues and I in Navy whites. As I went over the side, my request to chop the wing direct to AIRPAC as type wing was approved. No longer did the VP P-3 community have to be bothered by TACAMO; we had grown up at last.

The VQ-3 notion that the E-6 could connect the two coasts communications-wise came back to haunt us. The Joint Staff and the Secretary of Defense decided to retire all the Air Force Airborne Command Posts and give the mission to the E-6. We began the arduous task of adding this new, and little understood, mission to our operational plans and training. My old navigation instructor, Lew "Zig-Zag" McIntyre, and Gary Soldow, both then with a small company called GRD, produced a mountain of classified documents, updated our Personal Qualification System, which

Lew had written during his VQ-3 tour for the Herc, and took some of our people to Waco to familiarize them with the new communications suite. This suite added Milstar, a new satellite mission voice and data system transplanted from the EC-135, and a new message processing system. The transition of the EC-135 Looking Glass equipment to the newly designated E-6B was a crash program that went operational just as I was retiring. In the process, I almost got fired when an E-6B crew, with General Habiger aboard, landed at Offutt in a thunderstorm, a violation of Air Force procedure, but not an unsafe event. Armed with the facts, I defended the young aircraft commander's decision, using his authority to assess the weather and land safely. The Offutt leadership disagreed. I stood by my guns, telling them that unless they closed the field, the Navy could land there. No harm, no foul, but no Air Medal, either.

Looking back, I had been involved in support of all the TACAMO progression of professionalism from the resumption of 100 percent airborne coverage in VQ-4 in the 1970s, the buildup and assumption of 100 percent coverage in VQ-3 in the 1980s, the E-6 buy, the E-6 transition from the Hercs, the wing standup, the U.S. Strategic Command chop, and the E-6B, along the way becoming a TACAMO and Nuclear Command and Control Communications expert. The progression began when I had taken a leap of faith in TACAMO in 1980 for a second set of orders to an as-yet uncertain community. Nearly 20 years later, I retired at the top of the ladder, confident the professionalism so many had built would continue.

So I asked myself, "What now, Commodore?" The embassy in London had an opening and the Joint Staff was looking for help. With several lucrative offers from industry, I elected to take the advice of the E-6 Assistant Program Manager for Logistics, Ken Gray, who counseled in favor of Boeing, saying it was just like the Navy, big and with plenty of opportunity to grow.

Lew McIntyre

Prior to retiring, I decided I wanted to go into engineering, as I had always enjoyed tinkering. I sent out lots of resumés and landed a job with an old friend from VQ-4, an engineer from the Naval Electronics Systems Engineering and Test Facility named Wendell Metcalf, who had supported my first squadron two decades past in a trailer behind the maintenance department. He got me a job with a company in Albuquerque, United International Engineering, that would take me to the D.C. area doing electromagnetic pulse testing for the Naval Surface Warfare Center, White Oak, Maryland, with most of the testing done at Solomons Island on Sparrow missiles, F-14 Tomcats and F/A-18 Hornets. I also bid on a proposal to support the Program Office, and brought in Fil Baca, my old mentor and now a retired captain, as the prospective program manager. My first proposal and we came in first in technical, but third in cost! Of course, the competition won the cost shoot-out, aborting my early return to TACAMO. I had fun with the various projects, but the company left a lot to be desired and, when Wendell offered me a chance the following year to join his company, GRD, based in Warminster, on a tasking at Patuxent River, I took it and was quickly back to TACAMO.

I was supporting the Program Office, then still in Crystal City, under Dan Counts. Ed Hampshire was the Program Manager, Vinnie DiGirolamo, then a lieutenant commander, was the Avionics Systems Project Officer and I found myself immersed in TACAMO once again after a 10-year absence. My first project was an engineering review of Warminster's integration plan for the Airborne Command Post, which called for cross-decking mission-specific systems from the EC-135 to the E-6, upgrading the message processing system, and adding Milstar satellite communications. My time on the E-4 left me very familiar with the mission and mission-specific systems, many of which were also installed on the E-4.

I sketched a lot of drawings to explain how these new systems worked, then the drawings became PowerPoint slides. Vinny was a pilot without a lot of mission communications background. I gave him tables that listed all of our communications systems, from Very Low Frequency (VLF) to Milstar, their purpose, and some technical details. Then Vinny asked for some text and, before we knew it, the System Architecture Document was born. The birthing was not without a catfight. Mickey

DiPasquo did not see why anyone needed this information; it would just confuse them. I have always believed people work best when they know what a system does and what its purpose is. With a little help from Bill Okoniewski, now a lieutenant commander and the Chief of Naval Operations Staff (OPNAV) requirements officer, the document was published. The system architecture document has continued to this day, a unique document unlike any in all of NAVAIR, and the "go-to" text for any new modification to the jet. Even Mickey came to appreciate it!

I was involved in the test planning and test flight for the Milstar installation in 1995, my first ride in the E-6. The Milstar system worked beautifully. When I started, I had only a hazy idea how to use the system and I left out no detail on equipment set up. We had an operational system installed in the old Replacement Training Department Building 1652 and I was able to verify all my set-up procedures there, then train the crew. My test procedures were taken over by the operational evaluation team for their subsequent test flights and they were ultimately captured in the flight procedure documents; a good test plan ultimately should become a good operator's guide!

Dan Counts, my boss at GRD, began an expansion of our small office to support the E-6B via both PMA-271 and the wing, bringing on Dan Weis, a retired Air Force lieutenant colonel, communications officer and EC-135 veteran who taught me so much about the Airborne Command Post mission. He also helped me enormously, guiding me through political minefields. Dan Counts also brought in Gary Soldow and together we took on the major task of rewriting communications doctrine at various levels, adapting it from the EC-135 to the E-6B. We rewrote the Tactics Course for the wing to adapt it to the Airborne Command Post mission. We also upgraded their personal qualification system courses, little changed from what I had put together 20 years before in VQ-3, to reflect the E-6B and that new mission. I also got to attend the wing change of command. When Vern Lochausen took the helm in 1996, he spoke of his old navigator instructor, who had always emphasized the importance of maintaining a good dead reckoning position to check your fixes, and he charged them all to maintain a good dead reckoning position as we stepped into that new mission. He didn't know I was in the audience and I was deeply touched that something I had said so many decades before had stayed with him so long.

The crash of 151890 on the Eastern Shore of Maryland in 1972 had a positive impact that resonated down the years. The airframe was strike damaged and scrapped. The communications suite was undamaged, but unflyable because of the crash. Rather than simply scrap it also, VQ-4 had reassembled the communications racks and equipment in the Replacement Training Division, later to become a department, behind the hangar as a full-fidelity trainer, laid out exactly like the aircraft. Building such a trainer from scratch, for what was viewed to be an interim solution in 1972, would have been prohibitively expensive and out of the question. Reassembling it was not and, once we already had one, it was relatively easy to justify keeping it up-to-date. Down the years, when the squadron left, this moved across the street to become the System Integration Laboratory, "the E-6 without wings," no longer used for training, but for troubleshooting and pre-production installation. It is so much easier to install something in the Laboratory than on an operational aircraft. Changing even a light bulb can take up to a pound of paper to do it on the jet.

In 1997, I wound up working in the Laboratory, first assisting Joe Szmer to develop a five-year plan for keeping and upgrading the facility, thereby turning it into my own personal playpen. I have had a lot of interesting and productive projects conducted since, major mods to the aircraft mission avionics, all of which have been fielded successfully.

Epilogue

We all traveled many different paths through our careers in TACAMO, a career that seemed unthinkable when we began our journeys in the 1970s, pioneers by choice or by chance. At the end of our TACAMO service, however, we "True Believers" experienced various denouements: major commands, program management, or civilian careers as contractors, still supporting TACAMO. We made our mark on the community, each in our own way, but the community likewise shaped our lives, I believe in all cases, for the better.

Bob Downey

My next tour was initially in Washington, D.C., with Commander, Naval Telecommunications Command as N-3 Operations. It was a turbulent tour, with Captain Wes May as the deputy. He was the commanding officer of VQ-3 before me, and commanding officer of Naval Communication Area Master Station, Western Pacific. We never got along! Fortunately, I was selected for captain while I was at the Naval Telecommunications Command. 'Nuff said!

Subsequently, I was ordered to the Defense Communications Agency, Arlington Hall in Washington, working under Dr. Signori, a great leader. Soon after I reported to the Commanding General of Defense Communications, he tasked me to find out if TACAMO was a viable asset. I prepared a report for him with the assistance of the Applied Physics Laboratory, Johns Hopkins University, which had been evaluating TACAMO performance almost since its inception. That report convinced him to continue supporting TACAMO.

My last command was the Naval Communications Station Puerto Rico at Aguada, supporting the Very Low Frequency (VLF) submarine broadcast and high frequency broadcasts for ships at sea. We also helped the ships' crews take part in the excellent liberty in Puerto Rico, sending a team of radiomen aboard to take care of radio maintenance issues, while the crews enjoyed themselves ashore. We also had a detachment in Panama which I visited several times.

The communications station had two huge backup generators. Upon arrival, I decided to test them, planning to run them for two weeks, but they failed less than one day into the test due to rusted pipes. After major repairs, we did it again and they ran for 14 consecutive days with no further problems. This turned out to be very fortuitous as we got hit by Hurricane *Hugo* with winds over 150 miles per hour shortly thereafter. The generators ran port and starboard for over 30 days, keeping our communications on the air without a break. Power was out throughout the island, so we evacuated women with children to the States and billeted single women on cots on base. Our chief engineer, a lieutenant, took the initiative to go off base to bring back a generator to power up the Officers Club so it could serve meals to both officers and enlisted men through the crisis.

My last assignment was Deputy Chief of Staff for Communications at Special Operations Command, Tampa, Florida. There are some interesting stories there that must remain unsaid.

This was my journey, from a once-passed-over and bitter lieutenant in a community that had no future, to a "True Believer" who aspired to, and achieved, TACAMO command and beyond.

Mark Herkert

Upon standup of Strategic Communications Wing One under Commodore Andy Riddile, my team and I became members of the wing staff, each of us moving to our areas of expertise. I became the Wing's Comptroller and Executive Assistant from 1992 to 1994. As Shirley had settled well into the Edmond, Oklahoma, community and our children, Bryce and Ashley, were fully enmeshed in the Oklahoma school system, we elected to stay there and retire. Also, the Navy was downsizing, so staying on active duty after 20 years was not an option. I will always fondly remember my days on active duty and treasure being allowed to continue to serve my country and the Wing and the TACAMO mission as a defense contractor.

I was afforded the opportunity to participate in the transition from the E-6A to the E-6B as TACAMO assumed the Airborne Command Post mission from the U.S. Air Force, the importance of the TACAMO mission to the nation's defense highlighted by the Schlesinger Report.

It has been my pleasure to assist all of the commodores with coordination among various members of USSTRATCOM, COMNAVAIRPAC, COMNAVAIRLANT, and OPNAV staffs. I assisted with Command Brief formulation and preparation, crafting requirement documents and preparing executive correspondence. My most significant contribution is my role as the Wing's support agreement manager, coordinating over 100 agreements with different bases that support the TACAMO aircraft, both in the U.S. and overseas.

Looking toward the future, the Navy is beginning an effort to recapitalize its aircraft and the facilities. I currently am working to create new facilities for our west coast detachment and assisting with designs for new facilities for our central detachment at Offutt AFB.

It has been my pleasure to serve each of the TACAMO commodores. Each has added tremendously to the community and continued the transformation of TACAMO into a well-respected warfare specialty. The community well deserves its reputation for mission success. As with all tours, I have well enjoyed working with the sailors, civilians and other contractors that support this important Navy mission.

I truly believe in the vital strategic communications mission of TACAMO and am proud to have been a part of it over the years.

Bill Harsanyi

The plum for TACAMO officers, post-command, then as now, was a major command. Pretty much that meant commanding one of the Navy's Communications Area Master Stations. I was fortunate enough to draw the Naval Communications Area Master Station Eastern Pacific in Hawaii. During this tour, I was able to visit with another TACAMO retread, Vern Lochausen, while he was commanding VQ-3 and struggling with delayed delivery of the first E-6 Mercury jets. I provided him the best advice I could, saying "Just do the best you can," and telling him all of us had our unique challenges in our command tour.

Barry Coyle

From March 1987 to March 1988, I attended the Naval War College in Newport, Rhode Island. Then, from April 1988 to July 1991, I served as the Assistant for Communications Management on the staff of the Supreme Allied Commander Atlantic's Representative in Europe at NATO Headquarters in Brussels, Belgium. Here, there was no TACAMO-related work. I was completely involved in working on NATO maritime communications issues and budgeting. The only TACAMO connection during this time was through Commander Stu Bell, assigned to the staff as Air Operations Assistant. Stu was also an early "True Believer"; we had served two TACAMO tours together in both VQ-3 and VQ-4. He retired out of that job and stayed in Belgium. This was an extremely interesting tour, probably my best shore tour. The work was challenging, but the NATO Headquarters' work environment was much more relaxed and congenial than in a similar position at the Pentagon. I got to serve with outstanding officers and civilians from all NATO countries. My family and I got to travel extensively throughout Western Europe on both business and personal trips. Belgium was a fascinating small country, only an hour from six different nations, making even weekend trips cultural delights. The highlight of this tour was being assigned to NATO in 1989 when the Berlin Wall came down and the break-up of the Soviet Union began. These events set off a month-long party throughout both Eastern and Western Europe. NATO had been specifically created at the beginning of the Cold War to counter the Soviet Union, so the sense of victory and euphoria throughout the Headquarters building was extraordinary. Sadly, it would be short-lived, as Gulf War I would follow shortly after.

In April 1991, I was promoted to captain. Shortly after that year's captains list was approved, Andy Riddile was selected to become the first commodore of Strategic Communications Wing One. I was very happy to see Andy, a personal friend and the earliest of "True Believers," get this job. Of course, I was disappointed for myself. Since I had initiated the TACAMO wing concept, I had hoped the Navy would give me the chance to lead it. But the Navy sent me on a different path.

In July 1991, I completed my tour at NATO and reported to the staff of the Assistant Secretary of Navy for Research, Development and Acquisition. Here I served as Director, Resources and Evaluation. My division had three branches responsible for Acquisition Program Oversight, Budget, and Congressional Liaison. This was a very interesting and challenging high-level position in the Pentagon, but with little TACAMO connection, so I'll spare you the details of this job. I did participate in a couple of TACAMO activities during this two-year tour. While serving the previous four years in Newport and Brussels, I had been out of touch with TACAMO during those critical years of developing, testing and delivering the E-6A and constructing the new facilities at Tinker Air Force Base. It was good to be able to have the information available to get caught up on the program.

In our Program Oversight role, my staff was responsible for reviewing Navy acquisition programs and reporting status and problems to the Assistant Secretary of the Navy. Ed Hampshire was then TACAMO Program Manager. He was in the process of delivering the last lot of E-6As to VQ-4 and supporting the relocation of the squadrons to Tinker. I got to read his quarterly acquisition reports. His was an extremely well-run program, with deliveries going according to schedule and no major funding issues. He never needed any help from me! However, reading the reports helped me catch up on TACAMO developments.

In May 1992, I was invited to attend the commissioning ceremony for Strategic Communications Wing One at Tinker. John Keilty, then commanding officer of VQ-3, flew an E-6A to Andrews Air Force Base to pick up the Washington area dignitaries. This was my first flight in an E-6A, so I was like a kid in a candy shop. I got tours and briefings from the crew on both the trip out to Tinker and the return flight. John even let me sit in the pilot's seat for a little while.

The commissioning ceremony was a truly memorable event, a sparkling new hangar and wing headquarters building, a new bright-white E-6A parked just outside the hangar where the ceremony was held, a gigantic American flag behind the dais, which was packed with admirals, generals, members of congress, the mayor of Oklahoma City, etc. The keynote speaker was the Vice President of the United States, Dan Quayle, who also swore Andy in as the first wing commander. Wonderful! TACAMO had arrived in style at Tinker Air Force Base. TACAMO now had two original "True Believers" in key senior leadership positions—Andy as the operational commander and Ed as Program Manager—and the community had brand new E-6A airplanes and a purpose-built facility to support them. In the early 1970s, when the first "True Believers" rolled the dice to stay in the TACAMO community, we could not have imagined this outcome in our wildest dreams! Norm Tindall and Mark Herkert, who had led the small TACAMO pre-commissioning unit at Tinker, had done a spectacular job supervising the construction and coordinating with the Air Force and Navy on all aspects of the transition and relocation of VQ-3 and VQ-4 to Tinker. Of particular note, both squadrons completed the transition to the E-6A and the relocation to Tinker without a stand-down from operational commitments, and they did it without any accidents or significant incidents, an extraordinary and unprecedented accomplishment carried out by all hands in the TACAMO community. This was my first visit to the new Tinker Air Force Base facility, so I really enjoyed the various tours and events over the weekend. There were also a couple of receptions and a fine formal dinner. Around 30 prior TACAMO commanding officers attended the ceremony, providing great photo opportunities and the chance to catch up and tell sea stories.

However, too soon it was back to my real job at the Assistant Secretary of Defense office. In late 1992, I was selected to be commanding officer of a Major Shore Command and, after some negotiating with my detailer, was slated for the Naval Air Technical Training Center in Millington, Tennessee, just north of Memphis. This assignment was to begin in

August 1993 but required completion of several schools before reporting aboard. I completed my tour at the Assistant Secretary of the Navy slot in May 1992 and set off for my training.

The Naval Air Technical Training Center commanding officer job was particularly appealing because it was one of the few captain shore command positions that was also a flying job. I would get to fly the C-12 aircraft assigned to Naval Air Station Memphis as well as regular passenger and cargo missions assigned to these airplanes. My first training was in the C-12 Fleet Replacement Squadron at Naval Air Station North Island, California. It was nice to get back in the cockpit after six years away from flying. The Technical Training Center is the organization that trains all Navy enlisted men in the aviation ratings. It had "A" schools for initial training of sailors right out of Boot Camp, "C" schools for more advanced rate training, instructor schools, and some specialized training. The Technical Training Center also conducted Limited Duty Officer and Warrant Officer training for newly-minted officers in aviation specialties. It was a large command with a staff of over 1,000 that trained 16,000 students per year, with an average student load of about 4,000. There was also a detachment at Naval Air Station Lakehurst, New Jersey, that trained sailors on the operation and maintenance of aircraft carrier catapults and arresting gear, a big and complex leadership job. Commanding officers going to these large bases attended an Executive Leadership Course to give us some tips on managing them. Also, as if this big commanding officer job and the flying duties weren't enough responsibility, the Naval Air Technical Training Center, like many other Navy bases then, was also involved in a Base Realignment and Closure action. The Naval Air Technical Training Center project was the Navy's largest and most complex with a four-step plan. Step one was the closure of the Naval Aviation Depot in Pensacola, Florida. Step two was relocation of the Naval Air Technical Training Center from Millington to Pensacola using a combination of new construction and refurbished buildings. Step three was relocation of the Bureau of Naval Personnel from Arlington, Virginia, to Millington, which would require modification and refurbishment of many Naval Air Technical Training Center buildings as the training schools moved out. Step four was the demolishment of the old Navy

Annex facility in Arlington. I was designated team leader for this base realignment project. The planning for steps one and two was already well underway in 1993. All commanding officers also had to attend a two-week course related to Base Realignment and Closure planning, budgeting and execution.

After completing this training, I assumed command of the Naval Air Technical Training Center in August 1993. I will leave it to your imagination to guess how extraordinarily busy, demanding and challenging the next two years would be, worthy of a book of its own, but with only a couple of TACAMO connections during this tour. First, there were a number of TACAMO people at Millington. By 1993, thousands of people had served in the TACAMO community and you met old shipmates pretty much everywhere you went. Naval Air Technical Training Center was no exception: Commander Janine Igou Clemens was one of my department heads; Mike Clemens was Exec of the naval air station; Russ Noble was Exec of Naval Aviation Maintenance Training Group, a tenant command at the naval air station; Master Chief Russ Johnson was Department Master Chief for the Avionics School; and several TACAMO sailors served as instructors in different schools. There was plenty of opportunity to reminisce about the old days in TACAMO.

Second, in September 1994, Vern Lochausen, who was then Commander, Strategic Communications Wing One, asked me to serve as the TACAMO community representative on the Fiscal Year 1995 Aviation Command Screen Board to select the next crop of squadron commanders, including the TACAMO squadrons. I was happy to accept this extra duty as I had never served on a promotion or selection board and it would give me one final chance to support the TACAMO community. The Board took a couple of weeks and was a fascinating learning experience that also made a pretty big contribution to the Navy. One is sworn to secrecy for life about the deliberations of these boards, but it is no secret the Board that year selected Commander Sue Davies, who had served under my command at VQ-3, and Commander Bill Okoniewski, whom I did not know at that time. Both would be outstanding TACAMO commanding officers and Bill would also go on to be NAVAIR program manager for the E-6B. That turned out to be my final TACAMO chore while on active duty and it was a very satisfying one.

For a variety of reasons, I decided to retire at the completion of my Technical Training Center tour and became a civilian on July 1, 1995. But I was not done with TACAMO.

Our family relocated to Centreville, Virginia, in the suburbs outside Washington. We bought a small farm and settled into the second career routine, as a support contractor. I took a job with a small business working on acquisition of training programs for the Navy, but after just eight months, that company was essentially driven out of business by the government shutdown in 1995. In March 1996, I joined Camber Corporation and remained with them until my second and final retirement in October 2014. At Camber, I served as a Senior Acquisition Analyst and Program/Contract Manager supporting acquisition of training systems, major naval aircraft procurements, and chemical and biological defense systems. In all those years, I only worked on one TACAMO project, which was to facilitate development of a strategic plan for Naval Air Systems Command (NAVAIR) just after Bill Okoniewski took the helm there in 1998.

In the early and mid-1990s Bill Crowell, Mike Vos and others began hosting bi-annual TACAMO reunions in the Patuxent River area. These were well attended by the large TACAMO retired community near Naval Air Station Patuxent River, but also drew word-of-mouth attendees from all over the country. I attended a couple of these reunions, and discussions at these events led to the idea of forming an official TACAMO veteran's association. Bill Crowell and Mike Vos led the effort to begin a TACAMO veterans group. They recruited Franklin Forrest, Chris Skafidas and Lynn Zepik as initial Board of Directors members, then asked me to join and serve as the first president. I think they wanted someone who had been a senior officer to sign off on documents and lend some weight to future fund-raising efforts. Sue Davies joined the board a few years later after she retired from the Navy. The board chose TACAMO Survivors Association as the name of our organization and the members all knuckled down to complete initial organizing tasks. Chris Skafidas and I worked the paperwork to obtain tax-exempt status, so that contributions to the association would be tax-deductible. Mike Vos became executive director and webmaster, creating a great first website that included a nice database of TACAMO sailors, a chat room, and pages for news and events and history. As vice president, Bill Crowell concentrated on organizing reunions and activities. The association mostly concentrated on social activities: reconnecting TACAMO sailors through the web database and chat room; bi-annual reunions mostly held at Pax River, though there were two in Memphis, all successful and well-attended. Still, the association remained small and underfunded. We never attracted more than a few hundred dues-paying members and didn't succeed in gaining sponsorship support. It was difficult to expand into bigger activities without the needed seed money to start them. In addition, all the first board members had challenging jobs and homes to maintain, along with teenage children with all the attendant school and sports activities. In addition to the lack of funding, we didn't have the time necessary to really expand the TACAMO Survivors Association, so we continued as a small social-focused group.

About the same time as the TACAMO Survivors Association was being founded, Vern Lochausen started up his *Old TACAMO* website, which focused on TACAMO history and heritage, and began attracting a goodly number of retired TACAMO folks. Vern also led efforts to have TACAMO exhibits included in the Naval History Museum's Cold War display and within the new Patuxent River Aviation Museum.

The association and *Old TACAMO* operated in parallel for several years. TACAMO veterans associated with both organizations began to desire an organization with more activities and services than offered by the association. In 2010, a new slate of directors was elected and the association transitioned to the present TACAMO Community Veterans Association, with help from former skipper Bill Coyne, by now a lawyer, in drafting the charter. With Vern as president and historian, Mike Vos as executive director and webmaster, "Coach" Warren as VP, and Jim Gallagher as ship's store manager, the new association began to expand the scope of activities. Mike and Cheryl Vos broadened reunion sites to include locations of interest to TACAMO such as Seattle, Hawaii, Marietta and Oklahoma. History and heritage events were included in reunion schedules. Outreach efforts such as the Crew Four Quest were added to find and contact the families of those crewmembers who died in the crash off Wake Island in 1977. Vern and Coach initiated and nurtured the TACAMO Hall of Fame. History and heritage displays and collections were expanded. Corporate sponsorship was obtained to support these activities. Membership and participation increased greatly. The TACAMO Community Veterans Association has done a great job under the leadership of a team that has the time and dedication required to run such an organization. I'll continue to participate in that organization's activities for as long as I'm able. It's a great way to stay connected with former shipmates, learn new things about TACAMO, swap lies about our active-duty adventures and give back to the community. Always a "True Believer."

So that's my TACAMO "True Believer" story. I have tried to tell the story, not of just this one "True Believer," but how our small group in the 1970s was able to stay with the new mission and small nascent community and contribute to its growth and success over long careers of service to TACAMO and the Navy. The handful of original "True Believers" were able to train, mentor, and lead the next generations of dedicated officers which grew to hundreds, then thousands of dedicated professionals. We became the first group of TACAMO squadron commanding officers, wing commanders and NAVAIR Program Managers, and served in various senior staff positions, while continuing to develop the following generations and laying the groundwork for expansion of the mission and procurement of the E-6. In some ways, the "True Believers" story is unique to TACAMO, but in others, it exemplifies the story of the growth of any naval aviation community, whether TACAMO, fighters, or patrol.

I have tried to give shout-outs to people who served with me and made significant contributions to the community. I know I missed many, so please don't be offended if your name was omitted due to failing memory or lack of space. So many people contributed to the growth and success of TACAMO that it would be impossible to list them all in a work of this length. I would particularly like to acknowledge the contributions of the enlisted men and women who served in TACAMO over the years. Of course, there was a large cadre of early enlisted "True Believers," those who started with the early squadrons and returned for multiple tours. People like Cotton Hope, Rossie Coleman, Jeff Homewood, Jimmy Kugler, Don Woody, Dan Shore, Jim Mulligan, Ron Gray, Gary Nelson, "Red Dog" Summerday, Ken Whitten, and Ralph Burgoon taught me invaluable lessons about aircraft and mission systems, as well as deck plate leadership. These and hundreds of others trained and led the subsequent generations of TACAMO sailors and ensured the community continued to be successful. They flew all the long arduous missions. They developed and refined operational and communications procedures so that every mission hummed. They maintained and repaired the aircraft and systems on the ground and in the air; a wonderful community full of dedicated professionals and interesting characters. It was a great honor and pleasure to serve with them for so many years.

Mike Davidson

I elected to stay in Hawaii for a follow-on tour, partly due to a beach house that was too good to give up. I was assigned temporarily to the commodore's staff at Patrol Wing Two as the acting Chief Staff Officer. Commodore Norb Ryan is one of the most intelligent and operations-savvy flag officers in the Navy. His twin brother, Rear Admiral John Ryan, was already on the Pacific Command Headquarters staff, and we had interesting chats about the Navy and future of VP (patrol squadron) operations. He was equally qualified and as intelligent as his twin. They are a truly awesome pair that I would follow into battle anywhere, anytime.

At my final stop at Pacific Command Headquarters, I was initially assigned as branch chief for producing all the communications annexes for all operational plans and exercises. This included Noncombatant Evacuations Operations and unusual events such as transporting chemical weapons from Germany to Johnston Atoll for incineration. I moved up as Executive Assistant for the Deputy Chief of Staff for Communications, an Army major general in the Signal Corps. At the end of this tour, I was selected for promotion to captain, but my Senate approval was bogged down by the Tailhook scandal, even though I wasn't there.

I went back to Washington for a detailer visit and met with Vice Admiral Jerry Tuttle, that maverick in naval aviation. He had a program manager position open in the Space and Naval Warfare Systems Command. If I was interested in that position, he was adamant that I be frocked to captain before walking in the front door. Back in Hawaii, I learned he had called Admiral Larson and explained I was to be program manager for the Over-The-Horizon Targeting program, responsible for numerous senior officers and civilians. During this tour, I was designated an acquisition professional and handed off to a different detailer.

My final career assignment was as Deputy Commander and Commander of the Joint Interoperability Test Command at Fort Huachuca in southern Arizona, about 30 miles north of the U.S./Mexican border, responsible for certifying the joint interoperability of command, control and surveillance systems before they went to full funding. Despite the associated growing pains, we expanded exponentially, from a $1.5 million fee-for-service agency to a $32 million operation when I retired. In the meantime, my detailer laughed at my dream sheet, every line requesting to be volleyball officer on Tahiti.

His admiral laughed as well. Under 10 USC and Title IV of the Goldwater–Nichols Department of Defense Reorganization Act of 1986, an officer may not be appointed to the grade of rear admiral (lower half) unless the officer has been designated a joint qualified officer. With my four TACAMO squadron tours, my Atlantic and Pacific Command Headquarters assignments, long before being joint was "cool," I was selected as a joint-qualified officer. The admiral then directed my detailer to stick me somewhere in the Pentagon, where he had over a hundred unfilled billets there requiring a Joint Duty subspecialty and Acquisition Professional designation. Years later, *Navy Times* would feature me in an article discussing the importance of joint duty assignments and education.

My detailer offered me the choice of any ring in the Pentagon; I just needed to choose one. The forked-tongue devils exist even at the O-6 level! I told him I didn't need or want another D.C. tour, since I'd had plenty already. That's when he said, "You're experienced, just what we need." I wanted to sail into the sunset off Tahiti. He noted that particular job was not available to me, as he was going to take it himself. It broke the ice between us but, in the end, I would be ordered to Washington, based on the admiral's direction. Three months later I retired and became a defense contractor. The rest is history.

Despite my squabbling, I had a very successful naval career. Even if I had the chance, I wouldn't change a thing. I was given awesome responsibility that my civilian counterparts never saw at any age. I participated in mission upgrade requirements, development, implementation and deployments unheard of in any other naval community. Once I made the decision for a career as a regular officer, I dedicated my life to the TACAMO community. I went where I was asked to go and did what was expected, and more. I personally grew in my own life and in what's important. I made friendships I will cherish forever. I served under terrific skippers, wing commanders, supervisors and leaders, and had the best possible officers, men and women working under me. I flew an awesome plane for four assignments, and again after I retired from the Navy. The lessons and experiences were things I could, and did, carry on to my successes in the civilian world.

Before I close, I hold dear those shipmates we lost under various circumstances during my 26 years in the Navy, especially VQ-3 Crew Four lost off Wake Island in June 1977. They appreciated this mission's importance and gave their all for it. We are so much better for their energy, knowledge, experience, and contributions. I will always keep them in my thoughts and prayers. As General George S. Patton said, "It is foolish and wrong to mourn the men who died. Rather, we should thank God that such men lived."

For those who have served and made our community what it is today, thank you. For those who are now serving and will serve our community in the future—TACAMO!

Vern Lochausen

The Boeing ticket came with a lower salary than some of the others and at a cost; it meant moving to Seattle and right away, with the youngest daughter enrolled in and doing very well in a rural high school in Choctaw, Oklahoma. I went to Seattle as a geographic bachelor, with an attractive job title: E-6 Product Development Manager. Nice little office, without a window, and a nice room at the Residence Inn in Kent, Washington.

In my first week, I was vectored to the big flight training center built on a tract of land that was formerly Long Acres Horse Park. There I met Jerry Whites, the famous Boeing test pilot who had flown the E-6 in those test flights when the tail departed the jet while doing rudder kicks at the upper edge of the envelope. I knew him from my commanding officer days when NAVAIR had taken me to Seattle to hear about that event. He built my confidence in Boeing's ability to prevent that from ever happening to my little initial cadre of pilots about to fly the jet at Barbers. We entered and flew a 737 Next Generation simulator. Jerry knew my last cockpit was the wing C-12s as a qualified co-pilot. As we flew along, I found it really easy to fly and navigate during the approach, touch-and-go, and departure phases. The amount of pilot aids, like flight path vectors, visualization of the glide slope, navigation aids and other traffic, and the cool speed "tapes" and such, were nothing short of awesome. There was a guy behind us whom I assumed was the simulator controller just like we had in the Merc simulators at Oklahoma City. Later, I learned he was taking notes, not on my below-average performance trying to fly the thing, but my motor-mouth comments on how the glass cockpit and flight management system made flying it so much less work and so much safer. Then the light came on, not the Master Caution light but the "Here's Why They are Doing This" light. "Hey, Vern, you are the Product Development Manager." From that day on, my mission was to develop a glass cockpit value proposition for the Navy E-6.

Over the next year, I made contributions to the existing pitch and the unsolicited proposal that we presented to NAVAIR and the fleet. I hit my Rolodex and got some E-6 pilots interested and I went back and flew the simulator. I got the chance to use a prototype Heads Up Display in a pattern hop around SeaTac airport in the goo. In one of the many "gate reviews" for the proposal, a Boeing commercial manager asked me why we would want to put a new digital glass cockpit in an old 707 with lots of analog systems. He recommended we just sell them a 737 or 767. My answer? They can't afford a new jet and they don't need those jets. Long story short: the Navy bought the idea, on the basis of safety, reduced pilot workload, greatly reduced logistics support costs and box count, and commonality with the 737 Next Generation population.

As that project took a life of its own, I was next challenged to package and help write a proposal for an airborne internet connection using the Connexion by Boeing Ku Band satellite system. The airlines and the E-4B National Emergency Airborne Command Post were all signing up for Connexion By Boeing, so again part of the value proposition was being a part of that larger crowd, thereby allowing the Strategic Command Battle Staff Teams to connect to the Global Information Grid via this link. Again, the Navy bought the proposition. With two good wins on my scorecard, Boeing Space and Communications, then building the 737 Wedgetail airborne early warning and control system for the Australians, gave me a budget of almost a million dollars to develop another unsolicited proposal. This one was to rework the E-6B Airborne Command Post Battle Staff Team systems. This internal research and development project put a team of Boeing engineers and logisticians with me, to which I added Rockwell Collins and Long Wave to the team. We traveled to Omaha, Oklahoma City, submarine bases, and the Naval Undersea Warfare Center at Newport, Rhode Island. We interviewed some Battle Staff teams and TACAMO communications crews, surveyed the developing Common Submarine Radio Room and the U.S. Strategic Command center. The resulting proposal gave NAVAIR a vision of "the art of the possible" in giving the Battle Staff team the kind of automated and integrated displays they used in Strategic Command's command center, capitalizing on the "Looking Glass" idea of an airborne mirror image of that information and that kind of display presentation. It would replace the paper pads, maps, and grease pencil forms they used in the EC-135 and in the E-6B Airborne Command Post. We listed the issues presented by the Battle Staff team and our solutions sets. The Navy decided to go competitive, so the team disbanded and went off to write their own proposals. Vern's batting average just went from 1,000 to 667. With the wife looking for me to "come home" and Boeing recognizing that the Request for Proposal would be years away, Boeing offered me a return to Oklahoma City to be a Navy programs manager there.

Over the next two years, my portfolio was all Boeing Military Field Service worldwide, all services and all field service representatives. That meant more travel. The Navy piece included contract maintenance and logistics for the Top Gun program at Fallon, Nevada. Boeing, having merged with McDonnell Douglas just after I came aboard, was doing a poor job, and I was charged with "fixing" it. They had fired the site manager and sent me my own team. Long story short, I fired some more folks and hired some retired Hornet and Tomcat maintenance officers with the help of my fellow commodores that I had known through AIRPAC. That team turned the program around. The low point was during my status check with the customer at the beginning. The Top Gun Tomcat leader said "Vern, we are afraid to take a Boeing-maintained Tomcat up. We don't trust the maintenance." I regained their trust, our proposal in the re-compete was accepted, and we won that work for the next seven years.

When I reached a crisis in my marriage, I found it necessary to leave Boeing and Oklahoma, where I had been elected a city councilman in a small suburb and served on the board of a chamber of commerce. I needed a job in San Diego. As divine providence would have it, I got a call out of the blue from former VQ-3 commanding officer Joe Gerard who had led the efforts to get VQ-3 ready and on step for 100 percent coverage. He hired me for business development manager for TRW and its software-defined radio division. He had trusted me during the build-up and I delivered for him in TRW. But the marriage failed and Joe helped me get transferred back to Oklahoma in the same job there. Later, Boeing made me a decent offer to return as the Deputy E-6 Program Manager. Soon I was in Wichita, leading the whole E-6 program including that glass cockpit mod installation, the contractor logistics support program, and the service life assessment engineering contract. For five years, that was my job until Boeing promoted me to V-22 Osprey Sustainment Director. I had proven myself successful in the Tactical Air Top Gun support program and V-22 was a Boeing sore spot, about to go into combat. It succeeded and so did I. After five years of that, living first in Amarillo, where the V-22 is built, and then Pax River, where the NAVAIR program office resides, I retired from Boeing.

I found a way home to TACAMO with a contract vehicle and a belief in me by former VQ-3 commanding officer and NAVAIR E-6 Program Manager, Bill Okoniewski. Today, I still support the community, the program manager and the wing, as a subject matter expert and mentor to the newly assigned staff. Since I returned to Patuxent River in 2010, after having not lived there since 1977, I discovered the TACAMO Survivors Association, which Buff Crowell and Barry Coyle had put together with Mike Vos. My wife of then six years, Colleen, said to me after a reunion I helped plan and execute in Pax, "TACAMO is your family, this is where you belong."

Looking back on now 43 years of familiarity, sometimes hate, but much more often love, for something called TACAMO, I find that I believed in the mission and served and cared for the people and that is my fulfillment. Colleen was right; TACAMO is my family. I lived through some really tough but forthright leaders, and some not so good ones. I learned something from all of them. To paraphrase President John Kennedy, "I can imagine no more rewarding a career. And any man who may be asked in this century what he did to make his life worthwhile, I think he can respond with a good deal of pride and satisfaction: 'I served in the United States Navy—TACAMO!'"

Lew McIntyre

So, here I am, five decades into the "interim program" of TACAMO. This book is an attempt to capture the stories of the "True Believers" who, against advice to the contrary, returned to TACAMO and became its Founding Fathers. Today's "True Believers" are charged with the mission of carrying the torch onward, to ever higher heights. Keep 'em flying, keep 'em vertical, the world is counting on you to do your mission. Take Charge and Move Out!

List of Acronyms

ACO	Airborne Communications Officer
AIRLANT	Naval Air Forces, Atlantic (colloquial)
AIRPAC	Naval Air Forces, Pacific (colloquial)
CINCLANT	Commander-in-Chief, Atlantic
CINCLANTFLT	Commander-in-Chief, U.S. Atlantic Fleet
CINCPAC	Commander-in-Chief, Pacific
CNO	Chief of Naval Operations
NATOPS	Naval Aviation Training and Procedures Standardization
NAVAIR	Naval Air Systems Command (colloquial)
NEACP	National Emergency Airborne Command Post
NFO	Naval Flight Officer
NROTC	Naval Reserve Officer Training Corps
PLE	Prudent Limit of Endurance
PLOP	Pressure Line of Position
SAR	Search and Rescue
SARS	Selective Action Reports System
SLOP	Sun Line of Position
TACAMO	"Take Charge and Move Out"
VP	Patrol squadrons
VQ	Special Mission squadrons (general)
VQ-1	Fleet Air Reconnaissance Squadron One
VQ-2	Fleet Air Reconnaissance Squadron Two
VQ-3	Fleet Air Reconnaissance Squadron Three
VQ-4	Fleet Air Reconnaissance Squadron Four
VS	Carrier-based Anti-Submarine squadron

Index